T0122815

Get the eBook FREE!

(PDF, ePub, Kindle, and liveBook all included)

We believe that once you buy a book from us, you should be able to read it in any format we have available. To get electronic versions of this book at no additional cost to you, purchase and then register this book at the Manning website.

Go to https://www.manning.com/freebook and follow the instructions to complete your pBook registration.

That's it!
Thanks from Manning!

Application Security Program Handbook

A GUIDE FOR SOFTWARE ENGINEERS AND TEAM LEADERS

DEREK FISHER
FOREWORD BY MATT ROSE

MANNING
SHELTER ISLAND

For online information and ordering of this and other Manning books, please visit
www.manning.com. The publisher offers discounts on this book when ordered in quantity.
For more information, please contact

> Special Sales Department
> Manning Publications Co.
> 20 Baldwin Road
> PO Box 761
> Shelter Island, NY 11964
> Email: orders@manning.com

©2022 by Manning Publications Co. All rights reserved.

No part of this publication may be reproduced, stored in a retrieval system, or transmitted, in
any form or by means electronic, mechanical, photocopying, or otherwise, without prior written
permission of the publisher.

Many of the designations used by manufacturers and sellers to distinguish their products are
claimed as trademarks. Where those designations appear in the book, and Manning
Publications was aware of a trademark claim, the designations have been printed in initial caps
or all caps.

⊗ Recognizing the importance of preserving what has been written, it is Manning's policy to have
the books we publish printed on acid-free paper, and we exert our best efforts to that end.
Recognizing also our responsibility to conserve the resources of our planet, Manning books are
printed on paper that is at least 15 percent recycled and processed without the use of elemental
chlorine.

The author and publisher have made every effort to ensure that the information in this book
was correct at press time. The author and publisher do not assume and hereby disclaim any
liability to any party for any loss, damage, or disruption caused by errors or omissions, whether
such errors or omissions result from negligence, accident, or any other cause, or from any usage
of the information herein.

Manning Publications Co.	Development editor: Toni Arritola
20 Baldwin Road	Technical development editor: Michael Jensen
PO Box 761	Review editor: Adriana Sabo
Shelter Island, NY 11964	Production editor: Keri Hales
	Copy editor: Carrie Andrews
	Proofreader: Jason Everett
	Typesetter: Gordan Salinovic
	Cover designer: Marija Tudor

ISBN 9781633439818
Printed in the United States of America

brief contents

contents

foreword

I am a big fan of analogies as an interesting way to describe technical concepts like application security. I find it a straightforward way to get everyone on the same page and get to that "Aha, I get it" moment. I came up with a brand-new analogy for this book's foreword: application security is like the game Stratego. Stratego is a board game where the goal is to protect your hypothetical country's flag from your competitor with different types of defenses and strategies that you have access to. It is up to you to define and design the proper protections for your flag. There is no right or wrong way to protect your flag, but there are good and not-so-good ways. Just like application security programs that ensure the security of your applications, there are many ways to design them. Some application security program designs are excellent, and some need work. This book by Derek Fisher does a fantastic job of helping you understand what an effective application security program should look like for the modern applications your organization is developing today with aggressive CI/CD pipelines.

Let's face it: application security is difficult to do correctly. There are so many different variables associated with a practical application security program. Some examples of these variables include making the right decisions on tooling, methodologies, processes, and staff roles and responsibilities. Once you complete these decisions, you need a plan to operationalize the selected variable. For example, if you buy a best-of-breed application security testing tool, it does not mean your applications are now magically secure. The tool needs the correct configuration to look for the critical application security risk that most concerns your organization.

After being in application security for over 17 years, I was very impressed with the way Derek categorized and explained the multitude of concepts associated with application security. Without a clearly defined purpose and charter, application security programs will not be successful. The most simplistic way to define an application security program is to find security issues your organization cares about, remediate the problems, and then measure the results. Derek's approach to explaining application security through a define, develop, and deliver strategy is well thought out and complete.

One section of the book that I very much enjoyed, and I suggest people read multiple times, is section 1.4, which discusses shifting right versus shifting left in development. This section discusses how there are benefits in application security to shifting security left, but it is not the only way to properly implement an application security program.

Whether you are a veteran application security professional or a student looking to enter the application security industry, this is a foundational book for all application security principles, definitions, and concepts.

—MATT ROSE,
CHIEF ARCHITECT, BIONIC
FORMER LEADER AT CHECKMARX AND FORTIFY

preface

I spent a lot of time thinking about writing a book about the subject of application security. In my early career in security, it was clear that the resources, outside of OWASP, were few and far between as it relates to application security. Today, things are picking up and the resources are becoming more plentiful. However, there is still not a single resource for what an application security program looks like in an organization. I attempt to provide that resource with this book.

However, every organization is different—each with their own tools, technology stacks, ways of developing code, and varying size of the security organization. But even with this variance, the methods for tackling security are similar across organizations. Vulnerabilities still need to be found, tracked, and resolved. Training still needs to occur. Code still needs to be written securely. In this book, I wanted to capture the essential parts of application security that can work regardless of the size of the organization and the size of the application security team.

One of the goals I set out to tackle with this book was to attempt to give a blueprint for an organization that was looking to build an application security team from the ground floor up. Again, the resources for this are few and far between, and not generally in one location. My hope is that this book will give someone the help they need to start up an application security program in their organization by taking some of the learnings I've had throughout the years.

acknowledgments

First and foremost, I want to point out that we always stand on the shoulders of giants in technology and specifically in security. I did not break much new ground in this book in the sense of novel concepts but instead took the things that I have learned from numerous sources in the industry and based on my experience of what has, and hasn't, worked. So this is a blanket acknowledgment to all those who have been building the security protocols, standards, and technology that have gotten us this far.

I'd like to also thank all my friends, family, and coworkers for putting up with me talking about writing a book during the year that it's taken me to do so. There has been more than one occasion when I might have said, "I talk about that in my book," so I'm sorry for that.

I want to thank those who have kept me on target with this project and those who have provided valuable feedback to the content. It is often difficult and lonely to impart information that you may think is valuable into a book. It has been refreshing to see that much of what I have covered in this book has some value to those who have read and provided feedback.

A huge thanks to the staff at Manning who helped see this book through production: Brian Sawyer, Toni Arritola, Michael Jensen, Keri Hales, Carrie Andrews, Jason Everett, and all the rest of the folks behind the scenes.

I also appreciate Matt Rose taking the time to write the foreword for this book.

Finally, thank you to all the reviewers: Adonis Butufei, Ahmed Sammoud, Alex Lucas, Aliaksandra Sankova, Andrea Barisone, Bobby Lin, Claudia Maderthaner, Daniel Wanjohi, Fernando Bernardino, George Onofrei, Giampiero Granatella, Grzegorz

Bernas, Hugo Cruz, James Jardine, James Woodruff, Jens Gheerardyn, Jeremy Bryan, Jim Amrhein, John Bassil, Juan Guzman, Kosmas Chatzimichalis, Krishna Anipindi, Krzysztof Kamyczek, Lakshminarayanan AS, Malte, Manoj, Matt Borack, Mladen Knežić, Nikolaos Alexiou, Noah Krieger, Oscar Frink, Paul Grebenc, Paul Love, Richard Vaughan, Roman Zhuzha, Ron Lease, Rosalyn Williams, Ryan LaBouve, Sebastian Maldonado, Stanley Anozie, Steve Hill, Stuart Ellis, Teddy Hagos, Tim van Deurzen, Tim Wooldridge, and Valer Bocan. Your suggestions helped make this a better book.

about this book

When I first set out to write this book, I was thinking about someone who may be asked to stand up an application security program from scratch. They could be a consultant, or someone brought into an organization to create a program. As the book idea morphed and I added additional topics, it became clear that this book has value even to those who are in a mature organization that requires a reexamination of their application security program or concepts on additional approaches.

Who should read this book

You do not need to be technical to understand the concepts in this book. You do not need to have a robust background in security, either. This book is geared toward those who need to organize an approach to addressing vulnerabilities in developed software. This could be a leader, a program or project manager, a scrum master, an architect, a developer, or a tester. Even those in other disciplines of security will gain value, and maybe appreciation, for what an application security organization does.

This book will not teach you how to hack your friends, perform penetration tests, or other parlor tricks. It will, however, give you guidance on how best to approach building security into the software development life cycle, which is a far better way to impress people.

How this book is organized: A road map

This book is divided into three parts with three chapters each, as shown in the following image.

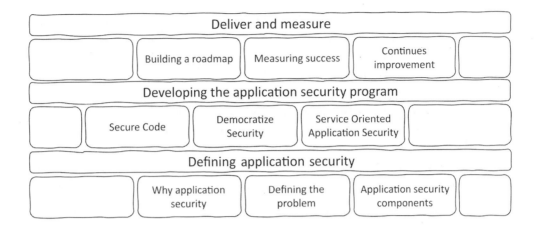

Defining application security

Part 1 looks at what an application security program is and its purpose in software development.

- Chapter 1 presents the reasons for creating an application security program and why is it important today.
- Chapter 2 identifies the risks, threats, and activities that impact our ability to create and deliver secure software.
- Chapter 3 covers the different components of application security and how they are applied in an organization.

Developing the application security program

Part 2 focuses on creating the application security program within an organization and the steps that should be followed.

- Chapter 4 shows how modern software development creates an opportunity for us to integrate security in a way that provides faster feedback to the development teams.
- Chapter 5 walks through the concept of a shared responsibility model that should exist between security and the engineering organization.
- Chapter 6 discusses the concept of making application security functions and tools as a callable service that can be leveraged at all stages of the software development life cycle.

Deliver and measure

Part 3 covers how to measure the effectiveness of the program and identify areas of improvement.

- Chapter 7 provides guidance on building out a roadmap to address building security into the software development life cycle.

- Chapter 8 will show what to measure and how to measure the effectiveness of your application security program.
- Chapter 9 covers more future and advanced topics in application security and how to keep your program on track.

This book should be read in order, as the concepts in the first part are the foundation for the future chapters. If you are already familiar with application security, you may skip this part, as some of it may cover information you already know. However, there are good exercises throughout the book that will get the reader more familiar with the various concepts in application security and will help reinforce the topics covered in the book.

liveBook discussion forum

Purchase of *Application Security Program Handbook* includes free access to liveBook, Manning's online reading platform. Using liveBook's exclusive discussion features, you can attach comments to the book globally or to specific sections or paragraphs. It's a snap to make notes for yourself, ask and answer technical questions, and receive help from the author and other users. To access the forum, go to https://livebook .manning.com/book/application-security-program-handbook/discussion. You can also learn more about Manning's forums and the rules of conduct at https://livebook .manning.com/discussion.

Manning's commitment to our readers is to provide a venue where a meaningful dialogue between individual readers and between readers and the author can take place. It is not a commitment to any specific amount of participation on the part of the author, whose contribution to the forum remains voluntary (and unpaid). We suggest you try asking the author some challenging questions lest his interest stray! The forum and the archives of previous discussions will be accessible from the publisher's website as long as the book is in print.

about the author

 **DEREK FISHER** has decades of technical experience in both hardware and software engineering while working in various companies and industries. Through his work in security as a developer, architect, and leader, he has provided his insights at development organizations attempting to create more secure code. Today, he performs many roles, including security evangelist, architect, mentor, speaker, and instructor, where he attempts to bring more secure development to the organizations he works with.

about the cover illustration

The figure on the cover of *Application Security Program Handbook* is "Homme Insulaire de Minorque," or "Man of Minorca, Balearic Islands, Spain," taken from a collection by Jacques Grasset de Saint-Sauveur, published in 1788. Each illustration is finely drawn and colored by hand.

In those days, it was easy to identify where people lived and what their trade or station in life was just by their dress. Manning celebrates the inventiveness and initiative of the computer business with book covers based on the rich diversity of regional culture centuries ago, brought back to life by pictures from collections such as this one.

Part 1

Defining application security

In the first part of this book, the groundwork will be laid for the purposes of an application security program. This all-important topic is critical to securing software that is developed in an organization.

In chapter 1, you'll see the how an application security program can be used to reduce the vulnerabilities that are developed in an application and why it can sometimes be a challenge and where some organizations have fallen short. In chapter 2, you'll start to learn about what the tenets of security are and how adversaries create risk to the defense of an organization's assets.

You'll round out this part with topics related to threat modeling, and the various tools that are used in an application security program. Each of these will identify risks and vulnerabilities that need to be collected and prioritized for remediations. We'll finish this part with pulling all the pieces together so that you can begin to see what makes up an application security program.

Why do we need
application security?

This chapter covers

- Exploring the current state of application security
- Going right or going left
- Looking at breaches caused by insecure applications
- Exploring the cost of inaction

Every company uses software to function. Whether they are a Fortune 500 technology company or a sole proprietor landscaping company, software is integral to businesses large and small. Software provides a means to track employees, customers, inventory, and scheduling. Data moves from a myriad of systems, networks, and software, providing insights to businesses looking to stay competitive. Some of that software used is built within the organization or it is purchased and integrated. What this means is that every organization, regardless of size and industry, has a software need. It enables organizations to move quickly and stay ahead of their competition. In the United States, the growth of software in various industries, including finance, sales, human resources, and supply chains, has seen a steady increase, and the trend is continuing. Over the next decade, these industries will see a steady increase in market size. For instance, in 2020, the market size of global business software and service was nearly 390 billion USD. This is expected to have an annual growth of 11% from 2021 to 2028. This expansion is based on the increasing need for automation and processing solutions in nearly every sector on the economy.

The shift to software-driven organizations can be seen in several prominent examples. Movies were rented at a physical store before Netflix began streaming them in 2007 directly to your television. Books were purchased in a shop before Amazon upended not just the book-buying experience but the overall retail market for any item you can think of. It used to take a phone call to order food; now a mobile app allows you to not only order your food but also track it from the restaurant to your front door. Moreover, software is used in all parts of the supply chain for every organization. Leaders in these organizations can get real-time updates on product as it moves around the world and to their customers' hands. This is no longer a nice-to-have for organizations but is critical to any organization's ability to compete.

In short, software is eating the world.

—Marc Andreessen

Each new piece of software brings new capabilities but also new challenges, especially when that software is available over a network where it is open to a wide audience. More capabilities mean more software. More software means more data. This data is intended to assist an organization and its customers to gain insight into the services the organization offers.

However, the additional software and data means more opportunity for bad actors to leverage weaknesses that might exist. Data is a lucrative target for attackers and difficult for organizations to protect, especially when the organization collects a large amount of it. By the beginning of 2020, the amount of data created worldwide had reached 44 zettabytes and this is expected to reach 463 exabytes per day by 2025 (https://techjury.net/blog/how-much-data-is-created-every-day).

> **FUN FACT**　1 exabyte is 10^{18} bytes and 1 zettabyte is 1,000 exabytes or a trillion gigabytes.

The increasing software landscape and the repository of data growing every second offers a target-rich environment for malicious actors looking for a way in and access to the data. There is constant background noise of malicious activity that pervades the internet. The moment that any software becomes available online, it is immediately probed and prodded. Some of that activity is from automated tools that will then alert when it finds software that can be compromised. Some of it is from bad actors waiting for the latest vulnerability to become public so they can hunt the internet for applications that are vulnerable to it and create exploitation software. Other activity comes from well-financed bad actors who are simply looking for any weaknesses so that they can gain a foothold in an organization in order to come back later for exploitation. If ever there was a more fitting metaphor for software on the internet, it would be the Wild West of the early United States, when lawlessness was rampant, and sheriffs were often overwhelmed and outgunned by the range of activity.

Software, data, attackers, oh my! When organizations don't take software security seriously, they run the risk of jeopardizing not only their client's data, but also the organization's future. Most organizations that are not in the software-building industry will often say that they are not a prime target, or that their data is not interesting to an attacker. They would be wrong. Almost all data that is collected and processed by an organization can be used and misused by an attacker. Nothing is too unimportant. And although many large organizations can weather a data breach, smaller companies often cannot while remaining in business.

It is often said that data is the new oil. Mining, processing, and selling data is a lucrative business both for the organizations that do so openly and the malicious actors who are looking for ways to profit off an organization's missteps. Building security into the software from the start is the first, and most important, step to ensuring that organizations have the means to protect their software, their data, and their livelihood.

1.1   The role of an application security program

Application security is the implementation of security through practices, tools, technology, people, and processes in the development life cycle. The rest of this book will cover how application security is used throughout the development life cycle to ensure that an organization has reduced the risk posed to its software and has done so in a way that does not impede an organization's ability to deliver that software in a timely manner. It is important to know that there is never a silver bullet to solving security issues. No one tool, process, or person can claim that, as attacks are constantly evolving and technology keeps moving. However, ensuring that you have a robust approach to application security that includes not just the fundamentals of an application security program but also the ability to adapt and evolve your approach on an ongoing basis is what sets apart a good program from a bad one. This is what we will discover throughout this book.

Products start as an idea in a client or someone at an organization's head. Transferring that idea from concept, to paper, to minimum viable product, to a production application that is brought to life takes a team of people from multiple disciplines. Most will think first about all the developers, testers, and product people that go into making a successful product, but what about those that make the product secure? The goal is to make a product that does what the customer wants and that is free from defects and security issues that would otherwise devalue the product and the organization as a whole.

1.1.1   *Software from concept to production*

The software development life cycle (SDLC) is defined differently in every organization, but in general, every organization has a similar path from concept to production. Figure 1.1 depicts a standard SDLC, where

- The client or product owner envisions a new feature or enhancement.
- Use cases and requirements are developed. The team determines where to slot the work for an upcoming release.
- The development team then makes decisions on how the requirements will be implemented through technology choices. Development begins and the code is integrated into a feature branch.
- The feature is then moved to a preproduction environment like a test or staging environment where tests can be performed. The product owner will accept the results of the test and agree to have it released to production for the clients to use.
- The feature is released to clients, and the organization manages the feature as a set of a larger application through client and technical support. Eventually, the feature is decommissioned in favor of a new release.

Phases of an SDLC

Figure 1.1   Phases of an SDLC

In the first step, the product may already exist, in which case the client would request an enhancement or a new feature. For instance, perhaps there's a new method of accessing reports within the application, or a new dataset becomes available in the user interface. Otherwise, the product owner may be collecting information from several clients and put in an enhancement request for a new feature. In either of these cases, an organization will gather the client needs in the form of use cases. A simple use case could be written as the following:

> *"As an administrator, I want to be able to create weekly reports that show the application usage among users in my organization."*

This is a simple use case for an application that is based on SaaS (software as a service) and is used by many organizations to provide some service. The details are not important in this case, as every organization is different regardless of the industry they are in. In most cases, a feature would include multiple use cases.

Once the client or product owner has the use case defined, this is then reviewed with the development leaders of the product. The architects, lead developers, and operational members of the development team review the use cases and determine the feasibility of the request.

This brings the use case to the next step in the process, where the functional and nonfunctional requirements are defined. Like having multiple use cases, each use case can have numerous requirements. Following is a functional and nonfunctional example of requirements for the previous use case:

- *Functional*—Application shall provide the ability to create a report of application usage by user.
- *Nonfunctional*—Report creation shall be available to only administrators.

This is not a book on writing requirements, but a simple explanation is that *functional requirements* describe what the feature should do, and *nonfunctional requirements* are how the feature should do it. Most information on requirements describe security as a nonfunctional requirement. However, it is not uncommon to find security features being described as functional requirements, especially when it comes to things like encryption, authentication, and access.

1.1.2 *Where does application security fit?*

The product owner will take the defined requirements and decide with the development team what priorities might need to shift and what the delivery dates are for the new feature. There is something missing so far. Where are the people, tools, and processes that bring security into a product? As mentioned, security is typically a nonfunctional requirement. However, those nonfunctional requirements should not be left up to the product owner and the development team to determine on their own. A more mature organization would bring in the application security team to not just review the use case and requirements, but also define security requirements that should be in place as part of the feature development. If the product team defines their requirements and begins coding before engaging the application security team, they run the risk of creating security issues that are more difficult to resolve once the feature is nearing completion or ready for release. For instance, a development team may know that they need to provide authorization and may decide to develop an internal solution to manage the authorization without looking at a more fitting solution that is used across the organization and is more industry aligned, like OAuth.

Fitting security in during the initial phases is done by taking industry and organizations standards and best practices and building them in to the process of creating requirements. For instance, using industry guidance on encryption would lead to setting requirements on key management and encryption strength. Or the organization may have standards that require the development to adhere to certain architecture or regulatory requirements like using a specific analysis tool. Additionally, when building these requirements, the team will take inputs from items like threat models and risk assessments to further develop requirements that align to the business requirements so that security can be built into the process as early as possible. We will discuss threat models and risk assessments more in depth in future chapters.

1.2   *The current state of application security*

As mentioned, application security is the implementation of security into an organization's development life cycle. The reality is that application security teams, if they exist in an organization at all, are often external to the engineering teams they work with. They can be found under an enterprise-wide function like the enterprise architecture organization, or under a broader security organization. The last one is the most typical. These application security teams will bring in tools, processes, and people to identify software vulnerabilities that are then backlogged for remediation. These vulnerabilities are found through several opportunities, including the following:

- Through the tools that are provided to engineering by the application security team.
- Through internal or external penetration tests completed by the application security team or an external vendor, respectively.
- Through identified issues from clients, or other external sources like a bug bounty program, or vulnerability disclosure policy. More on these in later chapters.

If the application security team and the organization are considered mature, these vulnerabilities, when found, will block builds. Most organizations that take this approach will set a threshold or vulnerability type that will trigger a block. For example, a vulnerability with a high or critical rating could block a build. You can see how this can cause issues between the engineering team that is working toward a release of code and is suddenly stopped by tools and processes that have been put in place by an external team. Blocking a build is by far the most preferred method for an application security team that wants to ensure a secure product, but this can become an instant point of contention. In less mature organizations, a process is in place to allow the engineering team to continue with their build and deployment by having the found vulnerability backlogged for future resolution.

The application security team is in regular competition with feature release. Every new release brings new features. New features bring new defects. New defects bring new security vulnerabilities. As mentioned previously, in some cases these vulnerabilities can break a build and block the release of a feature. However, most organizations will prioritize their feature release over a nebulous vulnerability. I will discuss this more later, but many scanning tools are noisy and produce results that are not easily consumed by developers. Furthermore, not all application security teams are great at translating results from tools and other tests into something that is understandable by engineering without having a meeting or work session to understand. This obviously doesn't scale well in large organizations.

The security issues are backlogged with an I-owe-you to address the issue in the future. But every new release brings the potential for more vulnerabilities to the growing backlog and the cycle continues. Most organizations will take a systematic approach to reducing vulnerabilities, such as focusing on only the high and critical ones or ones of a certain type, like SQL injection or cross-site scripting. Other organizations may focus on the riskiest vulnerabilities based on product capability and exposure, like a financial organization processing sensitive account information. Some organizations may even have a "security release," where their focus is on resolving a large number of security issues in a single release. These different methods help reduce vulnerabilities in burst but don't address the overall issue.

Like Jacob Marley from Charles Dickens's *A Christmas Carol*, these vulnerabilities become chains that weigh down the development team and will eventually haunt an organization. The continued accumulation of vulnerabilities adds to what is called *security debt*, where an organization continues to add new vulnerabilities to the old ones that were already existing. This security debt increases the risk level of the product being developed and the organization that is selling it. Eventually one, or several, of those vulnerabilities will lead to an exploitation of the application by a bad actor. This is similar to the concept of technical debt that builds when an organization takes a quick and easy path to getting features to their customers instead of choosing more sustainable design choices.

Further complicating the job of the application security team is the fact that they are often brought in too late in the development process. Usually, it is once the feature or product has gone through several design and architectural decisions. The code development may have already been well underway, or worse, nearly complete by the time the application security team gets involved. This means that many "one-way" decisions may have already been made, and it is up to the application security team to provide some blessing of the design and code or identify mitigations for discovered threats. This is not the case everywhere, but in a sufficiently large organization, this will happen. If the application security team has had the opportunity to provide guidance, requirements, and security tooling early in the process, potential vulnerabilities can be reduced. Unfortunately, the cases where the application security team is involved early are few and far between, despite it being effective. This leaves the application security team hampered with the decision to be "that person" by blocking a release in order to impose security requirements before production or face consequences from the broader organization for allowing code to be released with known weaknesses. Such is the current picture of application security where there exists a constant struggle between enabling the business and reducing the organization's overall risk.

1.3   Why building security in is challenging

> *There comes a point where we need to stop just pulling people out of the river. We need to go upstream and find out why they're falling in.*
>
> —Desmond Tutu

The application security team has at its disposal the most state-of-the-art tools that include technologies like machine learning, artificial intelligence, natural language processing, and automation. However, some of these tools detect issues once the code is written, and most likely checked in and on its way to a production environment near you. I will talk more about the various tools in future chapters, but as mentioned, there are several tools that are commonly found in a modern development pipeline related to security. Static application security testing (SAST) can scan written software looking for commonly found security issues like hardcoded passwords and SQL injection. Dynamic application security testing (DAST) will attempt to perform real-time security testing on a web application while it is running in an environment. Software composition analysis (SCA) tools will look for known security vulnerabilities and license concerns with third-party and open source software that is used to build the overall application. Additionally, there are cloud architecture, container, infrastructure template, and mobile security tools that can produce scan results that will identify vulnerabilities or other weaknesses in the code or deployment of the software.

DEFINITION *OWASP* (Open Web Application Security Project) is an open source community of application security professionals who develop standards, tools, and projects to assist organizations with the development of security in their applications.

> **Exercise 1.1**
>
> Take a look at OWASP's page on source code analysis tools and review some of the available tools. There are several that are "open source or free." One of these open source tools is the APIsecurity.io security audit (https://apisecurity.io/tools/audit/). You can use this tool to upload an OpenAPI JSON file to detect possible vulnerabilities. If you do not have your own OpenAPI JSON file to use, you can search for one online, or use a sample like this:
>
> http://mng.bz/Kxyj
>
> Look at the results that you get back from APIsecurity.io, and determine whether the issues are true positives or not. Begin to think about how to mitigate the issues that are found.

When a vulnerability is detected, the tools can open a ticket to the application security team and the engineering team, so long as the integration between security tool and the defect tracking tool is set up. The issue is then triaged with the application security and engineering teams, prioritized, and worked to closure.

1.3.1 *Trying to protect at runtime*

Although the aforementioned tools are detection tools, there are protection tools as well that will sit in front of a running application and attempt to block activity that looks malicious. Web application firewalls (WAF) provide protection against attackers looking to take advantage of weaknesses in a running web application. Run-time application security protection (RASP) will provide similar function as the WAF with the exception that RASP generally runs alongside, or even inside, the application. Both mitigation software and denial of service protection will attempt to stop volumetric attacks that send large quantities of malicious traffic that attempt to bring down the application or perform repeated tasks like brute-force activity. Secure gateways will provide similar protection by blocking unauthorized access and activity as well as provide real-time monitoring.

Again, these protection tools use all the latest and greatest techniques to attempt to provide protection like machine learning and artificial intelligence. Some of these tools are great at blocking unwanted activity by malicious actors but at the same time, some tools run the risk of blocking an organization's clients from using the software as it was intended if the tool is not properly tuned. A common example of this is when a batch job runs and calls an API or function hundreds or thousands of times in a short period of time. This could look like automated malicious activity to the protection tools and could block the legitimate traffic. To separate the two, the application security team and the engineering organization have to work together to pattern behavior into rulesets that block malicious traffic and allow the good traffic. This can come in the form of allowlists for certain URLs and IPs. There is a steep hill to climb to enable protection tools since many organizations, understandably, will be concerned with performance and possible interruptions of legitimate traffic.

1.3.2   Getting output from tools is not enough

Like a comfortable blanket, security tools that are layered in during the development process and pipeline can become reassuring to an organization. However, as with most tools, the effectiveness is determined by how well the tool integrates with the organization and how well it protects or provides legitimate results. Organizations that enable one or many of these tools simply to say they use them, or (*cringe*) say that they block the OWASP Top Ten, are not doing themselves or the organization any favors. Sure, during an audit the organization can say that they are using tool X or Y during their development life cycle. Regardless of whether the auditor's pencil gets to work checking a box, the organization may or may not actually be more secure.

The reality is that these tools can create a lot of noise for both the engineering team and the application security team. The scanning tools churn out findings that need to be triaged, rated, and assigned. Many are false positives. The blocking tools create false alarms and raise concerns about the impacts on legitimate activity. And many times, there is an overreliance on the security tools to provide protection, especially when there is a vulnerability that is long in the tooth with no plan to remediate. For instance, an organization may rely heavily on a WAF to provide protection for an SQL injection vulnerability found in an application that has been designated as a "sunset" with a multiyear decommission. We'll talk more about that as we get into vulnerability management.

1.3.3   Sifting signal from noise in security tools

Like any other tool, the security tools that are used in an organization can be expensive and misconfigured. Further, those tools that are not finely tuned will generate an abundance of false positives—like the ones that are turned on and walked away from.

This not only creates additional work on the application security and engineering teams, but also reduces the confidence level in those tools and, by extension, the application security team. When false positives become normal, they become an easy escape route for engineering teams looking to find a way to say that their application is not riddled with vulnerabilities. If the last ten SQL injection issues flagged by a tool were false positive, why would this new one not be? Which brings the application security and engineering teams to a standoff on proving a finding to be a true vulnerability or a false positive. This can be extremely challenging for the application security team, which typically does not have the extensive context that the engineering team has of their own application. It is also a time-consuming process to bring together the appropriate subject matter experts (SME) to pore over the details of the code in relation to the finding.

With the varying tools and the number of findings from each of them, mature application security teams focus on sifting the signal from the noise and providing quality results to the engineering teams. This raises the confidence level of the findings and establishes a more robust relationship between security and engineering.

The application security team will work closely with the engineering team and attempt to have as much application context as possible so as to take the burden of proof out of the engineering team's hands. In other words, the application security team's goal is to ensure the following:

- Results are true positives that have already been triaged by the application security team.
- The steps to remediate the vulnerability are clearly understood by the engineering team. If possible or applicable, the application security team should provide code samples that show exploitation and resolution.
- There are clear expectations on timeline to resolution based on the criticality of the vulnerability.

We will dive into this more in future chapters, but for now let's look at how security can be integrated into the development life cycle.

1.4   *Shifting right vs. shifting left in development*

Whereas every organization releases software in their own manner, for most organizations the path from idea to production is relatively the same. Figure 1.2 shows the common pattern to release.

The phrase *shift left* is the concept of moving security as close to the beginning of the software development life cycle as possible. In figure 1.2, that means during the initial stages of gathering and building requirements as well as in the development phase. The term has been used frequently in the application security space as a way to describe building practices and tools that can uncover security issues as soon as possible in the development life cycle. Many of them I've mentioned previously. Sticklers will tell you that the best way to accomplish this is to ensure that security is there when

Common stages of code development from client requirements to production release

Client needs	Product owner	Development team		QA	Product release	
⬤ (person icon)	Client requirements	Architectural decisions & design	Open source & technology used	Code test deployment	Production deployment	Product decommission
Client needs a feature	Functional/ nonfunctional requirements	Code development	Tool chain for integrations	Code testing	Client management	
	Slotting of work	Code debug	Code integration	Code acceptance		

①　②　③　④　⑤

Application security	Security requirements	Application security foundations		QA	Operational security	
Threat intelligence	Threat modeling	Standards and requirements	Scanning for OSS	IAST/DAST	Threat intelligence	WAF
Industry research	Risk assessment	IDE integration	Scanning for vulnerabilities	Penetration test	Client support	RASP
	Security requirements	Secure code review	Security training	Abuse cases	Vulnerability management	

Figure 1.2　Example of a development pipeline for code deployment

the developer's hands are on the keyboard creating that new function. Those sticklers would be right. The time to correct a security vulnerability is when it is being created.

Shifting left is less visible than shifting right. In the shift right model, tools are placed strategically throughout the development life cycle and production environment to ensure that vulnerabilities are identified and protected against. Penetration tests are executed to identify issues. You can verify that the tools are working, and you can generate reports that show you the effectiveness, or the ineffectiveness, of the tools that you implemented. This relies on a detect and respond paradigm that is very reactive and adds to the backlog of vulnerabilities that I talked about earlier where the critical and high ones are usually prioritized while others go to the backlog. This can also disrupt the DevOps model that looks to move quickly with changes and doesn't handle broken builds or gates very well.

Getting to the goal of developers creating more secure code usually means using controls like

- Security training
- Top-level security policies that are used to develop security procedures, processes, and standards

- Tools that are integrated into the development environments and pipeline that offer faster feedback
- Building reusable secure architecture

However, some of these can be circumvented. Like most training, security education can quickly be forgotten or pushed aside for the sake of speed of delivery of new features. Developers also change roles, jobs, and functions and are often overburdened with deadlines, tickets, requests, fires, and meetings, which favors moving fast as opposed to secure. This leaves even the most well-meaning, security-conscious developer to push security further down in priority, especially when there is a reliance on the protection tools, as described previously, that will detect and alert on security issues. Security quickly becomes someone else's problem. Additionally, the tools become a business blocker, which opens the opportunity for the product owner to request exceptions when a feature release is at risk due to a found security issue. Architecture is frequently misused or not well socialized across the organization, meaning that not all development teams are aware of frequently changing architectural patterns that offer more security.

1.4.1   *Shifting right in the development life cycle*

When an organization decides that their security posture will be mostly a shift-right one, they integrate tools into the development life cycle that will detect issues and open tickets to the security or development team (figure 1.3). Most of these tools are

When shifting right, tools are used to detect issues later in the development life cycle.

Figure 1.3   Security tools that are used in a shift-right approach

used to find issues in production, or late in the development process. These organizations will enable a few protection mechanisms like a WAF and primarily play defense by tracking the incoming vulnerabilities, triaging, and prioritizing them, and assigning them to teams to be resolved.

It is well known that resolving defects, in this case security vulnerabilities, costs more in terms of money and time than an issue that is resolved early in the life cycle. The effort and disruption that is required to resolve a defect that is already in a production environment can be multiple tens of times more expensive than resolving it at the requirements phase with each progressive phase of development becoming more expensive. There are also service-level agreements that could be at risk when a vulnerability gets resolved in production if an outage is incurred through resolving the vulnerability. This further exposes the organization to additional costs above and beyond the engineering cost of resolution. Security vulnerabilities have the added impact of potentially leading to a reportable event or even reputational damage should the vulnerability lead to a large-scale breach that exposes client data or takes an application offline.

However, shifting right does allow the development team to produce features at a rapid pace since security is largely a defensive position when the software is already running in production. This allows for the development team to spend less time resolving issues early, and instead rely on the protection mechanisms in place. The decision to rely on the right-sided tools and processes is one that is made by balancing risk versus reward since failing to deliver a feature on time has its own impacts on the organization's bottom line.

1.4.2 Shifting right fails

There is no shortage of stories where security controls were in place but failed to stop a larger breach or exposure. This happens for a myriad of reasons: alarm fatigue, people believing security is someone else's problem, or too many competing priorities. Those who work in the security industry know that there is always an open port, an insecure version of software, and a place where there is a lack of security controls. And attackers are just as in tune to this as the security workers. Attackers only need to be in the right place at the right time, once. Defenders need to be right every time.

If you're a fan of zombie stories, you'll be familiar with the individual or band of living humans that find themselves inside a building surrounded by the drooling, groaning undead. In most cases there are simply too many surfaces and weaknesses in whatever building they find themselves in. As the horde outside grows, the defenses become weaker and the living inside have fewer and fewer options to keep the zombies out. Working in the cybersecurity field can sometimes feel this way. Every time you shore up a weakness in your defenses, a new one is discovered, and your team is tasked with devising a plan to close the weakness and provide a meaningful defense. Additionally, attackers are not always the mindless zombies pressing your defenses; they are often smart, patient, and know exactly what they want. Good thing the defenders are too.

Bad actors are finding more ways to attack applications, and to the defenders of those applications, it continues to feel like there are more vulnerabilities than they can manage. More features mean more attack surfaces, which means more opportunities for a bad actor to find a way to steal data, impersonate a user, or perform fraud or other nefarious activity. Furthermore, more integration with internal or external applications and services means that there can be exposures that the organization can't control.

Case in point: In 2018, a vulnerability in Facebook led to the compromise of tens of millions of Facebook accounts. The flaw was in a feature that allowed a user to view their profile from the point of view of a different account. No surprise, this feature was called "View As." Bad actors were able to steal the access tokens of Facebook accounts that allowed them to then log in as the user that the access tokens were associated with. They started with their own connected friends and from there stole the access tokens from their friends' connections until they had collected several hundred thousand accounts and then several million. They were able to collect personal data, including the usual suspects of name, contact information, places the user checked in, and other private data.

This example shows the difficulty in providing a secure product that is open to millions of users with a multitude of features—even for a large organization that takes security seriously. The tools that we spoke of previously may have helped identify this issue prior to allowing the code to go out the door or would have detected and blocked it once it was running in production. However, one of the limitations with these tools is their inability to discover business logic, or workflow-related vulnerabilities. Furthermore, it can be challenging to rely on tools to uncover these issues quicker than end users do. This is where having the proper processes, requirements, and testing early in the development life cycle would raise the opportunities to uncover this issue early where the collective effort of tools, testing, and keen security eyes are brought to bear.

1.4.3   *Shifting left in the development life cycle*

Where shifting right means that the organization attempts to put as much effort into protecting and detecting security issues later in the life cycle, shifting left is pulling that effort earlier in the life cycle (figure 1.4). This is by far the preferred method of development security because it is less expensive and more effective than resolving issues in production. However, it is more difficult to implement and can be bypassed by the organization rather quickly if the need arises.

Imagine building a house. You have an architectural drawing, a bill of materials, and the actual building materials. You get a group of laborers together, and you get to work building the house. It is far more preferable to put the locks on the windows and doors, build the egress window, and install smoke alarms while you're building the house. Waiting until the house is built, or after the house has been robbed, or burned down, is too late. Yes, you will save time and money during the building process, but you are less secure for it. This example sounds silly when stated, but the reality is that this routinely happens in software development. Sometimes it is because newer security

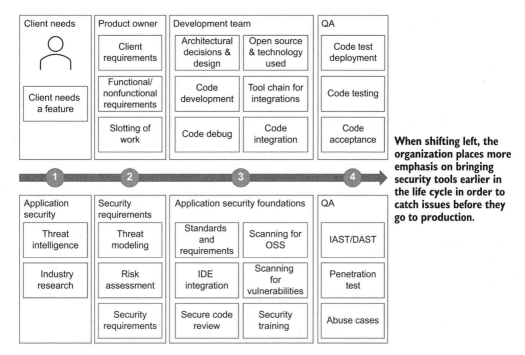

Figure 1.4 Shows the security tools that are used in a shift-left approach

patterns and architecture are discovered after the software is built, but it is commonly due to the lack of building security in at the beginning.

It is far more practical to layer in security throughout the development process, starting with the design decisions being made and requirements being gathered. When this approach is taken, the organization is taking the necessary steps to build better habits and have longer-lasting impacts. Take into consideration your personal health. Studies have shown that adjusting habits rather than going for a quick-fix diet is not only healthier for you but also provides a more sustainable path to better health. Shifting left builds those healthy security habits that will ensure the organization is on the right footing and can sustain a more secure overall posture.

A healthy secure development environment starts with making the right architecture and design decisions that take security into consideration. This means picking the right security controls in areas like session management, encryption, authorization, and the like. It also includes leveraging tried-and-true patterns and standards from well-regarded and vetted organizations like OWASP. For instance, the time for picking the right data protection scheme should be determined while architecture decisions around data flow and database technology are being made. Requirements for the encryption strategy should be well documented and provide the appropriate level of protection based on the data classification. Additionally, requirements like field-level encryption with proper encryption key life cycle management are much easier to develop before there is terabytes of data in the database that would require applying encryption to a large dataset. Where this can get complicated is with legacy applications where most organizations cannot provide encryption beyond the disk level due to older technology that may not support more granular, robust, and modern encryption. This is simply due to the fact that the application may never have been designed to work with encrypted data.

Even the language that is chosen can impact how secure an application will be. There are literally hundreds of development languages that developers can choose from, each with their own strengths and weaknesses for the given use cases. However, many modern languages provide some guardrails that can keep developers from producing insecure code. For instance, it should be no surprise that Java and C++ tend to rise to the top when it comes to vulnerable code. Much of this can be attributed to the power in each of these languages and the ability for developers to shoot themselves in the foot.

NOTE One of the most common issues with powerful languages like C++ is its ability to manually manage memory. Most modern languages will take this ability away from the developer as a convenience. One specific example with C++ is the ability to `call free()`, which allows the developer to free a memory address. If this is called twice with the same memory address, this becomes a doubly freeing issue. An attacker is able to leverage the memory leak that is made and inject code, possibly allowing the attacker to have an interactive shell with elevated privileges.

Additionally, these languages are widely used in billions of devices across the globe. An increased footprint means more opportunity to find security issues, as depicted in figure 1.5. Other languages such as Python, Ruby, and Go show fewer overall vulnerabilities but there are also fewer lines of code written in these languages.

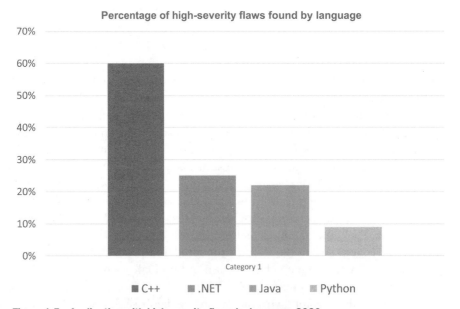

Figure 1.5   Application with high-severity flaws by language 2020

As much as language and design choices have an impact in the shift-left strategy, so, too, does testing. Unit, QA, integration, and system test can all be used to identify security issues early in the life cycle and allow time for the development team to correct an issue before it goes out to a production environment. This does assume that the appropriate security tests have been created, ideally automated, and are alerting the team when an issue is found. It further assumes that the findings do not disappear into the security vulnerability abyss of a backlog.

We will talk more about shifting left in the coming chapters, including items like threat modeling, measuring risk, creating abuse cases, using development tools, raising awareness and more. Make no mistake, shifting left is the most cost-effective and sustainable method of bringing application security to an organization near you.

1.4.4   *Shifting left fails*

Often, one or two members of a development team are designated as the "security person" (we won't call them champions; that comes later) for the team, with whom much of the security-related work is dumped. This person becomes responsible for being at the meetings where security decisions are being made, they perform code reviews on security-related changes, they have to make decisions for the team, and they are generally responsible for correcting or setting a direction on vulnerability management. By the way, this person also has a day job that is usually as a developer or architect for the team. They may not even want the role of the "security person," but they may have been voluntold. This has a huge impact not just on that individual but also on the team as a whole. This person is quickly overwhelmed without much opportunity for rest or objection.

This is generally where things like vulnerability management falls apart. A new vulnerability is discovered in one of the security tools, or in a penetration test. The vulnerability is placed in the defect-tracking tool and assigned to the security person, who then puts aside the regular development work that they were possibly working on to triage the security issue and attempt to resolve it. Meanwhile, several other vulnerabilities have been identified, building the security debt we talked about earlier. This is usually when the product owner, scrum master, or development manager comes in asking why a development deliverable is behind.

This type of failure has been seen several times in the past. One of the recent high-profile cases was with the Equifax breach that led to the exposure of over 143 million Americans' personal and financial information. Equifax is one of the big three credit bureaus in the United States providing consumer credit reporting to Americans. In March of 2017, a vulnerability was found in Apache Struts, a framework for developing web applications. A patch was released, and most organizations set out patching their software. This is generally easier said than done, as some framework upgrades may need additional development changes and testing. In worst cases, an application may need to be re-architected or have major development work completed. By May of 2017, two months after Apache released a patch, attackers had gained access to the

Equifax database and began to steal information. Equifax became aware of the breach in July. There were several failures in the security organization that led to the exposure of personally identifiable information (PII). Although the issue was internally identified, the email notifications for the known issue went to an old distribution list and therefore were never picked up by the appropriate team. Additionally, the databases were not segmented from the remaining network, allowing the attackers to pivot to other servers, where they found unencrypted credentials allowing them to escalate the attack.

It's easy for us to sit back and pick apart the lack of patching and other security controls in this case. However, two months from initial disclosure to exploit is a short window for many organizations. Some of these same organizations may have technology running that hasn't been patched in a much longer time frame. More importantly, the time to exploit these days is much shorter, where attackers are able to gather enough information to reverse-engineer patches and build exploits in days or even hours. But the security person in the development team has the responsibility to jockey with the rest of the features that are slotted for a release and ensure that the application is protected. Given that the Apache Struts vulnerability was only two months old when it was exploited, there were most likely older and more critical vulnerabilities that were already on the team's plate, ensconcing this Struts vulnerability in the annals of security history. This also highlights the earlier fact that every company is a software company. Equifax is not a technology company by trade but yet they find themselves in the software business due to being powered by layers of software that enable them and their customers.

1.5   *Is going left better than going right?*

As I mentioned, shifting security to the left will result in better outcomes for an organization. It allows the development teams to build a culture of security that is more sustainable and able to manage the "when" not "if" of security vulnerabilities that are sure to be introduced. No software in any organization can be written to be 100% secure for all time. There will be vulnerabilities. The organization needs to have the culture, processes, people, and technology in place to manage this.

There is no wrong or right (no pun intended) way of approaching application security. The people, process, and technology related to application security is needed throughout the life cycle regardless of the stage and its purpose. To put it into context, let me describe two different organizations and their approaches to application security.

The first organization, called Acme Services, has decided to engage the application security team prior to release to perform simple scanning and penetration testing to determine whether there are any vulnerabilities introduced into the product during development. This is the shift-right approach that has been described previously. The second company, Superior Products, knows that bringing in security earlier is not just easier, but is also more cost-effective than waiting until later. They requested that the application security team be engaged earlier. Even better, they have a security champion, Dashing Danielle, on their team who can provide guidance throughout the development process.

Superior Products has a mature application security team that keeps their finger on the pulse of the security industry. They've integrated a security champions team across the organization and maintain open communication with that team to ensure that they are kept informed of changes in the industry. With this information and structure, they are able to perform threat intelligence that informs decisions on new requirements and technology. In many cases, this allows them to implement security features ahead of client requests to do so. Acme Services is often caught off guard by requests for stricter security and privacy from their clients because they have decided to take the approach of implementing security later in the process.

Superior Products employs Dashing Danielle to review the use cases that come in from product ownership. She is able to perform a quick threat model on the feature to determine the open security concerns that impact the feature. Based on a risk assessment that she has done previously with the product and the application security team, she knows that the application and the information in the report is considered sensitive information for the organization. This means that she will want to create security requirements that maintain the confidentiality of the information that is contained with the data and ensure that access is limited to a small audience of users within the appropriate organization.

Dashing Danielle is able to raise these questions about the access to the reports during the review of the user stories and requirements based on the information she has. After she speaks with the application security team on what she feels are concerns with the new feature, she presents the following requirements that help protect the data in the generated reports as well as maintain access control:

- *Security requirement*—Application shall ensure that access to the report is limited to authenticated users of the organization that the report belongs to.
- *Security requirement*—Application shall log information related to the admin accounts that create and change the reports.

The development team agrees that these are important requirements and are capable of making them a reality without impacting the release time frame for the product feature. Dashing Danielle supports the development team in whiteboarding the workflow so that the requirements are clear and understood by the development team. Figure 1.6 shows how Dashing Danielle is able to take the product requirements along with her understanding of security to create security requirements.

Over at Acme Services, one of the developers raises some concerns about whether unauthenticated users could access the report. This is quickly dismissed since the product owner promised this feature in a short time window, and the development team doesn't know whether the data in the reports is actually considered sensitive. Everyone shrugs and moves on.

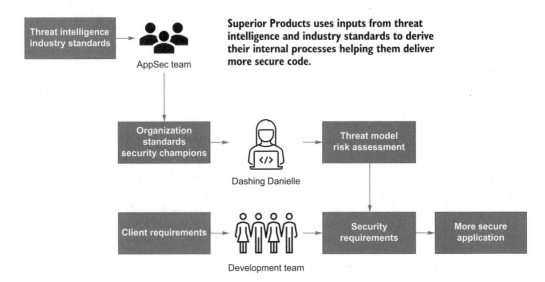

Figure 1.6   Superior Products' path to more secure code

This is a pretty clear distinction of where application security works and where it doesn't. It may seem like this story is far-fetched, but please understand that this type of story is typical. Picking up this book means that you want to be more like Superior Products.

1.6   *Application security needs you!*

It takes a village to do anything worthwhile. Security is no different. Generally, security teams are a slim percentage of the overall organization and rely mostly on automation and the goodwill of the engineering organization that it works with in order to scale to meet the demands. There is no "correct" size of the application security team, but size is not indicative of effectiveness. The variance in the size of application security to engineers varies from organization to organization.

> **DEFINITION**   Building Security in Maturity Model (BSIMM) is a study on the posture of software security initiatives and programs by quantifying the application security practices of different organizations across industries, sizes, and geographies. I will cover BSIMM more in-depth in chapter 5.

The BSIMM study defines the software security group (SSG) as the team that is focused on software security within an organization. They found that an SSG group can be as large as 160 or as small as 1 with the average size of the team being 13.9 people. This of course depends on the size of the organization and the amount of coverage that the software security group needs to manage. And it's no surprise that application security continues to be a smaller part of the overall engineering organization when you see the total spend for security relative to the overall IT budget. In most cases this is around 5% to 6%, based on a Gartner study in 2019 (http://mng.bz/Ayeo). Application security is yet a smaller portion of that security budget since much of the funding goes to perimeter defense, as well as to detection and response capabilities.

> ### Exercise 1.2
> Take a look at BSIMM's website for SSDL Touchpoints:
>
> http://mng.bz/95v7
>
> Based on what I've described about shifting left and shifting right, these touchpoints are all part of the shift-left model. If you were in an organization with a limited budget, where do you think the best place to put your and your team's focus in order to build security into the development life cycle? Think about the implications of the architecture analysis. This takes resources to be on the ground level. Security testing can scale but can be expensive and take time to implement.

1.6.1 Democratizing application security

Application security is less about a dedicated team and more about building the habits, culture, and infrastructure to support secure development. An application security team, regardless of size, relies heavily on others within the development organization to socialize and promote security within the broader organization. It is not possible for an application security team that is relatively small to be able to be integrated with every development team and be a part of every design decision. Without this borrowing of resources from the development organization, application security would rarely be integrated. It is critical for the advancement of application security to be able to find allies, build trust, and democratize security with the overall engineering organization. Throughout this book I will outline the methods used to achieve that advancement; however, to be clear, application security requires a culture of security and requires buy-in at all levels.

> **NOTE** It is important to remember that there are teams within the organization that are dedicated to security, whether formally part of the security organization, or security champions who are dispersed across the engineering teams. However, the organization will still require help from those who are not formally part of security. This means that resolving vulnerabilities, ensuring that security is designed into the application, and ensuring that architecture includes security best practices and that the formal security team is brought in at appropriate times rests on the engineering teams.

The critical part here is the helpers. Some organizations call them *champions*, *evangelists*, or *coaches*. The theme is the same regardless of what they are called. We will talk more about a champions program in future chapters; however, the basic principle is that these champions are the connection between the engineering organization and the application security program. They are there to represent the interests of the application security program and to ensure that security standards, designs, and architecture are properly implemented in the areas that they represent. The champion is usually a senior or well-seasoned engineering resource within an application or business unit and comes from within the engineering organization. It is important for the champion to be there because they want to, and not because they have to since a successful champion will be one who appreciates security.

These champions help the application security team advance security by being present where the application security team cannot be. Many decisions get made at the stand-ups, in the hallways, or in impromptu conversations between developers. Having eyes and ears that are closer to where the code is developed helps ensure that security is considered in every part of the software development life cycle.

One condition of a successful democratization of application security is to ensure that these champions are well versed in the organization's security culture; know where to find information related to requirements, standards, and architecture; and can ultimately feel comfortable speaking for the application security team. There may even be a formal training and assessment program before a champion can assume the role. To ensure these champions have the information that they need to be successful, the application security team needs to publicize their documentation and guidance and review and gain consensus on new items with the champions on a regular basis. This can be done in a formal, reoccurring forum, or through electronic forums. It depends on the organization's culture and the most practical way of reaching an audience.

1.6.2   *Users will be users*

Champions are not enough to augment the application security team. It's not that rare to hear a developer, an end user, a leader, or other technologist say, "We have a security team for that." We can build all the technical security controls into a system, but once a user contacts a system, an element of unpredictability is introduced. Users want to get their job done or find a way to complete some activity. We have all been in the situation where we were halted by system limitations due to security controls. Most of us do not throw up our hands and walk away. We look for other ways to complete what we set out to do. Users are doing the same thing with the applications you are building—they look for ways to accomplish their work, regardless of whether the application allows it. Additionally, malicious users are probing the application looking for weaknesses. They are not staying within the confines of the application that you developed. In fact, they are looking to do the exact opposite of what your application is designed to do in order to create an error condition that they can take advantage of. Application security is always working to keep up with the curious user and the malicious attacker, and no amount of tools will give us the level of comfort we are looking for. It requires a village dedicated to the security of the application that is devoted to building a secure application from the start.

I stated at the beginning that every company is a software company, which means that every company needs some level of software security. Likewise, software security is everyone's problem. This is a pretty common refrain, but what does this actually mean?

This is similar to the public service announcements urging people that if they "see something, say something." This doesn't mean that a traveler should attempt to open a bag that they find in an airport terminal that has wires hanging out of it and is beeping. This means that the traveler should alert the nearest authority so that they may investigate. Nobody in security is asking for an end user to triage an SQL injection flaw in a web application and write code to resolve it. They're simply asking to alert the nearest champion or security personnel. Leave the bomb disposal to the professionals!

1.7 Examples of failing to secure the software

The news is littered with examples of failures in security where applications were compromised for a slew of different reasons. The point of covering some examples is not so we can point and laugh at these organizations, but rather to focus on the how and why. Trust me, if your organization sells or uses software, it's not a question of *if* but *when* you will encounter a security incident. It might be a small and nonreportable event, but your organization will have a software security incident somewhere, sometime.

> ### Exercise 1.3
> Go to your favorite search engine and look up articles on the latest security breach. You can also go to sites like www.threatpost.com or www.securityweek.com for recent stories. I'm pretty sure that if you don't see one for today, you'll at least see one for this week. Dig into the article and put yourself in the shoes of the security organization. How would you have responded? Speculate on where things went wrong if they are not spelled out in the article. I often look at these stories and ask myself, "How could my team or I have avoided this?"

1.7.1 SolarWinds

SolarWinds was a chilling example that showed how a complex ecosystem of software, and the various components that make up that software, can lead to a massive and impactful breach. This type of compromise is commonly called a *supply-chain attack* for good reason. Attackers can compromise just one component used to build the overall software and have their malicious payload spread far and wide. This takes advantage of a fundamental complication with the supply chain, in that there is inherent trust between the developer of the primary software and the third-party software that is used to build the final product.

SolarWind's Orion product is a monitoring solution that is used to monitor an organization's network and applications. At the time of the attack in 2020, SolarWinds was being used by a majority of the top organizations across the United States, including most of the Fortune 500 companies, universities, many of the top government agencies, and the military.

Attackers were able to modify a plug-in called `SolarWinds.Orion.Core.Business-Layer.dll`. The attackers used a tool called SUNSPOT that allowed them to inject a malicious version of the `dll` and was digitally signed by SolarWinds and sent to thousands of customers. The malicious `dll` contained SUNBURST, which allowed the attackers to communicate with command and control (C2) servers. The attackers went to great pains to hide their activity by lying in wait for a period of time before retrieving and executing commands and by masquerading as legitimate Orion traffic and using block lists to identify forensic and antivirus tools so they could evade them.

Once the plug-in was within a target system, it would use a delete-create-execute-delete-create pattern that would hijack a legitimate task, run malicious activity, and then revert back to the legitimate task. This type of sophistication further shows how far the attackers went to keep their activity quiet.

The campaign went on for several months before it was eventually detected when the attackers compromised FireEye, one of the leading cybersecurity companies. The attackers gained access to FireEye's attack simulation and other security-related tools but were spotted, which led to the detection of the more widespread activity.

Attacks that are this sophisticated are difficult to defend against. Encrypting there and scrubbing here will not suffice. The vigilance of FireEye, the ability for SolarWinds to rapidly produce a patch, and the impacted organization's aggressive patch management shows how our digital world has changed to where we can no longer rely on putting our efforts into protecting our software; we need to pivot to a world where we always assume breach. It's how we respond and, more importantly, how rapidly we respond when something malicious is detected that makes the difference.

1.7.2   *Accellion*

For those of us who own a home or any other type of item that requires maintenance and constant attention, we sometimes willingly walk past that noisy appliance or creaky door thinking that one day we'll fix it.

Software is little different. There are many reasons to keep old software running. Clients insist on continuing to integrate with older software and make it difficult for organizations to decommission it. Organizations hold on to old software because it's cheaper to keep it running than to upgrade or replace it. Regardless of the reason, old software is prevalent in almost all organizations.

Accellion develops software for health care, financial, and education organizations. Their File Transfer Appliance (FTA) product is used by health care organizations to perform large file transfers. The product was almost 20 years old and nearing end of life when it was the target of a cyberattack at the end of 2020. The attackers first stole data from Accellion and then pivoted to attack Accellion clients directly with the goal of stealing data and extorting money. The initial attack was leveraged using an SQL injection attack against the document_root.html file, which allowed them to retrieve keys to generate legitimate access tokens. These tokens were then used to access the sftp_account_edit.php file, where the attacker was able to then exploit an OS command injection that allows the attacker to make commands to the host system. This last piece gave the attackers the ability to create a shell. The attackers at this point had the ability to upload more sophisticated tools and begin siphoning information and pivoting to customer servers.

Accellion's health care clients were left to notify the affected patients, the media, and the Department of Health and Human Services due to the HIPAA Breach Notification Rule. Lawsuits followed, and in the end, nearly 3.5 million patients had their protected health information (PHI) stolen. What made matters worse was the attackers then sent threatening emails to students at UC Davis after the university discovered that their information was part of the breach.

The impact of an organization's inability to decommission old software is wide. It is also not rare for organizations to be mostly running the latest and greatest version of software but have one client running a version of software that is several versions back. This is a failure of product ownership to move clients forward and leaves both the organization and the customers they provide service to at risk. It is critical for an organization to have, and stick to, a sunset and end-of-life policy. Two key takeaways are

- Decommission of software is the final stage of the software life cycle.
- Remember that technical debt is security debt.

FUN FACT Microsoft announced the end-of-life date for Windows 7 as January 14, 2020. When January 2020 came, the much-loved OS was still being used on 39% of PCs. Many speculate this was due to the lack of desire for end users to move to Windows 10. This shows that even Microsoft has issues coaxing users to newer versions. Instead, they take a more forceful approach by eliminating patches for the older versions. Even then, this doesn't stop users from using it, and Microsoft even allows users and corporations to pay a fee to continue to receive updates.

1.7.3 *Fake software*

SolarWinds showed how attackers can take advantage of the trust between components that are used to build a final product. However, this story is not unusual. Attackers are always looking for ways to get software into the supply chain in order to maximize their reach. Why try to compromise one organization by specifically targeting them when you can get into the supply chain and compromise multiple organizations?

There are other ways into the supply chain—bigger ways if you can believe it. In 2021, two students from the University of Minnesota released a research paper on what they called "hypocrite commits." These commits were supposedly intended to provide value to the Linux kernel but instead introduced critical issues—sort of like when your parents would hide vegetables in your meals to get you to eat them. Maybe you do this to your kids too. There is no shame in that!

This sort of commit was not well received, not only from Linux, but also from the broader security and engineering community. The Linux kernel is used by billions of systems around the world, from the smallest to largest computers. The two students' actions led to the ban of the university from contributing to the Linux kernel in the future. They also had their previous commits to Linux revoked.

The open source community depends on the submission of high-quality, well-vetted, and good-faith commits to its open branches. Although the example of what the two students from the university were able to accomplish shows that this system can be abused.

The explosion of open source software that is used to build an overall application further exacerbates this exposure for organizations. According to the Sonatype "State of the Software Supply Chain Report" in 2020, 1.5 trillion open source software components and containers will be requested by developers. Most software is an amalgamation of third-party libraries, code from software forums, and hand-coded logic by a small group of software engineers and architects. Per Synopsys's "Open Source Security and Risk Analysis" report in 2020, 70% of an average application is made up of open source software. Reliance on the third-party software leads to exposure to malicious actors getting into the supply chain and adding nefarious code. Organizations that have this level of third-party, open source software need to take a defensive approach to managing their SBOM (software bill of material).

> **DEFINITION** The SBOM is a list of components that are used to build an overall software product. This can be mix of open source and COTS (commercial off-the-shelf) software. In May of 2021, the White House released an executive order that specifically called out SBOM management as a key capability of an organization's cybersecurity. In the executive order, the White House requires the provision of an SBOM when purchasing software and requires particular agencies to publish an SBOM for their software.

Managing the security of an organization's supply chain can be done through the scanning of third-party libraries for vulnerabilities, only using libraries from a reputable source, and maintaining a robust patch management program that allows them to rapidly patch a vulnerable library as soon as a vulnerability has been identified.

Summary

- Application security teams are generally invited late to the party, which leads to findings that get moved to a backlog.
- This backlog continues to grow as security debt.
- Scanning tools used by the application security team are generally detection tools and do not remediate or block bad code.
- Protection tools can be enabled but are sometimes hard to sell to engineering due to concerns with blocking legitimate traffic.
- Shifting right will catch defects late, while shifting left will find them earlier.
- Shifting left involves more than just training and champions.
- Fixing issues in production is significantly more expensive than fixing prior to production.

Defining the problem

This chapter covers
- Defining the security tenants that software must adhere to
- Identifying and understanding risk that impacts software
- Exploring security in the software development life cycle

In the previous chapter, I used the example of building a house without the locks on the doors and windows. A house is a great example, as it allows you to think about the controls you use to limit your risk of the house being compromised due to break-in, fire, flooding, and so forth. We spend most of our time in security attempting to limit risk and counter threats, not eliminate them. A *risk* is the potential for loss of an asset or damage to an asset, whereas a *threat* is the activity that takes advantage of a weakness in an asset. Risk and threats can never be eliminated. Similar to a house, we can't eliminate the risk of fire, flood, or a break-in; we can only detect and respond while attempting to limit the risk and impact. To be clear, risk can never be eliminated, only reduced.

> **NOTE** In the case of a house fire, the fire is the threat, while the house burning down is the risk.

Whereas fire, flood, and break-in are risks that impact a house, our software has a different set of threats and risks. These range from the physical to the digital. Yes, physical threats exist that impact our software; a flood in a data center would be a physical risk to our running application.

In this chapter we will not dive into the various specific methods of protection, but rather outline the different places where our software and data need to be protected and some best practices to look out for.

2.1   The CIA triad

There are three basic tenets in security that all protection mechanisms that we integrate into our systems and software will come back to. It's commonly referred to as the *CIA triad—confidentiality*, *integrity*, and *availability*.

- *Confidentiality*—Protect data and allow only those who should have access.
- *Integrity*—Data is known to be correct and trusted.
- *Availability*—Systems and data should be available when requested by a trusted entity.

Most people in the security field are pretty familiar with these concepts, but I will provide further definition here to provide common ground for future topics in this book.

2.2   Confidentiality

Perhaps the most important security design consideration you can make when developing software is *confidentiality*, where you are designing the software to provide optimal protection of data. The reality is that this is much more difficult than it sounds. As I mentioned, data is the new commodity. This means that it is everywhere. Software may be processing data that it is not the custodian of.

> **NOTE**   Data custodians are responsible for the collection, processing, storage, and implementation of business rules related to the data.

Some data is transient, some data is not persistent in a system and resides in memory for only a period of time. Figure 2.1 uses a simple data flow diagram (DFD) to show you how data moves through your system and others.

As you can see in figure 2.1, once the customer completes an order, a series of other processes will coordinate with the payment company, process the order, and store the data. At each point, the protection of that data is paramount, especially if it is sensitive data like payment information. Today, we have methods to protect this information, primarily through encryption at rest when it resides in a database or other system, encryption in transit as it moves over the network, and encryption in use as it is processed in memory. These methods allow us to provide some protection of data as it traverses our systems, and in some cases even the services that your software sends data to.

Data flows through an example e-commerce site

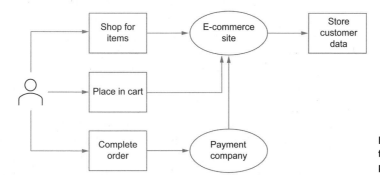

Figure 2.1   A basic data flow diagram (DFD) for purchasing online

2.2.1   *Data protection policy*

The first step an organization needs to take to maintain data protection is to create and maintain a policy that clearly outlines what data must be encrypted. Most organizations will call this their data protection policy and will define what data needs to be protected but will not get into the *how*, aside from a high-level direction. The data defined in this policy will follow the organization's data classification scheme (more on that later) and call out that data must be encrypted, and access is limited to only required personnel. Most policies will additionally include the following:

- Clear definition of what must be done at each location that data can reside, such as file system, end user devices, databases, and others
- Definition of the encryption key life cycle such as creation, distribution, and destruction
- Definition of algorithms for hashing and encryption
- Auditing of access to encryption keys

Once this policy is established, the organization can get to the business of mapping encryption standards and architecture to this policy but must give thought to two primary considerations when developing these standards and architecture:

- Although encryption provides extra protection, there is additional time that is incurred when you need to access a key, encrypt data, and send it on its way. This latency is usually measured in milliseconds, but for critical applications, this additional time needs to be considered.
- The system must also ensure that it is resilient enough to be able to overcome an outage that may occur due to the encryption keys being unavailable, or a failure in the encryption or decryption process such as the cryptographic service being offline.

This adds an additional layer of operational complexity and potential exposure to an availability issue and must be considered.

2.2.2   *Data at rest*

One of the first steps to protecting data at rest is to recognize that you have a problem—a data inventory problem. Put simply, data inventory is the ability to know where data is located in an organization. During a security incident, an organization needs to be able to know what data may have been compromised and whether there is a risk related to the data that was compromised. Is it critical client information that was on that database that was just breached? If this can't be answered, then there is a gap in understanding where the data is and what the nature of that data is. Review figure 2.1 again: Do you know what is happening to that information that is passed between your application and the payment company? Do you know whether they are sharing data with others, knowingly or not? Do you or the consumers of your application have a policy that disallows developers to copy data from a production environment to a lower environment? If so, is it enforced?

These examples are not intended to frighten, but to bring awareness to the fact that data is everywhere and that the first step in securing this data is to get an inventory. For smaller organizations, this can be done by keeping a catalog of data, location, and classification in a spreadsheet or database. More on classification in a bit.

For larger organizations, a tool may be more appropriate that can actively scan for data, classify it based on the organization's rules, and provide reporting and dashboards to track the organization's overall data. However, regardless of how you identify your data, there are still fundamental steps in order to have a robust data inventory, including the following:

1. Create an inventory using an automated tool or the manual process described previously.
2. Data inventory needs to include all data, structured and unstructured, across on-premises, cloud, and third-party locations.
3. De-duplicate the data and ensure accuracy.
4. Ensure that the inventory is maintained and kept up-to-date through the tools and processes used to initially gather the data.

Although there are tools available to assist with collecting a data inventory, creating this inventory is more of an organization and process problem than a technology problem. In lieu of a tool, one method is through surveys or questionnaires that are used to determine the type, classification, and location of the data. These questionnaires are simple in nature and should be completed by the data custodian who is responsible for the technical implementation and maintenance of data within the system. Each organization should create its own survey that attempts to determine the type of data that is moving through the system and should focus on the sensitivity of the data that aligns to the classification that the organization uses. They are also responsible for ensuring that this survey is kept up-to-date as the architecture changes and can incorporate that update during the development process. A sample of what a questionnaire might contains follows.

Does the application retain payment card information?	Y/N	If yes, list the locations where the data is stored.	Data encrypted at rest?
Does the application retain social security numbers?	Y/N	If yes, list the locations where the data is stored.	Data encrypted at rest?
Does the application retain protected health information?	Y/N	If yes, list the locations where the data is stored.	Data encrypted at rest?

If your organization is like many large organizations today, there will be a data lake or data warehouse that is a single location for most of your structured and unstructured data that all of the organization's applications can leverage. This certainly makes things much easier when attempting to locate and classify data considering that it is centralized and easier to apply tooling or processes to collect where sensitive data is located. In fact, many cloud providers offer the ability to automatically identify and classify data through the services they offer in their ecosystem.

> **NOTE** Macie is a service offered by Amazon Web Services (AWS) that uses techniques like machine learning and artificial learning to detect sensitive data in AWS. Currently it has some limitations on where it can find data within its services, but this is expected to improve over time.

However, there will always be legacy systems that are disconnected from the data lake and applications that need to maintain local copies of data in order to operate. It is hard to imagine any large organization having their data exclusively in a central location. This means that the organization will still have to rely on questionnaires or on-premises tools to locate and classify data.

Regardless of how an organization inventories data, it then needs to classify it. This allows the organization to provide the appropriate level of protection based on the classification of the data. Although it varies depending on the industry and needs, most organizations will have four ways that they classify data (table 2.1).

Table 2.1 Basic data classification in most organizations

Classification type	Classification description
Public	This is freely accessible to anyone, including individuals who are external to the company. An example might be information in a marketing release.
Internal	This information is intended for just individuals internal to the organization. This doesn't classify the access based on role; the individual just has to be a part of the organization. This could include communications regarding business plans.
Confidential	This is information that is sensitive and requires authorization to access. For instance, certain data that is in an internal database like social security or account numbers would not be accessible to everyone in the organization and is limited to those that require access. This should be a very limited audience.
Restricted	This is critical information that could lead to severe damage to the organization should it be released. This is something like source code or other intellectual property.

Having this level of classification allows the organization to apply, broadly, encryption methods based on the classification. For instance, the organization may require that all confidential data be encrypted at rest and in transit and that all restricted data be shared only with a small audience of people in the organization with a need to know.

2.2.3 *Applying encryption*

So, you've identified where your data is located, and you've used the methods described previously to classify it. Now what?

Encryption

We will talk more about encryption as we progress, but a simple way to think about it is the ability to change plain text to cipher text through an algorithm with an encryption key. One main point to remember is that encryption is reversible so that either the same key or a paired key will be able to decrypt. This is by no means a book on encryption. Trust me, I can't explain it like a cryptographer. However, one of the preeminent books on encryption as it applies to engineering is Bruce Schneier's *Applied Cryptography* (Wiley, 1996). If you are looking for some more basic information regarding encryption, look at the Wikipedia page on encryption, which follows the history, future, and uses of encryption (https://en.wikipedia.org/wiki/Encryption).

To encrypt properly, you need a few things. You need an encryption and decryption key (sometimes the same key), a secure method to create an encryption key, a secure location to store the key, and a way to distribute and access the key in a programmatic way. Depending on the architecture and deployment of your application, the ability to securely generate and store a key may be limited. Most legacy systems are limited in their ability to store an encryption and decryption key. The key or keys are often stored in a configuration file, or worse, hardcoded in software. More modern architectures will take advantage of a hardware security module (HSM) that allows the application to make secure API calls to a physical device that stores encryption keys and can be configured to auto expire, rotate, and generate keys as shown in figure 2.2.

Encrypting data with an HSM

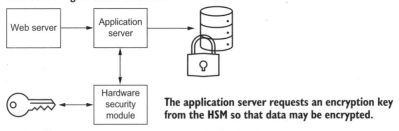

Figure 2.2 HSM in a simple workflow to encrypt a database

Today, many organizations are under regulatory or contractual obligations to provide better encryption methods such as the use of an HSM to encrypt sensitive data and even allow for their customers to manage their own keys. However, although an HSM will provide the highest level of secure access to data encryption and decryption keys, they are expensive and can be a single point of failure if the hardware becomes unavailable. There are cloud HSMs that are available that can reduce the need for the organization to maintain expensive hardware, but be aware that prices can vary and can increase as you add more encryption keys under management.

> **Exercise 2.1**
> Go through the assignment on symmetric encryption and get familiar with the way a single key can be used to encrypt and decrypt data (http://mng.bz/yvlB).You should also go through the assignment on public key encryption to get familiar with key generation, as well as encryption and decryption using a key pair (http://mng.bz/M5NW.

Depending on your organization and the industry you are in, you will most likely have to encrypt at least restricted and confidential data. For instance, in financial organizations, datasets that contain account numbers, social security numbers, and similar data will have to be encrypted based on compliance requirements. In the health care industry, you will have to encrypt insurance information and patient record information. One of the considerations for these organization is that information could be located outside of a database and could instead be in unstructured data like text documents, PDFs, or image files. For instance, a printed form from your doctor's office may have your social security number and would be scanned and uploaded to a health information exchange (HIE). Organizations have a few options when dealing with structured and unstructured data encryption:

- Full-disk encryption to provide encryption of the disk that the data sits on. However, this does not give you more granular encryption at the file level.
- File-level encryption that encrypts the individual files that hold sensitive information like confidential and restricted data.
- Column- or row-level encryption that encrypts a set of data in a database like the social security number or account number column.

Proper application of encryption is not as easy as waving a wand. Based on the location of the data, the ability to encrypt might be limited or infeasible. Legacy systems often struggle to access more modern encryption technology like HSMs. However, the organization needs to constantly consider what might occur if data is exposed. This can happen physically when a database drive is improperly disposed of and falls into the wrong hands, or digitally through an insider or malicious activity that is able to access the data in the database through the system. Some examples of data escaping the organization are

- Improper destruction or retirement of old drives that contain sensitive data
- An insider of the organization having access to the database through improper access management
- An attacker gaining access to the host where the application database resides
- A developer copying data from a production database to their local environment or a lower test environment instead of using mock data that is more suited for these nonproduction environments

With the mind-set that the data in the organization could be exposed to an adversary at any time means that the organization has to ensure that they have applied the appropriate level of encryption based on the classification of the data. If the physical drive that the database is on or a device with access to the database falls into the wrong hands, does the organization have enough confidence that its security controls will work? Can an adversary or competitor access the data on that database, or has the organization applied the proper level of encryption so that it cannot be accessed?

In addition to proper encryption techniques, the organization needs to ensure that there are proper access controls around the data at rest and access controls to the keys that can encrypt and decrypt. If a user has access to the database management tools, they will most likely have access to view the plain text of the data in the database. Additionally, if a user has access to the encryption or decryption keys, they are also able to view this data or encrypt data as if they were a legitimate service. Traceability of these sensitive activities can be met by using tools that provide access to the privileged account while also providing auditing capability. Usually, the auditing within the tool is completed through screen activity captures, keystroke logging, and auto filling passwords so that it's not accessible to the end user. In this scenario, an organization will know who performed sensitive activity and, more importantly, what they did while provided that access.

2.2.4   *Data in transit*

The job of protecting information would be much easier if we had to protect data only when it is sitting nice and still in a database or a filesystem. The reality is that data moves. In fact, the exchange of data is a way for organizations to make money. It's how organizations gain competitive advantages. In short, data needs to be in motion in order to be profitable.

It wasn't that long ago that most websites were using basic HTTP or FTP to transmit data. Using plain HTTP or FTP means that as the data moves from one location to another, it is in plain text and open to view by anyone who has access to see the traffic, as described in figure 2.3. Secure Sockets Layer (SSL) was the first attempt to bring encryption to data in transit, turning HTTP to HTTP over SSL (HTTPS). Although version 1.0 was never released due to security concerns, 2.0 was released in 1995. Since then, we have had many versions of SSL and then Transport Layer Security (TLS) replaced SSL. TLS is primarily used to protect HTTP and FTP traffic.

HTTPS ensures that an eavesdropper cannot read traffic to a web server

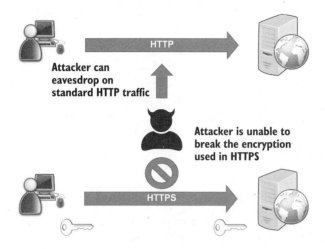

Attacker can
eavesdrop on
standard HTTP traffic

Attacker is unable to
break the encryption
used in HTTPS

Figure 2.3
HTTP vs. HTTPS

Prior to the time when everything was HTTPS, sites used the secure transit only during sensitive activities like login. Today, almost every website you go to is now TLS enabled, and you will be redirected to HTTPS if you attempt to go to a site with just HTTP. Several factors played into the adoption of TLS. The browsers played a large role in this as they began to mark sites "insecure" if they did not use TLS or even if they used a known weak version of TLS. Additionally, security over the years has become not just an obscure corner of an organization, but increasingly a concern for everyday users. Users may not know, or want to know, how TLS works. But they do want to know that when they input their credit card number into a website, that the number will be protected. Most users today are becoming accustomed to making sure that they see some version of a padlock or other indicator that the site they are on is using a secure connection.

Although the versions and ciphers associated with TLS often change as new vulnerabilities are discovered, TLS is easily enabled. This is completed through a simple configuration in the web server and a signed digital certificate from a trusted certificate authority (CA).

> **DEFINITION**   A public and private key pair, also known as *asymmetric key pair*, is a set of digital keys that are used to encrypt and decrypt data. These keys are generated together, but one is intended to be kept secret and private, where the other is used publicly. They are used to encrypt and decrypt and to provide digital signatures.

A private and public key pair is generated on the web server. The private key is retained by the web server and, ideally, never leaves the server. The public key is used to create a certificate signing request (CSR) that is then passed to the CA to sign with their private key. The product of this is a public certificate that is used to show that the web server has control of their private key and has been verified by the CA (figure 2.4).

Generating a certificate signing request

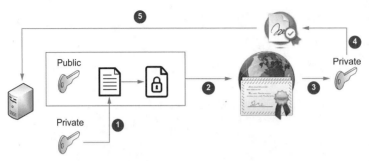

1. **Host creates a private and public key.**
2. **Host creates a signing request and signs it with the private key.**
3. **Host sends signed request to a certificate authority (CA).**

4. **CA signs the request with their private key.**
5. **CA returns the signed request as a public certificate.**

Figure 2.4   Generating a certificate for HTTPS using Entrust as the CA

Once this certificate is signed, it is used to announce to any user agent, like a web browser or command-line HTTP tool, that they can trust the web server. The user agent will look in its trust store and determine whether the certificate authority that signed the certificate can be trusted. If the certificate is signed by a well-known CA, the browser will already have a trust relationship and will accept that the web server is trusted. In some cases, if it is not a well-known CA, the user agent needs to establish the trust by placing the certificates in its trust store.

Certificate management is fun . . . said nobody ever. As you can tell, enabling TLS can be mostly simple, but there are operational costs. Similar to the key management problems discussed earlier, certificates have a life cycle and need to be renewed or replaced periodically. Additionally, some of the fundamental underpinnings of the technology can occasionally change and lead to the need to make drastic changes. In fact, in 2016, browsers began to display security warnings for certificates that were generated using the SHA-1 hashing algorithm with users being able to click through the message and continue to the site. By the end of 2018, browsers like Chrome were alerting users that they would disallow access to sites using the less secure SHA-1 at the beginning of 2019.

I had the pleasure of leading a project at a large organization with the directive to update all the certificates we had to SHA-2. This was no small task. Identifying all the use cases where these certifications were used—like single sign-on SAML certificates, TLS, FTP, digital signing, and others—was difficult. Additionally, locating where these certificates were stored was a further complication. They are found on filesystems, key stores, web servers, and databases. Changing them without creating an outage required tight coordination between the development, security, client, and operational teams. Inevitably, there were rollbacks when something did not go as planned.

Never fear, though, as with encryption keys, there are tools that can be used to manage, rotate, issue, and alert on the expiration of certificates. There are also protocols such as the Automated Certificate Management Environment (ACME) that can be used to create CSRs and manage keys and certificates. It is part of the business model for Let's Encrypt certificate authority, which allows them to issue certificates quickly and efficiently and provide short expirations of around 90 days. This short expiration date provides the ability for web servers to frequently change certificates and reduce the amount of time that a certificate is in circulation. Not that long ago, certificates would have an expiration of 5, 10, or even 30 years. For the sake of security, the industry has begun moving away from this practice and is looking for much shorter time frames to provide better security. This works effectively only if there is automation in place to make the rotation of expired certificates a smooth process.

2.2.5 *Encryption prior to transmission*

A method for ensuring that data is secure when sending between two organizations or two applications in an organization is to encrypt locally before sending the data. This does require the two parties to have either a shared encryption key that they have already determined or to use a key pair that allows one party to encrypt and the other to decrypt. The data will be transferred between the two entities and is protected regardless of whether it is transmitted over a nonsecure channel like HTTP. However, you still have a dependency on the key management. Transmitting the key opens each end to a possible compromise. Another consideration is if the key is compromised, there needs to be another exchange and rekeying effort by both entities.

PGP (pretty good privacy) is a well-known tool developed in 1991 that is used to provide encryption prior to transmission. It is now an encryption standard called OpenPGP and can be used for email and file transmission. PGP can use either a single encryption key or a private and public key pair. The latter offers the ability for two entities to send information to each other even if they never met or don't have the means to exchange a single key.

2.2.6 *Data in use*

While encryption in transit and rest get a lot of attention when it comes to protecting data, doing this for data in use is much more complex. Protection of data in use means when it is being accessed in nonpersistent states like memory or in the CPU. Additionally, this means that data is protected throughout its entire life cycle when combined with encryption of data at rest and transit. In general, well-designed systems will ensure that access to data in use is only accessible to the parts of the system that should have access. This will limit access to memory by malware and other processes. This should protect against not just writing and reading, but also executing of code when not allowed.

Many of the methods for protection are through the host level or operating system level controls like using segmentation, protection rings, or paged virtual memory. Additionally, address space layout randomization is set at the operating system level where memory is randomized to limit the ability of malicious activity from finding specific addresses to jump to.

Enclaves can be used at the system level that ensure the data in use is encrypted and available to the CPU or CPU cache only at read time, but at all other times it is encrypted and not readable to any other parts of the system. One other protection method worth mentioning is the ability for the CPU to manage encryption keys in a register as opposed to the keys being stored in RAM. This makes the window of opportunity smaller for an attacker or malicious code to access encryption keys.

2.2.7   *Not so confidential*

Hardly a day goes by where a breach or some type of cyber event occurs. A breach of confidentiality means that the data that was intended to stay confidential or restricted was released unintentionally. This can occur through malicious activity or accidental release.

Email is a quick and efficient method of leaking data. While information contained in an email can be concerning, it's also important to know that by most standards, an email address alone is considered PII. In February of 2020, the father of UK prime minister Boris Johnson caused a bit of an international stir when he accidentally copied the BBC on an email to British officials regarding the lack of contact between Boris Johnson and the Chinese state over the 2019 Novel Coronavirus (COVID-19) outbreak. Later that year, Australia's Department of Foreign Affairs and Trade exposed 1,000 citizens' personal data when an employee failed to use BCC to send information regarding emergency loans and reentry quotas for citizens stuck in other countries due to COVID-19 restrictions.

However, where email is an excellent avenue for leaking information, it tends to be smaller than the big breaches. In May of 2021, the company Peloton, which makes connected exercise equipment and is most famous for its high-end stationary bicycles, had to release a statement regarding an application program interface (API) that allowed anyone to pull private data from Peloton's servers, even if the user's profile was set to private. This API allowed unauthenticated access, meaning that you did not have to have an account or special access. Peloton initially only limited access to the API to users with a Peloton account; however, this only limited the audience, and anyone could sign up for a Peloton account and access the API to gather the personal information of other users. Eventually Peloton fully corrected the authentication issue, but they were not able to confirm or deny whether their over 3 million users had their data accessed or stolen due to the issue.

2.2.8   Do I even need this?

You may be familiar with Marie Kondo, who is famous for her show on Netflix called *Tidying Up with Marie Kondo*. She uses the KonMari Method to identify things that you should keep and things you should get rid of. Often, she asks the question: "Does this spark joy?" What does this have to do with security and specifically data security? One of the first things I usually ask when I get involved with reviewing security decisions and architecture that involves sensitive data is whether the data needs to actually be collected and retained. If you don't need to keep it or act upon it, then you don't need to worry about securing it. To be clear, securing it means more cost and effort. Something that not many product owners will be willing to spend if they don't need the data. Therefore, limiting the collection of this sensitive data is the best way to secure it. However, organizations and application development teams will err on the side of collecting more data because you may need it at some time, and storage is cheap.

Here are some questions that you need to ask regarding data:

- Do you need to store that data?
- Do you have regulations or contracts that require to maintain the data?
- Can you properly classify this data?
- Can you provide the appropriate level of protection for the collected data?
- Do you know when you no longer need it and can destroy it?

If you can answer these questions in the affirmative, then you are on the right path. If not, then follow the previous recommendations of classifying, inventorying, and encrypting the data.

> **Exercise 2.2**
>
> If you currently work on a development team or on a team that collects data, take a look at the database schema to identify at least one set of data, like a column in the database that contains sensitive information. Ask yourself or your team whether the data that is being collected is imperative to the operation of the application and whether or not having the data would impact the application. The answer might be yes—in fact, odds are it will be yes—but asking these questions regularly will get you into the habit of questioning whether you need to retain sensitive information.

2.3   Availability

Confidentiality takes the limelight when it comes to the CIA triad primarily because you can get the biggest bang for your buck by properly encrypting data. Availability sounds like something that is more for IT operations or site reliability engineering (SRE), which are primarily concerned with the uptime of the systems. The reality is that availability can be critical for applications where being down can be a matter of life and death. It's not hard to imagine scenarios where this is evident. Hospitals, emergency services, critical infrastructure, and so forth have high demands for uptime.

Not all uptime demands are for public safety. Organizations that are solely an online retailer stand to lose money should their systems be unavailable. In early 2021, Amazon was taking in roughly $830,000 per minute. It's pretty clear that an outage at Amazon would cost the company millions of dollars, depending on how long it persisted.

You may not be running Amazon or a hospital, but make no mistake that application uptime is still important for the organization and does have a financial impact. Organizations regularly report on their uptime, and it is a critical metric that needs to be met. Most organizations have contractual obligations that require them to meet service level agreements (SLAs) or penalties will be incurred, usually in the form of monetary compensation to the clients.

2.3.1   DoS and DDoS

Most people think of one thing when they hear about attacks that bring down a service or application. DoS, or denial of service, is an attack that purposely floods the service or application with a large number of requests. Its bigger brother is the DDoS, or distributed denial of service, where the requests are from many different sources instead of just one in the DoS model. The system is then overwhelmed and is unable to complete requests for other legitimate traffic. One of the greatest complications with protecting against DDoS attacks is that the traffic often looks legitimate, which makes the job of blocking this traffic difficult.

There is an old American television show called *I Love Lucy*. One of the most iconic episodes is when Lucy and her friend Ethel worked in a candy factory to make some money. They were assigned to the candy wrapping station where candy would pass by on a conveyor belt and the two would have to wrap each one. Naturally, at first the conveyor belt moved along at a reasonable pace, and the two friends were able to successfully wrap each piece of candy that went by. Soon the belt began to move much quicker, and with more candy. The two friends were quickly overwhelmed and began to stuff candy in their pockets and mouths while missing most of the candy that went by.

This is a simple example of a DoS attack, where the system can be tricked into accepting what appears to be normal traffic, at high volume, by a malicious actor. In other words, the candy coming down the belt is still legitimate and should be there, but the system setup to properly handle that candy is unable to handle the large amount being sent. Now, in this example, it's easy to laugh it off because it's a simple yet visually accurate example of a denial of service. In the real world, these attacks can be dire. Increasingly over the years these attacks have also grown in size. Early DDoS attacks were small in size and would use something like a SYN flood that would send a large number of TCP synchronize (SYN) packets without closing them out. It was simple, yet effective. More importantly, almost anyone could do this. Attacks today are much more sophisticated and larger, reaching over 2 terabits per second in some cases. To put that into perspective, that is 1,000,000,000,000 bits per second, or roughly 1,000 hours' worth of movies.

DDoS attacks are not limited to just network-level attacks. Layer 7, or application layer attacks, are common as well. These types of attacks are generally smaller in nature as they are targeted at disrupting the flow of the application or processing of data by going after the specific resources that serve up the application. This could be by targeting the database to make it unavailable or flooding the application with HTTP traffic that keeps it from processing legitimate requests from users.

2.3.2 Accidental outage

Not all availability issues are due to malicious activity. If the application is not built to be resilient, it is possible that something as benign as a software update could bring down an application. Other possible actions are system reboots, patches, or failed software installations. Most organizations will perform system maintenance during times where the client impact is low.

In 2019, while Britain was moving toward an exit from the European Union, many citizens of Britain who wanted to remain in the European Union attempted to sign a petition on the UK's Parliament website. The sudden spike in traffic that was unusual for the site presented many of the citizens with an HTTP 502 error signifying that the site was incapable of handling the large number of requests.

There are also cases where the protection mechanisms in use can create their own availability issues. Akamai is one of the leading companies in DDoS protection. They offer a content delivery network (CDN) that includes protection for many companies against volumetric-type attacks like DDoS. In June of 2021, an outage at Akamai led to several sites around the world becoming unavailable. Most were financial institutions in Australia and New Zealand; however, both Southwest and American Airlines were impacted as well. The cause of the outage was not due to a cyberattack, but rather a misconfiguration at Akamai related to a routing table value. This came shortly after similar outages at some of Akamai's rivals, Fastly and Cloudflare, showing that an overreliance on third parties to deliver protection can be an additional risk to an application.

2.3.3 The role of ransomware

Protecting against volumetric attacks that flood your network or application with legitimate or junk data is one thing, but an entirely different approach to availability chaos is by encrypting the devices or data that your application depends on. Ransomware is not new, but in the past few years it has gained popularity. We could spend an entire chapter on ransomware, but I'll summarize it here.

Ransomware is the outcome of a successful malware attack with the sole intention of encrypting a device (locker ransomware) or the more popular method of encrypting data (crypto ransomware). The methods of delivery of the malware vary from phishing to more sophisticated remote code execution. So, what does this mean for your web application or service? Obviously, an encrypted database will render your application useless in most cases. Returning to normal operations will typically mean paying a ransom to the attackers in the form of anonymous cryptocurrency in order to gain access to a decryption key that will unlock the data. Mature organizations may be able to overcome this disruption by restoring from backups that have not been encrypted.

Ransomware has continued to rise in the past several years and has catapulted cybersecurity to the mainstream with such famous attacks like WannaCry, the City of Atlanta, the Port of San Diego, and the Colonial Pipeline attacks. With ransomware as a service (RaaS) on the rise and affiliate attackers reusing popular ransomware software, the trend will continue to go against organizations.

Ransomware is a persistent and growing threat to organizations. The idea of having your data encrypted with no method of decryption is paralyzing to think about. The Cybersecurity and Infrastructure Security Agency (CISA) has several recommendations to avoid the risks of ransomware:

- Ensure that your organization has a procedure for patching software.
- Back up data on a regular basis and test the backups.
- Restrict access to systems and software following the principle of least privilege.

2.3.4   *Casino betting offline*

Not all organizations face DDoS attacks equally. Some, due to the nature of their business, face an increased risk. Imperva is a leading provider of application-layer DDoS protection through a suite of tools, including a web application firewall (WAF). Their Global DDoS Threat Landscape Report released in 2020 showed that the gaming industry and the gambling industry continue to be the most attacked websites on the internet. It is easy to see why this is the case. These sites need to be universally available especially during big events or risk losing revenue.

In 2020, an attacker used Datagram Congestion Control Protocol (DCCP) to slip past DDoS protections that are geared toward other network protocols like TCP and UDP in order to perpetrate one of the largest DDoS campaigns ever seen. They used the new attack vector to perform what is known as DDoS extortion or ransom. RDDoS (ransom DDoS) is, as it sounds, a way for the attacker to threaten an organization to either pay a fee or be the subject of a DDoS attack. By February of 2021, these attackers were able to muster over 800 Gbps of traffic to direct toward their victim—in this case, a gambling site in Europe.

2.3.5   *Health organizations are still fair game*

Despite a global pandemic, the health care industry was still too juicy of a target for attackers to ignore. Many of the most well-known cybercriminal gangs (more on these later) claimed that they would avoid attacking health organizations to show their sensitive side. However, there are plenty of fish in the sea, as it were, that did not feel the same.

There were countless attacks and attempted attacks against health organizations during the COVID-19 pandemic. Both the HHS (Health and Human Services) in the United States and the Paris AP-HP were in the crosshairs of DDoS attacks. In the case of the HHS, the threatened DDoS attack whose aim it was to create disruption in the pandemic response was thwarted. However, the Paris AP-HP, which operates dozens of hospitals across France and provides research and disease prevention, was impacted by a DDoS attack that was absorbed by the network provider.

One thing that is clear with the targeting of health care organizations is that attackers will always go for the lowest hanging fruit, the least amount of effort, and the most likely to pay a fee. Health care organizations are not engineering organizations. Their primary purpose is to provide health care services to patients in need. Any disruption to their capabilities puts lives at risk, which will drive decisions to move quickly to a resolution. With technology that is usually years behind the state of the art, and small or outsourced technology teams, the quickest resolution is usually processing a payment to an attacker.

2.3.6 *Building in resiliency*

Availability has one best friend in the world, and that's resiliency. One of the most iconic bridges in the world is San Francisco's Golden Gate Bridge. Known as one of the Wonders of the Modern World, the Golden Gate Bridge connects the San Francisco Bay with the Pacific Ocean. Construction began in 1933 and was completed four years later. The Golden Gate Bridge is a great real-world example of building for resiliency. Not only was the construction of the bridge an extreme modern marvel, but there are also unique considerations for places like San Francisco, namely earthquakes. The Golden Gate Bridge is within close proximity to the San Andreas Fault, which produces frequent seismic activity, some of which can be devastating to the area. It has survived several large earthquakes over its 80-plus years of existence, but not without the need of constant review and rework. Several projects are ongoing to make it more secure against not only earthquakes but also high winds. What does this have to do with software? Risk management in architecture is not much different whether you are building a bridge across a peninsula or developing an application to deliver value to your customers. Architecture, design, and development all need to consider the what-if scenarios and plan for possible attacks, failures, or errors, some of which could be intentional.

Your application should be designed and architected in a way that takes into consideration the type of risks and threat actors that may be looking for weaknesses in your specific application. Similar to the Golden Gate Bridge needing to be built to withstand winds as well as potentially large earthquakes, a health care application needs to be built to withstand a cyberattack that is attempting to ransomware your client data in order to turn the downtime into a profit. Your gambling application must consider criminals looking to DDoS your application to extort your organization. Your critical infrastructure application must be prepared to handle an advanced persistent threat looking to shut down your system to cripple key parts of a nation. We will talk more about these in the next sections.

One of the simple methods of building in resiliency is to add more processing power. Scaling vertically means you are creating bigger systems. Scaling horizontally means you are adding more systems. This is easier said than done. However, the migration to cloud-first architecture makes this easier, albeit expensive. Additionally, building segmentation into your architecture reduces the "blast radius" of a potential attack. If you always assume that one of your systems is compromised, you will look at your architecture much differently. Similarly, there have been books written on the principles of chaos engineering, which in its simplest form means injecting a bit of chaos into a system to identify issues in order to prevent full-on outages. Think of trying to find a pinhole in a tire. You might rub some soapy water around it and put it under pressure to look for where the bubbles show. This is similar to the concept of chaos engineering where the team develops a hypothesis, tests it, and then works to fix what was discovered in the test:

- *Develop a hypothesis*—The application will respond gracefully if an external service is not available.
- *Test the hypothesis*—Route HTTP from the application to a nonexistent service and observe the failure condition.
- *Fix*—If required, identify the issues, resolve them, and improve processes.

One last comment regarding building resiliency in. Things will break, processes will fail, systems will crash. What is done with that information is critical to improving the system long-term. Learning from mistakes and failures is the best method of building more resilient systems. A typical component of learning from failures is in a postmortem or a root cause analysis. Here, the team reviews what happened and where the failures were. From there they incorporate the findings into an action plan to ensure that controls, processes, and automation are in place to prevent the failures from occurring again.

2.4   *Integrity*

When we open a bottle of our favorite beverage, we expect to hear the sound of the cap snapping away from the protective top. Data is little different in the sense that we want to have confidence that it is correct when we view or process it. *Integrity* is the ability to know that data is known to be good and trusted. This requires the application to trust that data has not been tampered with whether in transit or at rest. Integrity needs to be confirmed in communication between two applications, in databases or filesystems, or a piece of hardware or software. Anywhere data resides or moves requires it to continue to be trusted by the applications that use it.

As with availability and confidentiality, integrity issues can be intentional or accidental. It can be from an attacker injecting junk into a business process that corrupts data that is then stored or processed, or it can be a write failure that then corrupts those backups you were planning on using to recover from a potential ransomware attack.

2.4.1 *Integrity starts with access*

Have you ever walked to your desk, got in your car, or entered a room in your house and noticed that something was moved that you *know* you didn't move? Your mind begins to walk back over the last time you were in that space. Did you really put that pen there? Was that book always on that side of the table? If it wasn't you, then who was it? If only you had a method to see who was in that room other than you and catch the perpetrator red-handed. I got news for you: It was probably you.

Think about a simple web request from your browser to a web server. The request leaves the browser in a GET or POST and traverses the network as a packet, which lands on several network devices. It is then received by a load balancer or proxy or a WAF, and it hits a web server, an application server, and a database. By the way, it's most likely been logged in a few of those locations and sent to a separate, centralized logging system. Not all paths through a system are the same, but in general this holds true for most HTTP requests made today and can be as simple as the diagram in figure 2.5. At each one of those steps there is the potential for a user or an account to gain access to view, copy, or corrupt the data through intentional or unintentional manipulation.

Reverse proxy flow

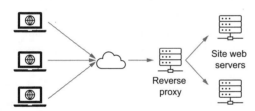

**End user devices making
a request to a site**

**Figure 2.5   Simple HTTP
request with a reverse proxy**

Access control and monitoring is primarily used to determine what accounts have had contact with data as it has gone through a system. It can be achieved through means as simple as providing a monitoring system for logging access to certain files, directories, and resources. Or it can be as complex as a privilege access management (PAM) system that requires a user to check out account access to sensitive systems where actions and keystrokes are logged. There are systems and security models in between that will provide varying level of access control. The key takeaway is to ensure that you can trace access, down to the individual file, to a physical person or user account. The moment that you have something like a shared account, you lose the ability to trace activity to a single account or individual. These accounts are ones that have a shared username and password that are used by a group of individuals.

Nonrepudiation is a form of access control that grants the application the ability to track an action or activity back to an identity. The most important concept with nonrepudiation and access control can be summarized by the FDA's definition of an *audit trail.*

> **DEFINITION**   An *audit trail* is a secure, computer-generated, timestamped electronic record that allows for reconstruction of the course of events relating to the creation, modification, or deletion of an electronic record.

Attackers may look for ways to ascribe their activity to a different account or otherwise pin the blame somewhere else. When an attacker performs an attack on an application, there is a goal in mind, perhaps data exfiltration or DoS. In these cases, they will also attempt to hide their activity through poisoning or corrupting the logs so that the team that reviews the incident is not able to piece together the attacker's activity. It is important to validate the input that is coming into your logs and make sure that access to logging workflows is tightly controlled. It is also important that enough information is logged to aid in the forensics of a potential incident. Without this audit trail, the ability to trace behavior back to an entity will leave the organization unable to determine the root cause of activity.

2.4.2   *The role of version control*

Version control offers the opportunity for a team of software personnel to work on a large application. Rarely is an application developed by one individual. It takes a team to build an application that is developed for commercial use. The use of a version control system (VCS) allows for the team to work simultaneously on the same application while providing the means to track code check-ins, resolve conflicts, and enable the ability to revert changes.

Version control is also a method for making certain that if data is corrupted, that there is a means to return to a good state. For those of us who have done any software development, we know that there have been times that, while coding, we broke something else in the process. Or maybe that only happened to me. You would usually attempt to roll back to a known good state or at least be able to view an older file and compare it to the current so that you can determine what broke. Version control software performs the function of providing control and visibility into files over time. As mentioned, this provides the ability to compare and roll back in the event of data becoming corrupted or deleted, or if there was just bad coding.

Many newer VCS include the ability to perform code reviews, track defects, and leverage task controls that can perform jobs related to continuous integration like merging code, running test suites, and creating a software package that can then be deployed to an environment where it can be tested. In relation to software security, the VCS that is used allows for the application security team to perform code reviews on sensitive code. For instance, a change may have been made in the code that impacts the authentication of the application. In this case, the engineering team may request that the application security team review the code for any increased risk due to the change. Additionally, if the VCS provides the ability to run tasks, the application security team can use this point to perform automated security testing to uncover vulnerabilities, like using a static analysis tool.

2.4.3 *Data validation*

An additional consideration when maintaining data integrity is to maintain the data as it is initially brought into your system through a user or service. In the application security space, we typically call this *data scrubbing* or *validation.*

> **NOTE** If there is only one thing that you remember from this book, let it be the fact that you can never trust your end users or the services your application works with to send you correct data. Whether intentional or not, data that is not properly validated can lead to failures in your application or a malicious actor being able to compromise it.

This means simple concepts like only accepting numeric values of certain length when expecting a phone number or social security number. It can be as complex as writing regular expressions that look for specific characters and other requirements. Many development frameworks may even have data validation built into the framework. However, ultimately, the validation strategy should ensure that the input data is both within the constraints of the value it is expecting and also makes sense from a logic perspective.

Depending on your development framework, validation techniques are natively available and can be leveraged to check common constraints on size, type, schema, and others. One consideration when developing validation, either using the native elements of your framework or developing your own, is that taking the allowlist approach is more effective than the deny list. What this means is that the application should specify what it allows, and not what it blocks. It is apparent that a deny list will need constant maintenance and will not always catch novel approaches to circumventing the validation. An allowlist will only permit the values that the application is expecting to work with and is a more secure method.

One last point on the input validation is that it is not sufficient to examine the input only on the client side. This check must also be done at the server side. Proxy tools, and projects like cURL, allow an attacker to manipulate an input or send requests to your application without needing to go through the UI. In other words, most attackers will easily circumvent your client-side validations that might be in place.

2.4.4 *Data replication*

Data replication is usually thought of, and incorrectly, as data backup. Data backup requires more than just replication, including testing and integrity checks. What replication does entail is making multiple copies of data in different locations to be able to absorb potential data loss or corruption in one copy. This provides not only better availability and lower latency but also the ability to restore to a known good state should something go wrong. Although there are file and system backups that should be in place, the application architecture should include the ability to distribute data through a clustered database. While in this scheme, data is split so that different fragments go to different nodes and are retrieved in a manner that will then consolidate the different fragments back to the original data. Replication of the data will provide the additional layer of making sure that a failure at one node does not limit the ability for the cluster to retrieve the data. There is one important caveat. Data replication can lead to the replication of bad data as well in the case where an attacker is able to corrupt the source that then gets replicated. It is critical to rely on a full backup strategy that does not depend on data replication exclusively.

2.4.5 *Data checks*

If you have worked in technology long enough, you are well aware of the concept behind checksums. These are values that provide a fingerprint for a given input. This is essentially a hash of an input, which means that it can only be done in one direction as shown in figure 2.6. In other words, the plain text is turned into a hash value, but the hash cannot be returned to the plain text. Checksums and hashes are not necessarily different from each other except for their purposes. Where hashes are an output of a mathematical function that is intended to create a unique value, a checksum is used to make a comparison and then decide whether a value has changed or not.

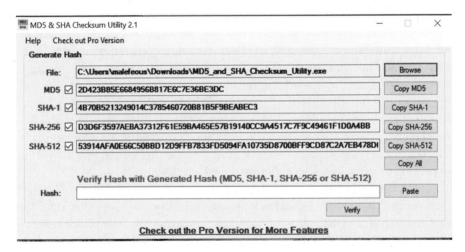

Figure 2.6   Hash validation utility

Another example of a generated code that provides data integrity assurance is the message authentication code (MAC). These are cryptographic checksums that are used to prove that data has not been tampered while it was saved or transmitted, and to provide a means to authenticate who it came from when a cryptographic key is used during the MAC generation.

2.5 *Authentication and authorization*

Authentication and authorization, as shown in figure 2.7, are two additional tenants that are vital to maintaining the security of an application. They are components of what is typically thought of more broadly as identity and access management (IAM). Diving deep on this topic is out of scope for this book, but it is important to know what they mean and their roles in security.

Authentication vs. authorization

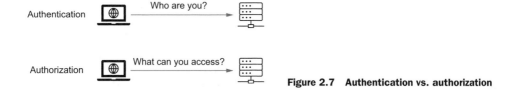

Figure 2.7 Authentication vs. authorization

2.5.1 *Authentication*

Authentication (or AuthN) is the practice of confirming that a user or account is who they say they are. This is accomplished by proving identity through the following:

- Username and password, which accounts for something you know
- A token through either a hardware device or software, which is something you have
- Biometrics like a fingerprint or retinal scan, which is known as something you are

In most cases, a single factor is enough to verify the account. Our username and password combination is widely used to allow us to log in to applications. More strict applications or services may require additional factors like token or biometrics (or all three) to provide enough verification of the account. The use of more than one factor is considered MFA (multifactor authentication). MFA is quickly becoming widely accepted as the minimum authentication for most applications, as the single-factor authentication is often easily circumvented. For instance, password combined with a token would be two factors that are used to provide authentication. It is important to point out that once an account has been authenticated, it does not grant access to everything within a system. That is an important distinction between authentication and authorization. Your ability to log in, and therefore authenticate, to a site like Amazon.com does not entitle you to access everything, including administrative functions.

2.5.2 *Authorization*

Authorization (or AuthZ) is the process of granting access to a user or account to certain features or activity within an application. This occurs during or after the authentication process. It's important to consider that during the authorization process, the least privilege approach is taken to ensure that the account has access only to the features that it needs to perform its tasks. That can be achieved through several access models:

- *MAC (mandatory access control)*—Gives the access control to the owner and custodian of the system or data
- *RBAC (role-based access control)*—Provides access based on the account's participation in a group or role
- *DAC (discretionary access control)*—Gives complete control of the access control to the owner of a system or data
- *Rule-based access control*—Defines access for an account that is defined by the custodian or system administrator

One common way to think of authorization and its role in identity is the common access card, passport, or license. These types of identifying items usually have a photo, your name, address, and other identifying information. Having one of these helps someone confirm your identity since you are the person in the picture. This is authentication. However, having that identifying item doesn't mean that you are granted access to certain locations. For instance, your license will not allow you access into sensitive areas of a military base. Sure, the picture and information on the license identifies you, but it by no means grants you access to off-limits areas.

2.6   Adversaries

One of the foundations to developing a defense-in-depth approach to addressing security is to know what types of attacks you should be expecting. The following is a popular quote that suits our needs here:

> *If you know the enemy and know yourself, you need not fear the result of a hundred battles.*
> *If you know yourself but not the enemy, for every victory gained you will also suffer a defeat.*
> *If you know neither the enemy nor yourself, you will succumb in every battle.*
>
> —Sun Tzu, *The Art of War*

Of course, we are not headed to battle every day when we head off to work, but this still works in the context of cybersecurity. Knowing the attackers, their methods, and what their targets are in your organization allows you to know where to spend your effort and money. We'll talk more about general risk next, but first let's talk about who the various adversaries are that you will likely encounter.

2.6.1   Script kiddies

One of the most prevalent adversaries that we can expect to see in the cybersecurity space is the "script kiddie." It's not a great name, but these are typically low-skill attackers who have little motivation outside of revenge or fame. They will look to purchase or reuse exploits that others have developed with no knowledge or understanding of how the exploit works. They simply want to point it to a target and click a button.

Although the skill level of these attackers is low, they are generally using automated-type attacks that allow them to run these attacks at scale. Make no mistake, organizations are under near constant, daily attacks. Some of this is noise from the general internet, and other activity is due to these adversaries who are just looking to test their skills or gain bragging rights with their friends. This type of motivation may make their attacks less impactful, but they are still widespread.

Botnets

Botnets are a common attack tool used by script kiddies. This is a method used to perform DDoS attacks at scale. These networks of bots are compromised devices that have malicious code injected into them so that they may be used in a future attack. Most of the time they are used to target organizations for volumetric types of attacks like DDoS. They can be Internet of Things (IoT) devices, laptops, desktops, printers, or any other device that has an internet connection and can be used to make web calls. Some of these botnets are even for sale or can be rented for a period of time. For this type of attack, most organizations are not equipped to mitigate it themselves and need to look for outside help in the form of firewalls both at the application and at the network layer. Other controls require your organization to know the type of traffic that it is expecting to see and where it comes from so that the controls can be put in place to limit activity to just those known locations. This might require geofencing that limits traffic to known good countries or locations.

2.6.2 Insider

The insider threat is an often-overlooked category. These are users who usually have privileges to data and systems that outsiders would not. Think about the system administrator for your organization's domain controller. Now that you have that person in your mind, think about that person being disgruntled. What about the back-office admin in a medical facility who has access to patient records? What if they are no longer "feeling" their job? These things do happen. Although it is fair to say that most insider leaks are accidental and not due to the activity of a malicious actor. An example is someone who leaves their laptop unlocked, opens a door for a stranger, or forwards an email accidentally to a wide audience. These actions are not considered malicious, but can leave an organization exposed to sensitive data leaks.

The numbers vary on insider threats since not everything is required to be reported. However, Ponemon Institute produced the "2020 Cost of Insider Threats: Global Report" that showed that criminal insiders accounted for around 23% of insider incidents and 14% were due to criminals posing as insiders. These types of attacks are usually thought of as a problem for the information security team to deal with, but keep in mind that software engineering teams not only have access to the organization's intellectual property in the form of proprietary code, but also usually have elevated rights to environments that may have sensitive information.

The motivations for an insider can vary. As mentioned, some leaks at the hands of an insider are accidental. This is due to the lack of controls around access to information like a lack of proper segmentation or a least privilege model that enforces access to only those that need it. Controls should also be in place to guarantee that sensitive data and production data is not able to be moved from a production environment to another location. When motivation is to take revenge on the organization for a perceived slight, this becomes more complicated to defend. However, getting to a zero-trust type of model means that you should, unfortunately, suspect that anyone who has access to your most sensitive data is malicious and provide the appropriate auditing and protections around access to that data.

2.6.3 *Cybercriminal*

Depending on the industry that you are working in, cybercriminals may be the most worrisome. Most organizations that are in industries like financial or health care perhaps face the most difficult challenges when it comes to cybercriminals. There is one thing that motivates cybercriminals—money.

As mentioned, many times, data is the new oil. It's a commodity, and organizations collect, trade, and monetize it. There is some folklore that attributes a comment to Willie Sutton, a famous bank robber in the 1900s. As the lore goes, Willie Sutton was once asked why he continues to rob banks. His famous reply supposedly is, "Because that's where the money is." Turns out that may not have been totally accurate according to Willie Sutton himself and was perhaps just an editor attempting to be pithy. Regardless, the statement is true and sums up, pretty well, why cybercriminals continue to target organizations and their data.

Their techniques vary: ransomware, DDoS, data exfiltration, or even physical theft of devices. The goal is to get to the data, put it on the black market, and make some quick money. Their technical abilities vary, but they are more adept at infiltrating an organization from the outside than the previously mentioned actors. They will use off-the-shelf or purchased tools, or they can go as far as developing and customizing their own exploits to target specific entities. They are more targeted in their approach and will look for low-hanging fruit in order to compromise an organization.

2.6.4 *Hacktivist and terrorist*

I don't mean to lump hacktivist and terrorist in the same category since they have different goals, but they are both propelled by the desire to publicly make an example of someone or some organization in order to advance an agenda. For both actors, this tends to be of a political nature. But that's where comparisons usually diverge.

Hacktivists will take up causes for people or movements aimed to effect change toward a shared goal. They are usually a loose band of individuals with a high level of skills. They will look to deface websites of organizations they don't agree with or even DDoS them. Their goal is to raise awareness around a cause, and their methods will vary.

Cyberterrorists move beyond political motivations and will often take up religious or ideological causes and target organizations accordingly. The targets can be individuals or organizations, and will often look to target key infrastructure of nations with the intent of causing physical harm.

2.6.5 Advanced persistent threat

Advanced persistent threats, or APTs, are gaining more recognition recently as nations such as Russia, China, North Korea, Israel, and the United States find their cyber differences (putting it mildly) out in the public space. APTs are deep-pocketed, nation-backed entities whose sole intention is to gain tactical and strategic advantage over adversaries. This shows up in their effort to gain access to organizations in specific industries, critical infrastructure, military entities, and so forth. In most cases, the APT will lie in wait and stay hidden until an order comes.

As mentioned, these are deep-pocketed groups and are the highest skilled adversary that any organization will face. APTs are usually branches of an already established organization within the nation such as intelligence services or the military. Their focus is to gain a foothold into another nation with the intention of creating domestic chaos, take out military capability, or cripple a nation's economy.

Defending against these types of attackers is not easy, and the best advice is often to do the basics of monitoring and protection. However, Rob Joyce, who led the National Security Agency's (NSA) elite Tailored Access Group (whose purpose was to break into adversaries' systems), summed up every organization's nightmare during a conference in 2016:

> *We put the time in . . . to know [that network] better than the people who designed it and the people who are securing it. You know the technologies you intended to use in that network. We know the technologies that are actually in use in that network. Subtle difference. You'd be surprised about the things that are running on a network vs. the things that you think are supposed to be there.*

It's important to highlight the last statement here. Systems are complex, and in any large organization, the amount of applications and services running can be immense. Sophisticated attackers are counting on large organizations not having the bandwidth, personnel, or tools to detect malicious activity quickly. They're often right.

2.6.6 Why do we care?

Defending against these threat actors requires varying techniques and difficulty, as shown in figure 2.8. Organizations often find themselves as victims to broader geopolitical attacks that have nothing to do with them, especially when it comes to hacktivists, cyberterrorists, and APTs.

Knowing your adversary is key to survival. Knowing that script kiddies will largely use already identified, automated attacks means that your off-the-shelf tools used for scanning and protection will usually suffice. Defending against more sophisticated attackers like the hacktivist, cyberterrorist, cybercriminal, and APT means that your defenses need to be more robust, and a plan for business continuity is required in order to recover from a potential attack. For these types of attackers, you need to augment the preventative mindset to include detection and response. In other words, the more sophisticated the attacker is, the more resources are needed to defend. Regardless of the attacker, the basics of security need to be integrated. Scanning, patching,

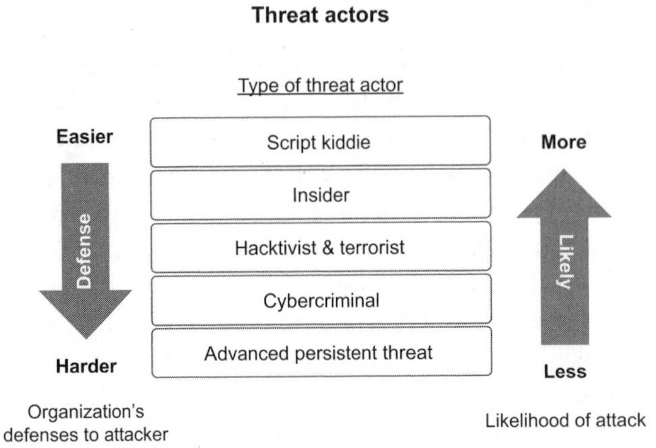

Threat actors

Type of threat actor

Easier	More
Script kiddie	
Insider	
Hacktivist & terrorist	
Cybercriminal	
Advanced persistent threat	
Harder	Less

Organization's
defenses to attacker

Likelihood of attack

**Figure 2.8   Relation of
threat actors vs. defense**

vulnerability management, visibility, and defense in depth are all required regardless of the threat actor.

2.7   *Measuring risk*

This book is not about risk, though it is an integral part of secure software development. There are plenty of resources available to help organizations understand and balance their risk. The goal of this section is to highlight some of the concepts with risk as it relates to an organization. Understanding this relationship will help application owners know why certain controls are used and needed. This leads to a stronger defense-in-depth model. Without knowing the risks that are posed, you run the risk of overcorrecting for risks that are not of a legitimate concern.

As mentioned, there are many different methods for measuring risk. For the purpose of this book, we will use the OWASP methodology, aptly named the OWASP Risk Rating Methodology, which allows you to identify risks through a series of steps. It uses a number range from 0 to 9 to assign a value to a particular rating. The lower the number, the lower the level and vice versa. Although this is not a perfect system, the goal is to create a means for scoring security issues.

OWASP
Throughout this book we will leverage many of the projects from OWASP. When it comes to application security, OWASP is generally the first stop for most application security professionals. It is an open source community of thought leaders who have built many of the foundational security practices used today. One of the most widely recognized application security projects is the OWASP Top Ten Web Application Security Risks. This documents the top ten most impactful security risks that a web application faces (https://owasp.org/).

Using the OWASP Risk Rating Methodology, the measured risk comes down to a simple equation:

$$Risk = Likelihood * Impact$$

The likelihood is calculated by asking questions related to the threat agent and the found vulnerability. More on this in a bit. The aim of these questions is to uncover how likely an exploitation of the found vulnerability may be. With the impact calculation, there are another eight questions that are geared toward identifying what will happen to the organization and technology should the exploit be successful. This will lead you to the ultimate rating of the risk, which allows you to prioritize and apply the appropriate controls to eliminate or mitigate the risk properly. Before diving into the risk rating methods with OWASP, it's important to call out that once a risk has been rated, there are several things that an organization can then do with that information and that risk.

2.7.1   *Remediate, mitigate, accept*

In general, there are three methods to managing an identified risk. The first is to remediate the risk. This requires the organization to take corrective action to fully implement risk elimination. An example would be a case where the application faces the risk of *formjacking*.

> **DEFINITION** *Formjacking* is an attack where an attacker is able to inject code that skims data from an HTML form. One of the most well-known types of formjacking is an attack called Magecart, which specifically targets checkout pages to steal users' information by injecting malicious code in third-party supplied code to a website.

This is where an attacker is capable of taking over a form on a website that allows them to inject code that steals information. To remediate this risk, the organization will need to perform regular testing through tools and penetration tests to identify opportunity of code injection into the forms they use. They will monitor traffic and create an allowlist that allows only outbound traffic to known good locations. Additionally, they may look to leverage subresource integrity (SRI) tags to create a hash of content that is used by the application and fetched by the browser so that it can determine whether the content has been tampered with. They may even go as far as eliminating forms if they are no longer needed.

If remediation is not feasible for business or technology reasons, the next step is to identify ways to mitigate the risk by placing in compensating controls. This can also be considered reducing the risk since it may not completely eliminate it, but instead makes it less likely and raises the bar for an attacker. In most cases, mitigation involves using additional tools like a WAF or by reducing the size of the attack surface by limiting the audience down to as few accounts as possible and monitoring those accounts closely. Again, the goal of mitigation is not to eliminate, if this isn't possible, but to reduce the attack surface to as small as possible.

The last option is to accept the open risk. This is a less-than-ideal option, as it means that the organization is aware of the risk but has chosen to leave it open and accept it. This should still be coupled with risk reduction so that the risk is as minimal as possible. A prime example of where risk is accepted is in the case of an older application that simply cannot be shut down. It may be due to the fact that the organization has been unsuccessful in getting clients to move to a new product or a new version of the given application, but whatever the case is, the organization requires the risk to remain open due to a business decision. In many cases, the acceptance of risk is taken when the impact to the business is low. In other words, the business is willing to accept a breach and knows that the total cost to the business would be low.

There are other facets of risk that can come into play such as cyber insurance and risk transfer. However, the purpose of this section is to cover the primary ways that organizations treat risk as it applies to the products and applications they create.

2.7.2   *Identify the risk*

The first step in rating the criticality of a risk using the OWASP Risk Rating Methodology is to identify what the actual risk is to the application or organization. This could come through due to the nature of the organization, the type of application in use, or geopolitical factors. Risk is ever evolving and may even be eliminated by doing nothing, as both risk and technology changes.

This is where knowledge of your threat actors (adversaries), a well-documented architecture, and strong knowledge of how your application is deployed and used will come in handy. Identifying risk can come from conversations with the business and technical people within the organization, it can be made apparent by a client who reports a risk they identified, it can come from fellow industry partners, or it can come from your internal tools. Regardless of the method of risk identification, the most important part is to know you have risk.

In the OWASP Risk Rating Methodology, there are scores associated with each component. The higher the score, the higher the risk. When performing a risk rating, it is important to have the right resources involved with the measurement. This includes not just technical resources, but also business resources that understand what the impact to the business and organization would be for a given risk. Measuring of the risk can take anywhere from a few minutes to a few hours, depending on the resources involved and the complexity of the risk. It is also important to highlight that much of the risk rating is subjective, where, depending on the resources involved, it is easy to go down a rabbit hole on conversations over the risk. An example of this is where participants in the process may differ on their perception of the risk or aspects of the mitigations that are available. Key to success here is to lay out ground rules, have previous examples handy, and keep the participants on topic.

2.7.3 *Estimating likelihood*

Likelihood is as simple as identifying when a risk may be exploited. We are all familiar with the statistics around driving a vehicle and the likelihood of a potential accident. Although many of us are aware of this risk, it doesn't stop us from getting into our vehicles on a regular basis. It's a risk we are willing to or need to take. The bottom line is that we never know when or even if an accident will occur on a commute to the office or another location; we simply know that statistically it may occur. Additionally, certain factors come in to play with this analogy. How fast we drive, other vehicles on the road, the safety of the route to our destination, and so on. The same applies with understanding the likelihood of a security risk. OWASP gives us eight factors for the threat actor and the vulnerability to help us measure the likelihood. The scores associated with each item is a weight that represents the impact of that item. This is used in the final calculation of the actual risk. The threat actor factors are

- *Skill level*—How technically skilled is this group of threat agents? No technical skills (1), some technical skills (3), advanced computer user (5), network and programming skills (6), security penetration skills (9).
- *Motive*—How motivated is this group of threat agents to find and exploit this vulnerability? Low or no reward (1), possible reward (4), high reward (9).
- *Opportunity*—What resources and opportunities are required for this group of threat agents to find and exploit this vulnerability? Full access or expensive resources required (0), special access or resources required (4), some access or resources required (7), no access or resources required (9).
- *Size*—How large is this group of threat agents? Developers (2), system administrators (2), intranet users (4), partners (5), authenticated users (6), anonymous internet users (9).

The vulnerability factors are

- *Ease of discovery*—How easy is it for this group of threat agents to discover this vulnerability? Practically impossible (1), difficult (3), easy (7), automated tools available (9).
- *Ease of exploit*—How easy is it for this group of threat agents to actually exploit this vulnerability? Theoretical (1), difficult (3), easy (5), automated tools available (9).
- *Awareness*—How well known is this vulnerability to this group of threat agents? Unknown (1), hidden (4), obvious (6), public knowledge (9).
- *Intrusion detection*—How likely is an exploit to be detected? Active detection in application (1), logged and reviewed (3), logged without review (8), not logged (9).

As you can see, the likelihood factors are looking at the threat actors as it relates to the vulnerability. The organization can then take this information to determine how likely a vulnerability is to be exploited based on the skill level and knowledge of the vulnerability.

2.7.4 Estimating impact

Impact is a bit different when it comes to measuring, as it is not based solely on what can be determined by just technical folks. Impact must leverage information related to the business considering that the impact is a measure of what is likely to happen to the organization should a vulnerability be exploited. One important consideration with impact is that there are two types of impact. *Technical impact* is a risk to our core security concerns of confidentiality, integrity, and availability. This focuses primarily on the systems that run and manage our application. Second is the *business impact*, which prioritizes what is important for the business that is running the application and is usually financial in nature. Technical impact factors are

- *Loss of confidentiality*—How much data could be disclosed and how sensitive is it? Minimal nonsensitive data disclosed (2), minimal critical data disclosed (6), extensive nonsensitive data disclosed (6), extensive critical data disclosed (7), all data disclosed (9).
- *Loss of integrity*—How much data could be corrupted and how damaged is it? Minimal slightly corrupt data (1), minimal seriously corrupt data (3), extensive slightly corrupt data (5), extensive seriously corrupt data (7), all data totally corrupt (9).
- *Loss of availability*—How much service could be lost and how vital is it? Minimal secondary services interrupted (1), minimal primary services interrupted (5), extensive secondary services interrupted (5), extensive primary services interrupted (7), all services completely lost (9).
- *Loss of accountability*—Are the threat agents' actions traceable to an individual? Fully traceable (1), possibly traceable (7), completely anonymous (9).

Business impact factors are

- *Financial damage*—How much financial damage will result from an exploit? Less than the cost to fix the vulnerability (1), minor effect on annual profit (3), significant effect on annual profit (7), bankruptcy (9).
- *Reputation damage*—Would an exploit result in reputation damage that would harm the business? Minimal damage (1), loss of major accounts (4), loss of goodwill (5), brand damage (9).
- *Noncompliance*—How much exposure does noncompliance introduce? Minor violation (2), clear violation (5), high-profile violation (7).
- *Privacy violation*—How much personally identifiable information could be disclosed? One individual (3), hundreds of people (5), thousands of people (7), millions of people (9).

2.7.5 Risk severity

Now that we identified the likelihood and impact factors, we can put it together to understand the overall severity. As mentioned previously, the higher the rating for each of the factors, the higher the overall risk.

Rating score	Rating level
0 to <3	Low
3 to <6	Medium
6 to 9	High

2.7.6   *Risk example*

Reusing the formjacking example from earlier, we can make some assumptions and walk through a scenario. I will use the example organization from the previous chapter, Superior Products. Dashing Danielle has been made aware of the formjacking issue impacting one of their flagship products that was raised up by an internal penetration test that was recently completed. After some research, she knows that this issue is significant; however, completing a risk rating will help her prioritize the issue with the engineering team. The impacted application has a section for making purchases and submitting reviews. There is a form in the section where the user can provide their credit card details in order to make purchases.

Given this basic information, we can make some assumptions about the threat actors and vulnerability in order to come up with the overall likelihood. For this example, the ability to perform a successful attack requires moderate skill for a big reward in the form of stealing credit card information. The threat actor category would be cybercriminals and would be generally widespread. For the vulnerability itself, the ability to act on it is determined by the fact that automated tools are available to not only detect but to also create the script that can be used for the attack. As of now, Superior Products has minimal ability to detect an attack. With this in mind, we can determine the likelihood in table 2.2.

Table 2.2   Sample of a threat likelihood using a formjacking attack

Threat agent factors				Vulnerability factors			
Skill level	Motive	Opportunity	Size	Ease of discovery	Ease of exploit	Awareness	Intrusion detection
4	8	6	6	7	7	5	3

Overall likelihood = 5.75

For the impact, we will break this into two parts, one for the technical impact and one for the business impact as described in table 2.3. Looking at this particular risk, the loss of confidentiality is high because the threat actor can gain credit card information. There is no impact to integrity, or availability. Accountability would be difficult since the attacker can perform this attack without being known to the application. For the business impact, this would be significant given that if this is not well detected, it could go on for a long period of time before being noticed. Although financial impact would be low, the reputational and compliance impacts would be high, as would the possibility of this being a privacy violation, depending on what information would be stolen.

Table 2.3   Sample of a threat impact using a formjacking attack

Technical impact				Business impact			
Loss of confidentiality	Loss of integrity	Loss of availability	Loss of accountability	Financial damage	Reputation damage	Noncompliance	Privacy violation
8	1	1	8	7	7	7	3
Overall technical impact = 4.5				Overall business impact = 6			
Overall impact = 5.25							

What does this example show us? The likelihood of occurrence and the impact are both medium. However, the business impact is high. This allows Superior Products to take the approach that although there is a lower technical impact, the cost of the risk to the business is high and they would approach the resolution differently. Dashing Danielle works with the product owner and security organization to prioritize this vulnerability as high based on the business impact and opens a ticket with the appropriate development team with all the information needed for them to resolve.

Having this type of methodology will allow the organization to look at the risk and define a remediation or mitigation strategy that could eliminate or at least reduce the risk and properly prioritize the resolution.

Exercise 2.3

Use the online version of OWASP Risk Rating (www.owasp-risk-rating.com/). Use a scenario from a cyberattack news story. Take a particular threat from the story and walk through the Risk Rating calculator. Document your scenario, the final score, and what you learned. You will have to use your imagination to fill in the unknown data. This is a chance to be creative.

2.7.7   Other methodologies

While the focus in this section is on OWASP Risk Rating Methodology, there are several other well-known methodologies that should be considered. The goal here is not to say that one is better than another but to simply outline that there are multiple options when it comes to risk rating methodologies.

Two of the other methodologies worth mentioning are the National Institute of Standards and Technology (NIST) Guide for Conducting Risk Assessments in Special Publication 800-30 and the Mozilla Rapid Risk Assessment. For those who are familiar with NIST, you will know that this is a well-documented and thorough approach to risk assessment. The NIST approach is broader and encompasses more than a simple activity and instead focuses on the overall ability of an organization to frame the risk, then monitor, assess, and respond.

> **DEFINITION** NIST is another organization that has contributed greatly to the advancement of security. It is an organization based in the United States and is tasked with providing innovation and technical advancement. Through this effort, NIST has defined many of the practices that are used not just in application security but in organizations who want to raise their overall security practices. (https://www.nist.gov/)

The Mozilla RRA (Rapid Risk Assessment) takes a similar approach to measuring risk as OWASP does in the sense that it aims to be discrete and quick. It looks at the risk from the point of view of whether the given platform has the appropriate level of security controls to host specific data. The input into an RRA is a data flow diagram that includes the type of data that is used by the service being assessed, as well as an understanding or documentation, of how the service works. From here, the process is similar to a threat model (we'll talk about these later) where basic discussions occur on the service and its purpose. Data is highlighted with attention on how it's stored and used. Then a methodical approach is taken to review possible threat scenarios that focus on the confidentiality, integrity, and availability of the data. Once this is complete, recommendations are made on how best to provide protection.

Identifying risks allows the organization to prioritize and frame vulnerabilities that are presented. This means the organization can focus on the risks that have the biggest impact on what matters most to them.

Summary

- The CIA triad (confidentiality, integrity, and availability) is the foundation for every decision that is made in protecting data and ensuring that our systems are available when needed.
- Knowing your potential threat actors will assist in the definition of the appropriate level of protection that is needed. You don't need military-grade protection if your only adversary is a script kiddie.
- Attacks get stronger as the threat actors get better. Defenses need to align with the threats that they are protecting against.
- Organizations such as NIST and OWASP are great resources for standards and projects to help with ensuring your applications build security in.
- The OWASP Risk Rating Methodology provides a means to define the risk posed to an organization through a calculation that takes into consideration the technical and business impacts, as well as the threat actors.
- Risks can be remediated, mitigated, or accepted. Each have their own benefits and disadvantages.

Components of application security 3

So, you have seen the issues that are caused by not having application security integrated into your life cycle and you're starting to ask the great question of where to start. There is not a one-size-fits-all package that works for all organizations. A lot depends on the following:

- Size of the organization
- The industry and the regulations impacting the organization
- The culture of the organization
- The security budget at the organization

It's often easy to overlook the organization's culture having an impact on the effectiveness of the application security being applied, but this is a huge component. You cannot effect change if the engineering organization and the broader organization does not want to be more secure or is passive about security. Building security into the development life cycle depends on the organization's ability to rally its engineers to the cause. But people in the organization can only do so much on their own. Providing the right tools and processes is critical to successful application security. In this chapter, I discuss several of the more common tools and processes that make up a successful application security program. This is by no means an exhaustive list, and new tools and novel ways of solving application security issues are coming each year. However, the basic tools and processes are outlined here to give you an understanding of where it fits in the overall application security picture.

3.1 Threat modeling

There are many books that have been written on *threat modeling*. The intention of this section is to familiarize you with the different techniques and tools that are used to perform a threat model.

DEFINITION *Threat modeling* is a structured approach to identify, quantify, and address the security threats and risks associated with an application. It is an investigative technique used for identifying application security risks/hazards that are technical (and even implementation specific). Threat modeling is an early-stage activity that is used to define security requirements for a design. Ideally, threat modeling would occur during the initial stages of the architecture development.

Threat modeling is one of the most fundamental parts of security. It is not just a specific part of application security but is used in all parts of engineering and security, including in networking and operational teams. It can be as simple as asking a question like, "What could happen if a malicious user does this?" and can be as elaborate as gathering the appropriate subject matter experts to review a complex architecture with clear action items and takeaways with a list of associated risks and vulnerabilities.

NOTE Some additional reading that is helpful with threat modeling is *Threat Modeling: Designing for Security* by Adam Shostack (Wiley, 2014; http://mng.bz/gRrV) and the Threat Modeling Manifesto (www.threatmodelingmanifesto.org/).

The purpose of threat modeling is to identify the potential threats that might impact a system or architecture and define the countermeasure that can be used to address the found risks. This activity should be completed as early in the development life cycle as possible, as shown in figure 3.1. As I mentioned, it can be as simple as just asking what could happen, but more complex architecture needs more attention. Most modern architecture includes multiple external connections that are coming in and going out of the application. It may also have reusable components from other internal applications within the organizations. This represents a large set of moving parts that are often changing and present a unique challenge when completing a threat model, as the attack surface is much larger than a simpler architecture. For these more complex architectures, there are tools that can be used such as *blockatecture* tools like Microsoft Visio or another graphical tool that allows you to drag and drop blocks down on a canvas and draw lines. There are also specialized commercial tools that can be used to not only draw the architecture, but to also help identify the risks that can impact the drawn architecture. One of the most comprehensive methods of threat modeling is more manual and requires time and resources to spend the effort to whiteboard the architecture and manually identify the risks. Each of these methods have their strengths and weaknesses.

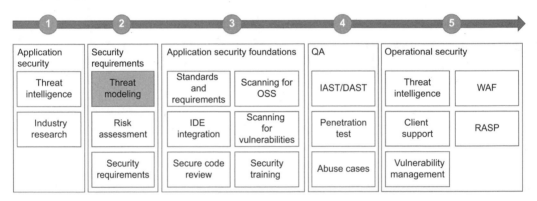

Figure 3.1   Threat modeling in the secure SDLC

3.1.1 *Basic threat modeling terminology*

Before we get into actually performing a threat model, you need to know a few terms that are used during the process:

- *Attacker*—Those who intentionally or unintentionally misuse an element of the system under consideration. This could be one of the threat actors I spoke of earlier, like a script kiddie, hacktivist, or others.
- *Asset*—Anything you deem to have value and something that the system must protect from an attacker. Some physical examples are money and precious metals. Digital examples are data, especially sensitive data like protected health information or personally identifiable information.
- *Threat*—A means by which an attacker might compromise an asset that has potential for success. Threats can include everything from hackers and malware, to earthquakes and wars. Additionally, intention is not a factor when

considering threats. A mechanical failure of a hard drive in a data center is an equal threat to a coordinated attack by an attacker.

- *Risk*—The potential for loss, damage, or destruction of an asset as a result of a threat exploiting a vulnerability. In the previous example about the mechanical failure of a hard drive and an attack by an attacker, the mechanical failure is a lower overall risk since there is usually redundancy built into an architecture to manage a failure, meaning the impact is smaller.

When you want to understand risk and threats, it's important to ensure that you take emotion and gut feeling out of the equation. Take the two visuals in figure 3.2. Many people have a very visceral reaction to the bear and view the stairs as just another daily activity, but what are the actual risks?

What's the higher risk?

   vs

Figure 3.2   A set of perfectly normal stairs and a grizzly bear

The reality is that stairs kill far more people than bears do. On average, 12,000 people a year die from falling down the stairs. A few dozen people are killed per year by bears. However, most people will feel instant fear when faced with a bear due to many different factors. What does this have to do with risk and security? When we look at the risks that impact our organization and software, it's important to put our risks in perspective. Most people who fall down the stairs may get right back up with some bumps and bruises, while the off chance of being attacked by a bear is likely to be much more fatal. Being under attack by an advanced persistent threat (APT) is of course concerning for any organization. However, most organizations should be more concerned about the daily noise that comes from automated attacks and less sophisticated attackers. Although this is not as flashy as the attacks that come from an APT, the organization is more likely to see automated attacks.

Now that we understand some basic terminology and have some perspective on risk, let's turn to threat modeling. For many, it's easier to understand the concept of threat modeling by first looking at the manual method.

3.1.2   *Manual threat modeling*

Imagine that an organization has determined that they need to identify potential threats and risks to a new feature that they want to deliver to their clients. Although threat models can be done later in the development life cycle, as with most security tools and techniques, the most benefit will come from performing this activity as early as possible. There are several inputs that are required for a successful threat model:

- A completed architecture diagram and description of the feature
- A data-flow diagram that shows how data will flow through the system
- A software bill of materials (SBOM) that provides a list of the software components used in the development of the application
- Web service integration points such as APIs and other web services with third-party or internal systems

Once these items have been gathered, members of the engineering team, security team, and business representatives would set aside time, potentially several hours or even days, depending on the complexity. To make these sessions as effective as possible, the right people need to be involved. The engineering representatives need to be familiar with the overall architecture and the way the application is used in normal activity. More importantly, they should be familiar with the data flows. The security representatives should have knowledge of which vulnerabilities and risks the organization is most concerned about and should have familiarity with the application and the issues and risks that impact the technology stack that is used. This should include the web server, database, deployment methodology, and coding language. The business representative should be there to help identify the way the application is being used in the real world and should weigh in on the identified risks and their impact to the business.

With materials in hand, the appropriate people will locate a room with a whiteboard. Although this can work in remote settings using virtual conference technology, it is far more effective to be physically together. For this exercise, they will be using STRIDE (spoofing, tampering, repudiation, information disclosure, denial of service, and elevation of privilege) to identify the risks that can impact the application. STRIDE is a threat modeling methodology developed by Microsoft (http://mng.bz/5m4a) and is used in their free Threat Modeling Tool.

Other threat modeling techniques

I will use STRIDE throughout this book since it is one of the more familiar ones used today and in use at organizations such as Microsoft. However, there are several other methods that can be used like OCTAVE, PASTA, Trike, and VAST. Which one to use really depends on the organization and the goals.

Threat modeling methods like Operational Critical Threat Asset and Vulnerability Evaluation (OCTAVE) focus on the nontechnical risk that resulted from breached data and was developed by Carnegie Mellon University.

In this method, assets are identified and classified, which helps define the scope. Through three stages, this method develops requirements, identifies vulnerabilities and gaps in policy or practices, and then develops an overall strategy to address the security risk.

In the Process for Attack Simulation and Threat Analysis (PASTA) method, the organization takes an attacker view and then develops a threat management, enumeration, and scoring process. This can then be elevated to key decision makers to determine what risk to tackle as opposed to developing requirements at the SDLC level. This method is primarily asset focused, especially with the mitigation strategies.

Again, there are several options when it comes to using a threat model methodology; however, the STRIDE method is broad and is a good way to learn about threat modeling. Additionally, the Microsoft Threat Modeling Tool uses STRIDE when it classifies threats.

3.1.3 Starting the manual process

The organization has the information gathered and the appropriate stakeholders, and has found a room with a whiteboard so that they may begin the process. Although the security representative does not have to lead the exercise, they are usually the most appropriate person to keep the team focused on the task and make sure it is working toward the appropriate risks. There are not a lot of ground rules for this effort, with a few exceptions:

- *Don't assume that your environment is secure or reliable.* Hardware and software fail. Attackers will be pushing on your defenses. It is better to assume that your environment is neither secure nor stable.
- *Don't assume that your environment is properly configured.* Similar to the secure and reliable, configuration drift is real, and not all systems are configured the same way.
- *Don't assume that your defense in depth will catch everything.* Not all security tools are evenly applied or configured.
- *Keep the conversation only to realistic scenarios and not "Hollywood" ones.* It's fun to think that secret agents from an underground organization will physically breach your defenses with a stolen truck and steal your servers. This is extremely unlikely. Stick to the more practical and likely scenarios like a hardware failure, an injection attack, or elevation of privilege.

With the ground rules understood, the security representative starts to draw on the whiteboard. They begin by drawing a few items:

- A simple copy of the architecture as blocks representing the different assets and technology in the architecture. This should include any third-party services. The purpose of this is to have a visual map that everyone can see.
- The acronym STRIDE with each spelled out as spoofing, tampering, repudiation, information disclosure, denial of service, elevation of privilege.

- Some exercises will put a "Hollywood" box on the whiteboard as well for any scenarios deemed too extreme.
- A grid with column headers and space to add items:

What	Who	Why	How	Impact	Countermeasure

The grid serves as the working area for the remainder of the exercise. The group will begin by identifying a risk and completing the rows below the header. The headers are defined as the following:

- *What*—What is at risk in a given scenario. This should be specific, such as "credit card numbers in the database."
- *Who*—What threat actors can potentially impact the identified object in the "What?" This should be specific, such as "A developer with access to the production database."
- *Why*—What is the motivation of the "Who" to put the "What" at risk. Such as: "The developer wants to sell the credit card numbers on the dark web."
- *How*—This is a bit more difficult and should avoid unrealistic scenarios. A plausible scenario would be "The developer copies the production data to their developer device."

3.1.4   *Threat modeling with linking bank accounts*

We can use our examples from previous chapters of Superior Products, which is launching a new feature in their e-commerce site that allows users to link their bank account in the application so that they can get paid for reselling items within the application. Dashing Danielle, the security representative in Superior Products for this application, begins by gathering the items needed as inputs from that development team. She reviews the architecture and data-flow diagram, as well as the software bill of materials to understand how the application is built and used. She follows up with the development team on a few outstanding questions and then organizes a work session with the development team's lead architect, two developers who have been working on the feature, and the product owner.

Dashing Danielle begins the session by drawing the simple architecture for the application along with STRIDE, "Hollywood," and the grid on a whiteboard. The group agrees that the architecture is complete and includes the critical components of the new feature. She then asks a basic question: "What are we trying to protect?" The obvious first answer is that the organization must protect the bank account information that is sent and stored. Dashing Danielle adds bank account information in the "What" column.

What	Who	Why	How	Impact	Countermeasure
Bank account numbers					

Next, Dashing Danielle asks, "Who would want this information?" Similar to the question of "What?" there is little debate on "Who." Clearly the attackers would be motivated by the financial gain they would achieve by stealing bank account numbers. With this information, attackers would be able to access the bank accounts of the users of the application, gain additional information on the user, and potentially link the bank account to an attacker-owned account. With this in mind, Dashing Danielle adds the information into the "Who" and "Why" columns.

What	Who	Why	How	Impact	Countermeasure
Bank account numbers	Cybercriminals	Financial gains with the information			

With the easy part done, it is now up for the group to determine how an attacker could steal bank account information and what impact it would have on the organization. Additionally, they will consider what countermeasures they could put in place to protect against this specific attack, and whether those already exist. If they do already exist, then Dashing Danielle will cross it off the list under "Countermeasures."

This is where the team has to get creative. There are several ways an attacker can gain access to this information, so it's good to start with higher-level themes. Here are a few cases they think about:

- Someone could accidentally, or intentionally, move the data to a developer environment for testing with live data.
- The data could be stolen directly in the database by an attacker who manages to deploy malicious code within the network to gain access to the database.
- The application could be susceptible to attacks that leak data like a SQL injection, cross-site scripting, or cross-frame scripting (XFS).
- The bank account information could get logged to a logging system in plain text.

For the purposes of this exercise, the team decides to first focus on the ability of the attacker to take advantage of a weakness in the application by leveraging XFS. The other attack opportunities can be reviewed in sequence after the first one.

What	Who	Why	How	Impact	Countermeasure
Bank account numbers	Cybercriminals	Financial gains with the information	XFS		

3.1.5   *What to do with the found threats*

Dashing Danielle turns to the product owner to understand what the impact would be of a breach of this information with regards to any contractual stipulations that might require the company to pay a fee to clients. The product owner acknowledges that there are clear financial impacts directly linked with data loss, and also raises the concern of brand damage that might be difficult to overcome since there are other vendors and solutions in the market that are direct competitors with Superior Products' application. Dashing Danielle also raises the likely support and recover cost associated with the attack, as well as the potential for having to purchase credit monitoring for the impacted accounts.

What	Who	Why	How	Impact	Countermeasure
Bank account numbers	Cybercriminals	Financial gains with the information	XFS	Financial payments to clients, credit monitoring, support and recover costs, brand damage	

Since the team is not familiar with the specifics of an XFS attack, Dashing Danielle is able to describe it to them. In this case, an attacker will use malicious JavaScript in an iframe that loads a page with the intent of stealing data. There are several mitigation techniques that can be used to protect against XFS. Considering that it is similar to a clickjacking attack, Dashing Danielle suggests the following mitigations:

- Preventing the browser from loading the page in frame using the X-Frame-Options or Content Security Policy (frame-ancestors) HTTP headers.
- Preventing session cookies from being included when the page is loaded in a frame using the `SameSite` cookie attribute.
- Implementing JavaScript code in the page to attempt to prevent it being loaded in a frame (known as a *frame-buster*).

Dashing Danielle puts the mitigations on the board in the "Countermeasures" column. The team discusses these mitigation techniques and reviews the current coding and architecture in place.

What	Who	Why	How	Impact	Countermeasure
Bank account numbers	Cybercriminals	Financial gains with the information	XFS	Financial payments to clients, credit monitoring, support and recover costs, brand damage	X-Frame-Options, `SameSite` cookie attribute, frame-busting

After reviewing the architecture and code, it was recognized that the application already sets its session cookies with the `SameSite` attribute set to strict:

```
Set-Cookie: CookieName=CookieValue; SameSite=Strict;
```

However, the other mitigations are not in place and require a resolution. The product owner asks whether the proposed additional countermeasures will be sufficient to resolve the open issue and whether the likelihood of an attack is high enough to warrant the additional effort. Dashing Danielle is able to produce research that shows automated tools that are used to attack their competitors. The product owner agrees to proceed, and Dashing Danielle describes and documents the steps that are needed to set the X-Frame-Options to "Deny" and set the Content Security Policy setting frame-ancestors to "None." Dashing Danielle also works with the development team to create proof of concept code that can be implemented in the code to deny the framing of the feature into another site.

The team is satisfied with the results from the threat model for this issue related to the stealing of bank account numbers. However, they don't stop here and instead move on to the next possible threat. Although the manual method of threat modeling is time-consuming, you can see that it can be pretty thorough, especially when compared to the method using a tool, which we will talk about next.

3.1.6   *Threat modeling using a tool*

Just like with the manual method of threat modeling, there are several options when it comes to tools that can be used to develop a threat model. Each of these tools has their own benefits and drawbacks. Some are free, some are commercial, some can even be as simple as using a graphical tool to just draw the architecture and annotate the potential threats. One of the biggest benefits of using a threat modeling tool that is purpose built to define threats is that it will identify the threats for you, making this tool more efficient at identifying issues. The results should still be reviewed with the appropriate stakeholders to ensure that the findings are indeed valid.

> **Threat modeling tools**
>
> Take some time to review the available tools that are out there for threat modeling. There are several commercial ones Like SecuriCAD, ThreatModeler, and IriusRisk. However, this corner of application security has fewer tools and less mature ones than in other spaces. Two threat modeling tools that are freely available are the Microsoft Threat Modeling Tool and Threat Dragon by OWASP.

Both Microsoft Threat Modeling Tool (http://mng.bz/69OA) and Threat Dragon by OWASP (https://owasp.org/www-project-threat-dragon/) offer the ability to drag and drop items to a board in order to build the architecture out and show the data flow. From there, each will generate a list of potential threats to the architecture. A simple diagram from OWASP Threat Dragon is in figure 3.3.

Threat Dragon can place threats in the STRIDE model, and with this basic diagram there are two simple threats identified automatically by the tool. One is related to spoofing and the other repudiation. Both are on the interaction between the actor and the process. What this means is that there is potential for the actor to impersonate

OWASP threat dragon—simple diagram

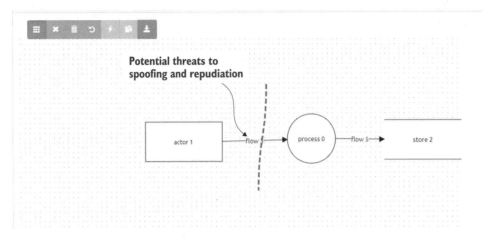

Figure 3.3   Simple diagram from OWASP Threat Dragon

another user and potentially access components of the system that they would not typically be allowed to do. To fix this, the application must put in place a means of authenticating the user and knowing that it is indeed the correct user.

I won't go through the steps of the threat model using one of these tools since the effort is similar to what I described in the previous section using the manual method. With a tool in hand, the organization can scale the threat modeling process and centralize the review and storage of the threat model. This also allows the organization to threat model reusable components once. For instance, many of the applications in an organization may use the same authentication architecture. In this case the organization can threat model the authentication once and reuse that threat model for each application.

Using the example of Superior Products, Dashing Danielle has reviewed several commercial tools for threat modeling and has decided that the best tool for the job, and budget, is OWASP's Threat Dragon. She has created a process diagram and documentation that walks the developer through the use of Threat Dragon. She created a repository where all threat models from Threat Dragon will be stored.

> ### Side notes about using a threat model tool
> This approach to decentralizing and democratizing threat modeling with a tool allows for most technical resources in the organization to create a threat model using something like Threat Dragon. If an application security resource creates it, they will review their model with the engineering team. If a resource from the engineering team creates their own threat model, then it will be assigned to the application security team for review in the repository.

Dashing Danielle begins to gather the information on the common architecture that is used in Superior Products so that she can threat model those architectures and determine the open threats in order to get them remediated. Once she completes the threat modeling of the common architectures, she works with some of the resources in the engineering organization to evaluate her findings to make sure she's not missing anything. She also discusses the remediation options for the open threats that are found. Taking the feature that was used in the manual threat modeling session, she works with the appropriate engineering team to define the architecture in the tool. She generates the threats and compares that with what she found in the manual effort.

Chances are, in this story, that Dashing Danielle will find discrepancies between what Threat Dragon found and what the team found in the manual process. This is to be expected, as they are very different processes. Furthermore, the findings from the manual process will tend to be more specific and tailored to the architecture. The findings in Threat Dragon will be more generic. The use of both methods may need to be used to first identify the broad picture using Threat Dragon, and then diving into the details with a manual session using the output from Threat Dragon as an input into the manual effort. Threat modeling is an early tool that can be used in the secure SDLC, but I'll cover how to identify security issues while coding next.

> **Exercise 3.1**
>
> Download either the Microsoft Threat Modeling Tool or OWASP's Threat Dragon from their respective download sites.
>
> Get familiar with the tool and how to navigate through it.
>
> Create a simple model similar to what you see in figure 3.3.
>
> Once your model is complete with several stencils and drawn interactions between them, locate the threats identified by the tool.
>
> Take some time to think about the suggested mitigations and whether you agree that they would be effective. If not, what would be stronger mitigations against the threats?
>
> You can document your mitigation strategies in the tool.

3.2 Security analysis tools

During development, there is potential for security issues to be introduced unintentionally and, less commonly, intentionally. These security issues can come in all levels of risk and technical implications. However, organizations do not need to rely solely on penetration testing and other tools and techniques to uncover issues later in the development life cycle. There is an abundance of tools that development teams are able to use in order to locate an issue before it becomes a production incident as shown in figure 3.4.

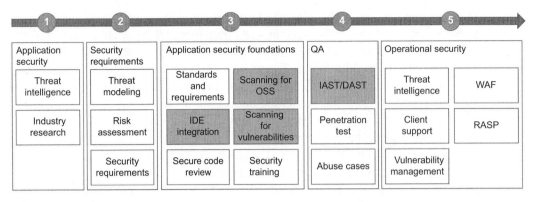

Figure 3.4   Scanning tools in the secure SDLC

Before we jump into the available tools, you should first know that a lot of tools on the market are *noisy*. This means there is a lot more noise than signal, and it is up to the organization to ensure that they have reduced the noise or run the risk of a failed adoption of the tool. This noise is often referred to as *false positives,* which means that the issue identified by the tool is not an actual security issue. Determining whether output from a scanning tool is indeed a security issue versus a false positive takes effort by the security team and the development team. For example, a tool may identify an SQL injection issue from the scanning tool. Depending on how the team manages results from the tool, the development team or security team will first triage the issue to understand whether it is indeed an issue. If you've ever worked on a software support team or otherwise have been involved with reviewing defects or bugs in an application, you will be familiar with this process. It requires knowledge of how the application is actually being used as well as the access to the code to follow the logic.

> **NOTE** False positives may seem like it's just a matter of working through the issues and closing the false positives while keeping the true positives. The truth is that false positives have a larger impact on the organization. Time is spent identifying them instead of working on other priorities. Additionally, a large number of false positives will reduce the confidence in the tools being used, and by extension, the confidence of the security team.

Similar to false positives, *false negatives* need to be considered when using analysis tools. This is where the tool failed to identify a true positive. Consider that you have integrated an analysis tool into your development pipeline. This will give your development team and your security team the confidence that issues will be identified and resolved. However, down the road, perhaps a penetration test is completed on the application and a cross-site scripting (XSS) issue is found. Depending on the analysis tool, this most likely should have been found earlier and resolved. This is an example of a false negative.

NOTE Make no mistake, false negatives can be as bad as, if not worse than, false positives. Whereas false positives will grind teams down with the amount of work that is required to filter out the issues, false negatives have the result of giving the organization a false sense of security. You expect your tools to provide the comfort that they are uncovering the issues so that you may resolve them.

There are many different tools out there to analyze code and applications, and many of them fall into more than one category. However, when it comes to security analysis tools, there are three main ones: static application security testing, dynamic application security testing, and software composition analysis. We'll cover static analysis first.

3.2.1 *Static application security testing*

Static application security testing (SAST) tools look at code as it sits. In other words, it is doing a code analysis on the source code and is looking for security issues. One common finding with SAST tools is plain text passwords that are hardcoded in the code. SAST will do this by source code by using techniques such as *taint analysis* and *data flow analysis.*

- *Taint analysis*—This allows the analysis tool to follow user input throughout the application to determine whether it is ever sanitized before it is used.
- *Data flow analysis*—This is where the analysis tool attempts to gather run-time information while the code is static.

SAST tools are primarily used at the time of development so that issues can be uncovered and resolved earlier in the development life cycle. Many of the SAST vendors today have integrated development environment (IDE) plug-ins that allow the developer to run a scan when code is being written. Some of these plug-ins are free, but I often say, "You get what you pay for," so always take the free tools with some healthy skepticism. These free tools are often offered without support or are not as frequently updated as a commercial tool.

Many of the tools I will talk about are used in conjunction with one another, as there is no silver bullet tool that will solve all of your security issues. For instance, static analysis tools are great to get an understanding of "hot spots" where the application appears to be weak from a security point of view. It can also be input into threat modeling exercises to allow the participants to focus on mitigations in trouble areas. Each SAST vendor has a different way of scanning; however, most follow a pattern of compile, model extraction, pattern matching, and flow analysis, as shown in figure 3.5.

There are certainly strengths and weaknesses with SAST tools. Some of the primary considerations are that SAST tools are usually bound by limitations in the languages that they cover, which means that if you work in most large organizations, you will have several languages that are used by the different teams. You may be forced to use more than one SAST product to get coverage of all the languages in the organization. Additionally, SAST products are the most notorious products for producing a lot of

Generic static application security testing flow

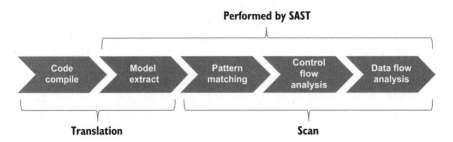

Figure 3.5   **High-level SAST process**

false positives. You may be able to tune the product to reduce this noise, but this will take time and coordination with the security and engineering teams. Lastly, the SAST tools are only able to see the static code and cannot see how it runs in an environment. This limits its ability to locate potential run-time security issues like parameter tampering.

There are a few things that SAST does well. It is ideal for locating low-hanging fruit like hardcoded secrets or passwords, as well as locating poor secure code practices like SQL injection type flaws or poor encryption methods. It can also pinpoint exactly in the code where an issue will manifest and give recommendations on how to fix it. This is extremely helpful for developers, and security folks, who want to fix a security issue as close to the code as possible.

Ultimately, SAST tools are as close to the developer as it gets. For those, myself included, who want to ensure that the right tools are available to the developer while they are creating the code, nothing really beats SAST. This needs to be weighed with the strengths and weaknesses mentioned above. Static analysis tools are decent at finding vulnerabilities early, but in order to get information to the developers as early as possible, you need to go to where they are.

3.2.2   *Tools in the development environment*

When we look at the development pipeline, the goal is to identify and resolve potential security issues before they are deployed to a production environment. This requires that tools are available and properly tuned, and that the developers know how to resolve a found issue when it's been identified. This also means that the organization should strive to find issues as early in the development pipeline as possible in order to provide the appropriate mitigations before it becomes a production vulnerability that puts the organization at risk.

To make this a reality, many of the tools that I mentioned previously have developed plug-ins or other tools to provide developers guidance on secure code as early as possible. For instance, many vendors will have an integration with development environments that developers work in to write code. Others will have standalone tools that developers will be able to leverage to do things like locate secure third-party libraries before they use them in their project. This can come in the form of internet browser plug-ins or other services.

As with the other tools in the develop pipeline I covered earlier, there are commercially developed ones as well as free and open source ones. However, you get what you pay for. The free ones, in general, will have fewer features and less support but will still create a quick feedback loop for developers and identify the low-hanging fruit.

The goal of these developer tools is to enable the developer to get in front of a potential vulnerability while they are in the process of writing the code. There is one tool that we can look at as an example here. It's a plug-in called `FindSecBugs` that can be enabled in several well-known IDEs like Eclipse, IntelliJ, and NetBeans (figure 3.6). This plug-in provides a general static analysis security scan to locate potential vulnerabilities in the code. Developers can initiate the scan, and `FindSecBugs` will produce a listing of the vulnerabilities that were found. When the developer clicks on the finding, `FindSecBugs` will take them to the line of code in the IDE.

Figure 3.6   `FindSecBugs` in Eclipse

Along with showing the line of code that has the vulnerability, `FindSecBugs` will provide reasons why it is vulnerable and possible solutions. There is a myriad of other similar tools, and as mentioned, most vendors with security solutions, especially in the SAST and SCA space, have developer tools.

The goal here is to provide the developers the resources to resolve a potential vulnerability prior to them checking the code in to the code branch. Other tools in the pipeline, like the ones I outlined previously, are still needed; however, having the ability to catch an issue before it goes to a code branch means that there is less reliance on these tools to find vulnerabilities when the code has already moved out of the developer IDE and may reduce the amount of effort spent in these other tools to find and resolve issues.

3.2.3 *Dynamic application security testing*

Where SAST and IDE integration tools are looking at the code in its static form, dynamic application security testing (DAST) will scan the application as it is running in an environment. It can be thought of as a penetration test that is performed by a tool considering that it is a security test that is looking from the outside in and attempts to locate weaknesses such as parameter tampering, cross-site scripting, improper redirects, and so forth. DAST tools are often used by penetration testers to identify low-hanging fruit in a running application and take some of the manual work out of a penetration test.

DAST tools are mostly technology independent since they are looking at the running application and attempting to find weaknesses. They are taking the outside-in approach and rely on the HTTP conversation as the common ground and therefore are not concerned about the underlying language or framework.

DAST tools rely on being language independent and being able to scan running applications to deliver the ability to scan applications in production environments and even applications that are not owned by the organization. However, both of these require prior approval from the application owner since these scans can be destructive and create disruption for the application. Additionally, DAST tends to produce fewer false positives over SAST tools since many of the findings are identified in the running application.

However, with the additional flexibility that DAST provides over SAST, there are some drawbacks. For instance, DAST tools will not be able to tell you the line of code where an issue is found unless it has been instrumented into the application. More on that in a moment. DAST also tends to be run later in the development life cycle, meaning that the issues are found farther right in the life cycle as opposed to SAST. It is possible to run DAST earlier on a developer's local environment, but this is not frequently done. DAST will also not discover code-specific issues such as hardcoded passwords. Lastly, the findings from DAST still need to be triaged by a security subject matter expert to determine whether it is a true positive.

There is another variation on DAST called interactive application security testing (IAST). The uniqueness of IAST is that it combines the strengths of SAST and DAST. It assesses the application from within through instrumenting the code. This means that the vendor will provide a library that the application then uses in its overall build of their application so that the IAST tool is running as part of the application. This allows it to have access to the code, the HTTP conversation, library information, back-end connections, and configuration information.

Open source DAST

There is an open source DAST tool available from, surprise, OWASP. It is called Zed Attack Proxy (ZAP; www.zaproxy.org/). It is free to download and use and is a great way to get your feet wet with a DAST tool. You can usually set it up to run an un-authenticated scan against an application in under a few minutes by just providing a URL. However, the real power of ZAP comes from using an authenticated session that crawls the site, determines the site map, and then begins to run through common attack patterns to report on vulnerabilities. It is a great tool to learn with, but many organizations use ZAP as their sole DAST tool as well.

One of the drawbacks of IAST is that some tools require the application to actually be attacked in order to detect a vulnerability. This may not be a huge deal for the organization so long as they have robust testing that enables the bulk of the application to be tested. Failing to have this robust testing means that a vulnerability could go undetected until that feature is exercised. A prime example of this would be the case where a reporting function is only periodically run. If this is not run as part of normal quality assurance or regression testing, then it is possible that a vulnerability in the report function would pass through to production. In this case, if the organization has good integration with its logging and reporting functions, the vulnerability would be picked up in production and allow the organization to respond accordingly.

Where IAST shines is the ability to work well in a DevOps model. I will cover DevOps, and more specifically DevSecOps in chapter 4, but for now just know that IAST provides constant monitoring of the application for vulnerabilities, and a much lower case of false positives. You are also able to tailor IAST to focus on specific areas if time is a factor. This means that you can focus on a small section of the application for testing and review the results from the IAST tool.

It's not all great news, though. IAST means more complexity with your build. That library that you integrate into your software needs to be updated periodically and could cause build failures. This means more development and deployment work by the engineering team. As mentioned, IAST can only report on what it sees. If the part of the application is not exercised, then the tool will not uncover any issues.

DAST and IAST are great ways to uncover issues in a running application and can augment the overall tool chain in a secure software development life cycle by testing the application while it is running, therefore exposing vulnerabilities that would not be found in tools farther to the left of the SDLC. It's important to remember that these tools are only a component of the defense-in-depth model and are not used to provide assurance that all vulnerabilities have been found. What about finding vulnerabilities in software that you use to build your application, but it's not actually owned by you? That is where software composition analysis comes in.

3.2.4 *Software composition analysis*

A house or a car from the outside looks well put together and looks like one object. We all know, however, that there are multiple components that are used in building that final product. Some of them are small and discreet items like screws, bolts, and nails. Others are more complex individual systems like assemblies with electronic systems that are sold as a total package.

Software is no different. A small percentage of code is actually written by a developer. In most cases, the developer pulls libraries and packages into their overall project that meet a need, as shown in figure 3.7. For instance, a developer is not going to create their own project that handles math equations; there is already a library for that either existing in their framework or from another source. This is convenient, but it becomes difficult to manage the sprawl of libraries that are used in an overall project. How do you know the libraries being used are secure or are not running afoul of license use?

Standard dependency structure

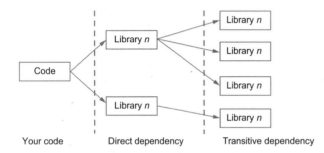

Figure 3.7 Example dependency structure

That's where software composition analysis (SCA) can help. Most typical SCA software is used to manage open source component use and tracking of the licenses. SCA tools perform

- Scans of an application's code base, including related artifacts such as containers and registries
- Identification of all open source components to help build a software bill of materials
- The library's license compliance data and any security vulnerabilities that may be known

Some SCA tools also help fix open source vulnerabilities through prioritization and auto remediation. Sounds pretty good. However, one of the issues with using an SCA tool is that it can often flag a library after it is running in production. Imagine that you built and deployed your application in January of this year, and in July your SCA tool flags one of the libraries you used as being insecure. At the time you initially built the software there was no issue. It gets even more complicated. What if the library requires you to upgrade other libraries or otherwise make a larger change to the architecture in order to resolve the finding? Another possible scenario is that the library that is flagged by the SCA may itself not be insecure, but rather a library that it depends on.

> **DEFINITION** A *direct dependency* is functionality exported by a library, or API, or any software component that is referenced directly by the program itself. A *transitive dependency* is a functional dependency, which has an indirect relationship with other dependencies.

SCA can be a huge benefit to the development team in identifying potential issues with third-party libraries. However, without the means to provide an updated library in a short period of time, the development team will be stuck knowingly running a vulnerable library. Finding out whether something is vulnerable in a direct dependency or a transitive dependency can by difficult and often requires the development team to debug or do a thorough code review to determine whether the application is truly vulnerable. Once the vulnerability has been confirmed, the most likely resolution is to upgrade to the latest release of the library. Rarely is it possible to "neuter" the library so that the application is no longer susceptible.

One other drawback of SCA is that the majority of them rely on known weaknesses, primarily from sources like the National Vulnerability Database (NVD), which catalogs known vulnerabilities through a common language called the Common Vulnerability Enumeration (CVE). These identified vulnerabilities are submitted through various sources and made available for consumption by tools. You can see more by going to https://nvd.nist.gov/ and reviewing the latest opened vulnerabilities, reviewing older ones, and searching by component.

What needs to be considered with SCA tools that report CVEs is that this is only for the known vulnerabilities and does not cover zero-day vulnerabilities in a library. This is where the vulnerability has not been reported and therefore there is no fix that can be released.

As mentioned, this is all great information, but without being able to act on the information the organization is only able to know that they are running in a vulnerable state. We'll talk more about DevSecOps in future chapters, but the critical takeaway here for SCA is to know that once a library has been detected as being insecure, a path to deliver the newer and more secure version of the software needs to be quick and clearly defined.

SCA is one critical component in the defense-in-depth model to not only provide security scanning, but also to aid in the collection and cataloging of the various libraries used by an application.

Exercise 3.2

Find a CVE on the NVD (https://nvd.nist.gov/). You can find CVEs by browsing by year and month. Click on an individual CVE to get the information on that specific vulnerability.

(continued)
Use the CVSS Scoring Calculator (www.first.org/cvss/calculator/3.0) to determine the CVSS v3.0 Base Score.

Document your finding using the following format on the CVS Examples Site: www.first.org/cvss/v3.0/examples.

- What's the vulnerability?
- What's the attack?
- What is the CVSS v3.0 Base Score?

3.3   Penetration testing

One thing about the tools that I just covered is that they will never replace a good old-fashioned penetration test. These are performed by highly skilled researchers and security professionals who are skilled at finding ways into a system and application. They are not limited to the confines of the rules that govern the tools that we previously talked about.

Exercise 3.3

Do a quick search for a job description of a penetration tester. The range of skills needed is quite impressive. Not only do you need to have technical abilities, but you will also be able to perform social engineering and physical security testing. It's no surprise that these jobs are in high demand.

There are several types of penetration tests. At the high level, there are penetration tests that occur from an internal team, like a red team within the security organization. There is also a penetration test that can be coordinated with an external party. This is typically an activity that is done in a testing environment, as depicted in figure 3.8, but can also be done in production with the right guardrails for the testers.

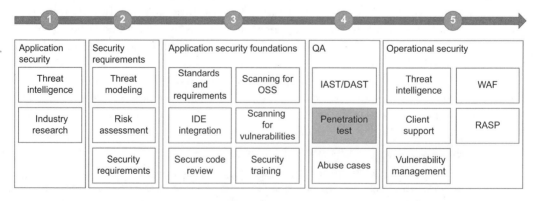

Figure 3.8   Penetration testing in the secure SDLC

DEFINITION Internal penetration testing is completed by a team inside the organization that is employed at the target company. This is a team/group that has other duties at the company but is engaged for a period of time to target a specific system/application. External penetration testing is an external party that is engaged to test the system/application. The scope is defined, and the party is given a time frame for completion.

Which testing path the organization takes depends on a few factors. In many cases, the organization is not staffed to support a full- or part-time internal penetration testing team, which makes it difficult to complete internal testing. Additionally, the organization may be required for compliance or contractual reasons to complete a penetration test from an external organization. Most organizations will opt for the external source of penetration testing, which allows them to pull a vendor in when needed. Regardless of the direction, there are several high-level approaches to penetration testing.

DEFINITION *White box testing* is where the organization provides information about the system to the tester. This can include code, credentials, network maps, and other system information. *Black box testing* is where the organization provides little to no system information. This resembles a typical attack where the information that can be gathered is generally only public information. *Gray box testing* is the in-between state. Some information is offered, but it is limited to just essential information.

Each of the approaches can be used whether it is an internal or external test. The outcome is more important. For instance, in a black box test, the tester is given no information to start with, which will closely mimic an outside attacker. This is much harder to achieve with an internal team given their alignment within the organization. This testing tends to be more closely associated with a gray box test, where the attacker has some, but not all information. Most testing that is done through an engagement with an external vendor, or with the internal team, is a white box test. Especially if the output from that test is used to meet an obligation such as compliance and contractual agreements. There is no right answer on which is best. Each type needs to be considered against the goals of the organization. However, as mentioned, white box testing tends to be more for compliance and black box is generally more for a true understanding of the security of the application and organization.

The great thing about penetration testing is that the findings tend to be true positives that are actionable, considering it was found by a simulated attack. However, in the case of white box testing, the true external security controls may not have been in place. For instance, it may be required that to exploit a particular vulnerability, the attacker would need access to an elevated account. If that elevated account information was given to the attacker at the time of the test, which is well within the parameters of a white box attack, this means that a true attacker would need to compromise that account. Perhaps there is good privilege access controls and multifactor authentication that are associated with that account and therefore the risk is very low.

Other benefits of a penetration test are that they can be scoped to specific areas and time. This means that you can request that a test focus only on a particular feature for a set amount of time, like 24 hours. The penetration test can also be used in combination with other security methods like threat modeling and scan reports. Providing this information to the penetration tester will help them cut down on steps and provide them a map to weaker areas of the application so that they may be able to focus their time and effort there. Additionally, some of the work that was done in your threat model can then be verified through the penetration test, like the security controls that you described as being in place to mitigate a found threat.

3.4   *Run-time protection tools*

Where the tools and processes that I talked about before are geared toward identifying vulnerabilities and risks, there are tools that are used to provide protection against application-level attacks during run-time in a production environment.

Run-time application security protection (RASP) is a security technology that uses run-time instrumentation to detect and block computer attacks by taking advantage of information from inside the running software. This will sound very similar to IAST, where the tool has the ability to see into the application and watch attacks as they happen. There is not a lot of difference between RASP and IAST, with the exception that RASP functions as a run-time protection tool and IAST is focused on observing and reporting on found vulnerabilities.

RASP technology can improve the security of software by monitoring its inputs, and blocking those that could allow attacks, while protecting the run-time environment from unwanted changes and tampering. RASP can also prevent exploitation and possibly take other actions, including terminating a user's session, shutting the application down, alerting security personnel, and sending a warning to the user.

Another common tool used to provide run-time protection is a web application firewall (WAF), sometimes referred to as application security manager (ASM). A WAF, shown in figure 3.9, is an application firewall for HTTP applications that applies a set of rules to an HTTP conversation and analyzes bidirectional web-based traffic. Generally, these rules cover common attacks such as cross-site scripting (XSS) and SQL injection. When the WAF recognizes a pattern that looks malicious, it will either report or block the attack depending on the configuration. Most WAF vendors also offer protection against robotic attacks (bots) like DDoS. This is largely a volumetric

Web application firewall (WAF) flow

**WAF can block malicious traffic in
the HTTP request like XSS, SQLi**

End user   WAF   Web
                                                   server   **Figure 3.9   WAF integration with web servers**

protection, but many vendors are becoming savvier by including machine learning and artificial intelligence to be more proactive in its overall protection against bots and other abusive behavior.

This is similar to RASP in the spirit of blocking malicious traffic. However, where RASP is typically run within the application itself or on the same host system, WAF can be cloud-based or otherwise external to the application. Most organizations today are moving to a cloud-based solution for WAF so that they have a managed platform for protection and a much faster adoption path. WAFs may come in the form of an appliance, server plug-in, or filter. Both RASP and WAF are run in the operational environment as shown in figure 3.10.

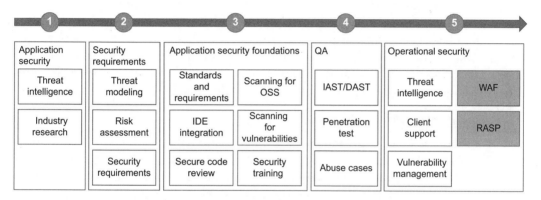

Figure 3.10   Run-time tools in the secure SDLC

These protection tools, whether WAF or RASP, help the organization by providing the run-time reporting and blocking when an attack is discovered in real time. The drawbacks are few and simple. First, the tools need to see something malicious happening in order to report or block. This means that a vulnerability needs to be detected by the tool so that it can alert, and then an action, like blocking the malicious activity, can be taken. There is also the very real potential for one of these tools to block legitimate traffic. There are plenty of scenarios where a customer may be using the system within the parameters and still trigger an alert or a block, especially when volumetric types of activity are detected, like running large batch jobs.

Another consideration when running any of these protection tools is that the rules that govern these tools need to be well vetted and managed. Both WAF and RASP require rules to be configured that tell the tools what to look for and what to do when it sees something that has been configured. For instance, if the WAF sees an HTTP conversation that includes patterns matching an SQL injection attack, should it alert or block? If it alerts, where does the alert go and what is the expected action? If it blocks, what is the user experience? Taking the out-of-the-box rules that come with the tool are often too broad and will alert on everything that it sees. Most organizations are not prepared for the flood of potential alerts. Additionally, some behavior that looks suspicious for one application may be completely legitimate for another. The rules for these tools must be well understood, tested, and managed between the application security team and the application development team.

3.5 *Vulnerability collection and prioritization*

All the tools have been integrated, and you are successfully running penetration testing. Great! You now have, most likely, a ton of vulnerabilities to process, each from a different tool, found in a different part of the process. You may not even know whether they are true positives or false ones. In most organizations, you are running at least two to three of the tools that I discussed. For instance, the organization is probably running a SAST, an SCA, and a DAST tool at the least. Others might be running just an SCA, a DAST, and a WAF. Some may be running all of them. Each of these can be noisy if they are not properly tuned to the organization's needs and processes. Additionally, they may each have their own user interface with a dashboard of some sort. This means that the development and security team will have to log in to multiple tools just to get the vulnerability information that they need.

3.5.1 *Integrating with defect tracking*

In order to be effective at managing vulnerabilities, the first thing that most organizations will do is integrate the security tools with their defect tracking tool. That might be Jira, or Bugzilla, DefectDojo from OWASP, or something else, but in any case, this will allow the developers to see the vulnerability information as it becomes known from the various scanning tools in the organization. For instance, the DAST tool that is integrated with the testing environment may detect a vulnerability when the developer's code was deployed to the testing environment. This DAST tool can then call an API with the defect tracking tool and open an issue to either the application security team to triage or directly to the development team to resolve. Which one depends on the confidence of the security tool that detected the vulnerability and the maturity of the organization.

Opening defects on teams will help get the organization to resolution on the open vulnerabilities, but being able to have visibility into all the open vulnerabilities across an organization can be challenging. There are usually different defect tracking tools being used unless the organization has tried to standardize. This means that the application security team cannot necessarily rely on building a dashboard in a single defect tracking tool. Often the application security team will build their own dashboards that pull information from the different defect tracking tools, or the security analysis tools that are being used. The application security team is then on the hook for managing this dashboard and enhancing it along the way as technology changes.

Assuming that the organization has access to a centralized dashboard that shows the various open vulnerabilities, the hard part becomes apparent:

- How do you get these vulnerabilities closed?
- How do you prioritize the vulnerabilities?

- Who owns the vulnerabilities?
- What if the vulnerability cannot be closed?
- Is there enough information for the development team to provide mitigation?

These are all questions that each application security team faces when they begin to review the open vulnerabilities. One of the most critical questions above is regarding ownership. Software is complex and is pieced together by several different components as I discussed earlier. When a vulnerability is found, for instance, in a specific part of an application, it is often difficult to locate the team that has developed that code. This is especially true where an organization has something like a team that develops common components that are leveraged by most of the applications in the organization. The application security team needs to have an inventory of the applications in the organization, as well as resources to contact that are responsible for resolving found vulnerabilities. This may be not just the engineering leader for the application like the technical manager, but also the project manager and even the product owner. Both of the latter resources typically maintain the control over what gets worked on in a given time frame, not the engineering leader.

3.5.2 *Prioritizing vulnerabilities*

Before even being able to request that the engineering team tackle a vulnerability, it's important to ensure that the organization has clear direction on time frames for resolution. Although every organization is different, and there is not a well-established industry standard on time frames, the organization should strive for resolving critical and high vulnerabilities as quickly as possible, while still having expectations on closing the medium and low ones. Table 3.1 shows generally what is seen in the industry for time-to-close timelines. Each organization may have different closure expectations and may even be directed by regulation, contracts, and other external pressures to have tighter timelines.

Table 3.1 **Vulnerability severity mapped to time to closure**

Severity	Time to closure
Critical	< 30 days
High	< 60 days
Medium	< 90 days
Low	< 365 days

Keep in mind that these vulnerabilities require code changes. This is separate from vulnerabilities that are found at the host level, like a Windows patch, which might have much shorter time frames for resolution. However, without clearly describing the expectations on closure, the organization will have a difficult time giving the engineering organization a target with the open vulnerabilities.

3.5.3   *Closing vulnerabilities*

Getting to resolution on the open vulnerabilities will take a very close partnership with the engineering teams that are responsible for resolving them. Frequent touch points to review the vulnerabilities and ensuring that they are true positives, have clear expectations on timeline for closure, clear steps to resolve, and a method in place to retest are the responsibility of the application security team. Application security will help the engineering team prioritize what is the highest risk to the organization using the methods I talked about before with a risk rating process. This can be done through weekly meetings between the application security team and the engineering team, where consensus will be reached on when the vulnerabilities will be resolved in an upcoming release. To accomplish this, the engineering team may take on a burst of effort to resolve a batch of issues like in a bug blitz or a security defect release, which are concentrated and focused efforts to remediate open vulnerabilities.

It is important for the application security team to identify common threads in the vulnerability data that they are collecting. For instance, are there frequent issues with encryption that should be addressed holistically by a more general approach like a centralized encryption program that addresses the key management, and sets standards on how, where, and when data should be encrypted? With this type of approach, it is possible to eliminate several vulnerabilities on a larger project while creating a more sustainable security model going forward.

The most important component of being able to successfully tackle the abundance of vulnerabilities that will be produced from the security tools that are integrated is getting senior leadership buy-in on the resolution effort. To facilitate this, it is critical to provide data that is trustworthy, complete, and shows the impact to the organization. One pitfall to avoid with bringing vulnerability information to senior leadership is to ensure that there is confidence in the data that is being presented. Nothing will hurt your cause more than having numbers that are frequently different with little explanation. Numbers will change as you resolve issues and bring on more or different tools. But if your method of gathering information is unreliable, your data will become unreliable, and therefore undermine your effort to convince senior leadership that you need them to help you drive down vulnerabilities. If the senior leaders feel that you will be wasting their team's time and resources, they will be less likely to support your effort.

3.6   *Bug bounty and vulnerability disclosure program*

Vulnerabilities that you generated from your tools and processes are pouring in, but what if you are looking for a different set of eyes and hands on your application? A common method for mature organizations to receive vulnerabilities from a broad audience is through a bug bounty program (BBP) or a vulnerability disclosure program (VDP). Both programs open the organization to receive vulnerabilities from external sources that are not affiliated with the organization. For instance, in a VDP, the organization will create the boundaries, communication paths, and expectations for individuals who want to locate security issues with the organization's applications. The organization will post their policy on their main website, usually on a security page, so that it is easy to locate for those who find issues within the organization's applications. These individuals, often called *security researchers*, will be able to look for security issues in the organization's applications and then submit them through the appropriate channels in order to get a resolution. This differs from the BBP, where researchers are paid a bounty for issues that they find in the application, sometimes by an intermediary organization.

3.6.1 Vulnerability disclosure program

VDPs follow the simple idea of "see something, say something" and allow for researchers to uncover security vulnerabilities without the fear of retribution. Additionally, a VDP simplifies the process of getting this security information to the right team. One of the issues that many researchers have is knowing where to send information. Additionally, once the information has been submitted, the path to resolution is often opaque to the researcher. In many cases, the researcher may not even get a response from the organization. The VDP attempts to solve this by providing five components of the policy, as shown in table 3.2.

Table 3.2 Components of a VDP

Component	Details
Purpose of the policy	This section should include the purpose of the VDP for your organization and demonstrate the commitment to more secure applications.
Scope	Probably the most important part of the policy. This is where the organization sets the boundaries for what is allowed and what is out of scope for any issues reported. For instance, the policy could specify that client data is never to be accessed or removed from the applications and that only certain parts of the application are allowed to be tested.
Safe harbor	This provides assurances to the researcher that they will not be prosecuted or have legal actions taken against them by the organization as long as they stay within the scope identified within the VDP.
Process for submission	This section sets the expectations for how the researcher should submit their findings as well as the expected quality and content that is expected in the report.
Expectations	This is what the researcher should expect from the organization as it responds to the submitted report. Examples would be the time between submission and response, when the finder may publicly disclose their finding, and what the communication will look like between the researcher and the organization.

3.6.2 Bug bounty program

The BBP builds on the VDP by providing an incentive structure to the submitted vulnerabilities. In the BBP, the organization will pay based on a predefined set of guidance. This will put a price on specific vulnerabilities like SQL injection, or the organization may structure the cost by severity where critical issues are priced higher than low ones. Regardless of the structure, this needs to be determined ahead of time and the leadership team needs to be ready to provide periodic payouts for bounties. The common BBP has two options: private BBP and public BBP.

> **DEFINITION**   *Private BBP* is a VDP program that is available only to researchers who are invited to the program. A *public BBP* opens the program to any researcher who wants to participate.

As vulnerabilities are submitted, the organization will need to triage them. This is typically completed by the application security team in conjunction with the engineering team. The vulnerability should be determined to be a true positive, and the severity agreed upon. Depending on how the policy is written, it may allow for the public disclosure of the vulnerability should it pass the allowed time frames. This means that it is imperative that the organization has a clear process for resolving the issue within the time frames that are in their policy and maintain communication and coordination with the researcher. The news is littered with cases of a vulnerability disclosed to an organization where that organization failed to stick to their own policy, and it instead became a very public matter.

3.6.3   *Third-party help with vulnerabilities*

There are several third-party programs that will assist the organization with setting up and maintaining both a VDP and BBP. These services will assist you in creating the VDP and host it on their site. They will also be the middleperson that accepts reports and checks them for quality, and in some cases they will de-duplicate them against a list of vulnerabilities that you may have already identified through your internal tools. For instance, a researcher may uncover a XSS issue in your application. In this case, the third party will match that against vulnerabilities that you have already identified and provided to them in order to determine whether this is a new or existing issue. They will then respond to the researcher that the issue is already identified and provide expectations for remediation.

There are several prominent companies that provide this type of service like HackerOne and Bugcrowd. However, there are also many companies that run their own bug bounty like Intel, Facebook, Google, Apple, Microsoft, and many others. In these cases, the payouts and rules of engagement are clear and provide these organizations with the ability to have another channel for getting vulnerability information.

> **Exercise 3.4**
>
> Take a look at Microsoft's www.microsoft.com/en-us/msrc/bounty?rtc=1 and Google's www.google.com/about/appsecurity/reward-program/ Bug Bounty Program (BBP). Understand the scope and the rules of engagement, and think about how this would work in your own organization.

3.7 Putting it together

I covered a lot of ground in this chapter on the different tools and processes that may be used during the secure development life cycle. You may be wondering how all of these fit in and where they make the most amount of sense. As I mentioned previously, security is the business of applying the right amount of mitigation to reduce risk to as low as possible for an organization. It's critical to ensure that you are not overspending. A simple example that most of us can relate to is a car repair. Most of us would never pay for a repair that cost more than the actual vehicle worth. Security is no different. You can apply every tool that I mentioned in this chapter, every process, build a massive application security team, and pay for a massive BBP. Will that make you more secure? Yes. Will it cost you more than what it is that you're actually trying to protect? Most likely.

In previous examples, I showed the development life cycle, the various components, and where you can apply technology, process, and people. Taking another look at that example SDLC with the tools from this chapter integrated looks like figure 3.11.

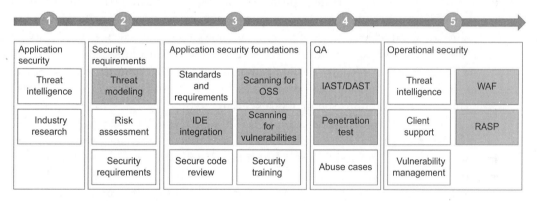

Figure 3.11   SDCL with tool integration

In figure 3.11, the tools I identified in this chapter are highlighted. We can use the example of Superior Products from earlier to help illustrate how these tools should be integrated.

Remember that Dashing Danielle from Superior Products was able to perform a threat model with the development team in order to identify open threats. Based on that threat model, the development team was able to define several requirements that will mitigate against the identified threats. Superior Products then begins the coding effort on the feature that will allow users to link their bank account in the application so that they can get paid for selling items. While coding, the developers take advantage of IDE plug-ins that show them when code that they are developing might potentially introduce a security issue. This reduces the introduction of additional vulnerabilities that may not be caught until further in the development life cycle. One developer has additional questions regarding a found vulnerability from the IDE tool, and Dashing Danielle is dispatched to work with the developer to determine a more secure approach.

The developers are able to use the browser plug-in available from their SCA tool to determine whether the library they are preparing to use is secure or not. The SCA tool integrated with the developer's local build identifies a few old components that are being used in the application. Although these findings are already existing and are not related to the current coding, the developer now has the opportunity to locate a more secure version of the components and integrate them.

The code is now moving to a testing environment where test analysts are able to run predefined test plans. In this stage, security tools that test the application in a running state like IAST and DAST will be used to identify security issues that need to be resolved before an application gets moved to a production environment. Superior Products has decided to use a free and open source DAST tool to determine run-time issues with the application. This tool identified several issues that need resolution. Because this was located in a test environment, the development team has an opportunity to resolve it before code is pushed to production. Dashing Danielle is alerted of the findings when the DAST tool opens three vulnerabilities in the development team's defect tracking tool. She takes some time to triage the issues in order to determine whether the issues are true positives. Luckily, only one of them was determined to be a true positive; however, it will take time to fix and may delay the release. She does a risk rating on the issue and builds out the recommended solution with an approximate time to resolution. She then takes this to the product owner to get it prioritized.

There is some discussion regarding the issue found in the DAST tool with the product owner and the engineering manager. Resolving the issue will require rewriting a component related to how authorization is managed in the application. This is not a small task, but to not do it means that a user may be able to link another user's bank account. This is too significant of an issue to allow in the product. The product owner makes the decision to prioritize the vulnerability and leave another feature out of the release in order to balance the remaining work.

The new features are available in a pre-production environment, and Superior Products has engaged with a third party to complete a penetration test. They use the threats that were identified in the threat model as the basis for the scope of the penetration test, as well as the authorization finding in the DAST tool. The penetration test is completed with no significant findings, and the team is able to validate that the countermeasures they identified in their threat model are indeed providing mitigation.

The features are finally ready to be deployed to a production environment. Given the vulnerabilities that were identified and the team's ability to remediate them, Dashing Danielle recommends that integrating with the enterprise WAF will provide sufficient run-time protection against what they deem are the most likely threats that they will face.

The product goes to production behind the WAF, and the customers are now using the features in the most secure manner that Superior Products could provide. All is well!

Summary

- Threat modeling is the process of identifying threats that may impact an architecture. It's used to understand the who, what, why, how, and countermeasures as it relates to threats.

- There are two prominent methods to performing threat models: one through a manual process, the other by using tools.

- Analysis tools throughout the software development life cycle provide feedback to the development team as early as possible. These tools are used to find issues in static code, running applications, and in the software components that are used to build the final product.

- Developer security tools are used to give developers quick access to potential vulnerabilities as early as possible. Many of these are available as plug-ins within the developers IDE.

- Run-time protection tools are used to provide protection when an application has been deployed to a production environment. Two of these tools are RASP and WAF.

- Penetration testing is the closest method to mimic an actual attack by a threat actor. These tests are performed by skilled people who are able to locate weaknesses in the application within scope.

- Vulnerability management becomes quickly overwhelming when multiple tools are finding vulnerabilities. The organization needs a common approach that builds confidence in the data and enables developers to act on the information. This gives the organization the greatest chance of getting ahead of the vulnerabilities.

- Bug bounty and vulnerability disclosure programs provide an avenue for researchers who are external to the organization to submit reports that identify vulnerabilities within the scope that the organization has provided. In the BBP, researchers are paid for their findings.

Part 2

Developing the application security program

Now that you understand the basic building blocks of application security, it's time to put those concepts to the test in developing an overall program that can be used in an organization to develop more secure software. First, you'll learn about the different deployment models that are available, and how each one can be used to introduce security into the development life cycle. Different models like Waterfall, Agile, Lean, and DevOps bring their own approaches to integrating security. However, the security tools and processes that are used in each of these methodologies is still valid and useful regardless of which one is chosen, as long as a feedback loop is present that provides information to the development team in a timely manner.

In chapter 5, you'll learn about how to spread the security responsibility beyond the security organization to achieve greater scale. Moving beyond the security team means educating the development teams and providing them the information they need to integrate security into the developed applications. Additionally, maturity modes can be used to measure the security successes and achievements of the organization.

Chapter 6 will dive into how to provide a paved road to production through tooling and services. These services should be created by application security and made available to the development organization through callable application programming interfaces (API) so that they can be called during most stages of the development life cycle. This chapter will also cover how to identify the risk of a release and ensure that it meets the risk tolerance of the organization.

Releasing secure code

4

This chapter covers

- Exploring how organizations can release secure code
- Explaining what a DevSecOps pipeline looks like
- Looking at why DevSecOps supports security better than other release methods
- Differentiating a DevOps model compared to other models
- Discovering how to use a fast feedback loop for security issues

In this chapter, I will show some release methods that are in practice in most organizations. While each has its pros and cons, release methods such as DevOps can support a more secure method of delivering software. If you are not familiar with DevOps, it is a set of practices that bring together development and operations to deliver software in an efficient manner.

> **DEFINITION** Microsoft defines *DevOps* as a compound of development (Dev) and operations (Ops). DevOps is the union of people, process, and technology to continually provide value to customers.

What has been historically the case for software development and release is that there is a product team, a development team, a testing team, and an operational team that all take part in the delivery of features and products to a production environment. This is typically done in a way where each team has gates that start and finish their part of the process. DevOps intends to streamline that process and reduce or eliminate the hand-offs between teams. Most organizations will accomplish this by creating a single team that owns not just the development of the code, but the testing and delivery as well. In some smaller organizations, there may only be a few people on the team who do all of these activities themselves; in larger organizations, specialists would be used to perform specific tasks within the team. For instance, in these larger teams, there would be one or more people focused solely on the deployment, or just the testing, as well as having developers focused on the code. However, in all of these cases, the team would share the work items as one team.

DevOps is primarily a function of automation, tooling, and processes. This model works best when there is little to no manual work or processes. Some of the most successful organizations that use a DevOps model are able to deploy code from a development environment to a production environment in minutes. And they can do this multiple times a day. To achieve this level of speed and confidence, the organization will build a CI/CD pipeline.

> **DEFINITION** A *CI/CD pipeline* is where code is continuously integrated (CI) using an integration tool like Jenkins, and continuously delivered or deployed (CD) using deployment tools like Octopus or Ansible. Code is built into packages that are automatically pushed to a production environment (continuously deployed) or could require a manual step to push code to production (continuously delivered).

The confidence in deployment is built in through strong controls around how source code is tracked, merged, and versioned. Testing must occur all throughout this model, from the developer's unit test at the lowest level, up to the testing of API integration and system testing. Lastly, monitoring of the application in production for potential issues and having a rapid feedback loop to the development team will reduce the time to fix issues as they are found. This gives greater confidence to the development team that they can deploy and fix code rapidly. This certainly enables the developer to feel empowered, but where does security fit?

> **NOTE** There needs to be a clarification between DevOps and CI/CD. Although there is some overlap in the implementation, CI/CD focuses on the automation and the tools that deliver software to an environment. DevOps focuses on culture and process in order to produce software.

4.1   Security in DevOps

The general appeal of DevOps is that it allows for a rapid resolution of discovered issues. As an application security person myself, this makes me happy. This means that if the developer has the right information and knows how to resolve a vulnerability, then they can fix a vulnerability and have it running in production in a short period of time—maybe even within a day! But getting to this point requires a few things to be in place and working well. Without getting into the specific tools, a successful DevSecOps pipeline provides the following capabilities:

- Educating, enabling, and empowering the development team to make security decisions during the development process
- Fewer security gates in favor of faster, more targeted testing using automation
- Vulnerability management that provides a fast discover>triage>report>resolve process

I'll break each of these down here in this chapter. But first it's important to understand that the basic security tools and processes that I've covered in the previous chapters still hold true even in a DevOps model. There is still room for threat modeling, static application security testing (SAST), and penetration testing, for example. However, where they are integrated and by whom changes.

4.1.1 DevOps pipelines

As described previously, a DevOps pipeline consists of automation that integrates and delivers code to a production environment. The tools that are part of that pipeline vary in each organization, but the fundamental pipeline for code to be delivered will resemble figure 4.1.

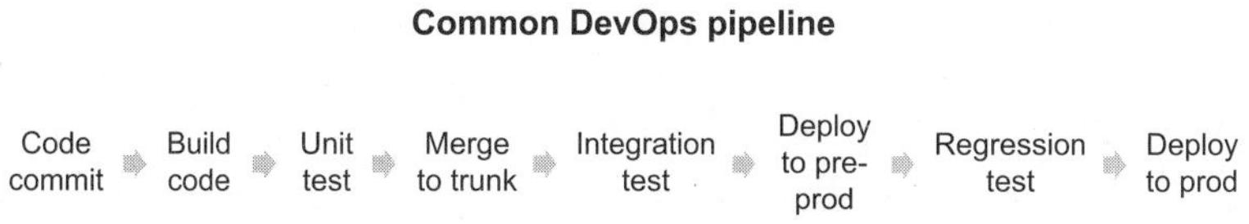

Common DevOps pipeline

Code commit ➡ Build code ➡ Unit test ➡ Merge to trunk ➡ Integration test ➡ Deploy to pre-prod ➡ Regression test ➡ Deploy to prod

Figure 4.1 Standard components of a DevOps pipeline

In figure 4.1, the automation occurs at every step unless the organization has decided to add a manual step for deployment. For simplicity, in the rest of this chapter we will assume continuous deployment where the code is sent to production automatically as long as it has cleared all automated testing and checks.

For the pipeline as shown in figure 4.1, the code goes through the following process:

- The code is committed by the developer once they have completed development.
- It enters a build process that pulls together the different libraries and components together in order to create the application.
- The unit tests are run that test the code changes for any potential regression issues.

- If the build and test complete on the local level, the code is merged to a trunk where additional tests are initiated in order to perform tests with the code change in the context of other components of the overall system, like APIs and other products in the organization.

- If the merge and integration testing complete without failure, then the artifact like a jar or war file is deployed to a preproduction environment where additional testing is run as the final stage prior to production.

- Lastly, assuming that there are no issues found in the preproduction environment, the artifact is delivered to a production environment and is now live for customer interaction.

At each stage of the pipeline, the processes and tools ensure that all checks are complete before the code is moved to the next stage. For instance, if the build breaks in the developer's environment, then unit tests are not triggered. Likewise, if integration tests fail, then the code is not delivered to a preproduction environment. This model moves code rapidly through the system with each component tied to the next through automation. Although there are many steps in figure 4.1, some organizations can accomplish most or all of these steps through one platform and can do so rapidly.

> **NOTE**   GitLab is a common platform that can perform most of these components, allowing organizations to build, test, deploy, and monitor their application.

This process of code deployment can occur many times a week, a day, or an hour, with each release bringing new features to customers at a rapid pace.

4.2   *DevOps isn't the only game in town*

There are many different processes and models to release software. Similar to choosing the right security controls that align to the actual risk it is attempting to protect, the right release methodology needs to be in line with the organization's goals. If you are an organization that needs to release software multiple times a day like Facebook, Amazon, Netflix, or Google do, then a DevOps model works well. If you are an organization that requires more strict control over your code releases, like a health care or critical infrastructure organization, a Lean or Waterfall methodology may work better. The important takeaway with these different methods is that every organization approaches their release cycle differently. In fact, in many organizations, they will not follow just one approach across the organization and may even combine different ones to gain efficiency. For example, some teams may follow a DevOps model while others are Lean, and others may use a CI model while working in a Waterfall methodology. I will describe these methodologies next.

4.2.1   *Waterfall*

Waterfall is a methodology that depends on each part of the process acting as a checkpoint where formal sign-off must be achieved before the next part of the process can begin. This, of course, leads to a long deployment process and can have the impact of the organization releasing features that are no longer considered cutting edge.

In a typical Waterfall model, there are several stages (figure 4.2). Much of this will sound familiar to what has been described in previous chapters. This is largely because many organizations built their application security programs while their engineering teams still worked in a Waterfall methodology.

- *Requirements phase*—Where product requirements from the client or internally within the organization are defined and documented.
- *Analysis phase*—Where the scaffolding of the application is defined, including the database schema and business rules that will govern the way the application works. For instance, the application requires authorization from an administrator for certain critical functions.
- *Design phase*—Begins to build the architecture of the application and makes key decisions on technology.
- *Implementation phase*—Where the real fun begins. Everything to this stage has been to clearly define what needs to be created while coding.
- *Testing phase*—When code has been considered complete and begins to go through the process of testing which is likely to uncover defects that will need to be resolved before the final product reaches production.
- *Operations phase*—Where the operations team takes over and ensures the uptime and patching of the application as it's running.

Waterfall methodology

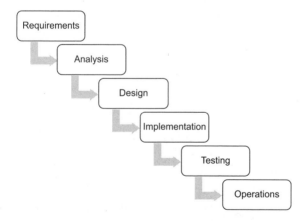

Figure 4.2   Waterfall methodology

Once these phases are complete and the code is running in production, the process starts again with a new set of requirements. The release could have been a monthly, quarterly, or even a biannual release. These releases tend to be large with many features, hence the heavy process to ensure that everything is accounted for and production-ready. However, in this process, there is typically a part of the development team that is needed to manage the incoming production defects. They process these defects and push fixes to production in something like a fix pack, but still with the proper oversight of a *change control* entity that ensures that changes are properly considered by an audience of stakeholders.

Security in Waterfall is handled primarily through two avenues. One is through the methodology itself during the requirements gathering, the design phase, and the testing phase where the security team or tools within the organization will impose security. Some of the requirements that are pressed may be part of regulatory, compliance, or contractual needs. New security technology will also be required by the security team if it provides better protection for the organization. The security tools that are either integrated with the development environment or during the testing phase will uncover different security issues that will be treated as defects where they will be triaged, assigned, and resolved.

The second way that security makes it into the Waterfall methodology is through the support path. If a vulnerability is found in production, the support team will typically be alerted and will be required to triage and resolve it in a fix release. This is true for not only issues that may be reported by external parties, like clients, but also for issues that are discovered when components that are used in the application become vulnerable. This can happen when a weakness is discovered in something like the web server or a parsing library that has a newly discovered vulnerability that needs to be resolved quickly. Waiting for the next release cycle for a critical or high vulnerability to be resolved is unlikely to win over any fans.

Although Waterfall can create latency in the process of releasing software, the lines for injecting security in the process are pretty clear. Need to get security requirements in? Do that during the early phases. Found a vulnerability after the code is in production? Open a ticket with the support team. What happens when the process is kicked up another notch?

4.2.2   Agile

Agile is another methodology that allows for development teams to deliver software to clients. However, in this case the process is continuous and has the intent of getting software to the client often and quickly, as shown in figure 4.3. Agile methodology is typically associated with Scrum and Kanban frameworks, where there are short iterations and clear work items outlined for a given time frame.

Agile methodology focuses on delivering software quickly through collaboration within the organization as well as with the client. Agile is also able to adapt to changes without impacting the delivery of software, hence the name. Unlike Waterfall, which requires a more structured approach to intake new requirements, Agile allows for changes to be integrated in a short period of time. If the development organization is using something like Scrum in their Agile methodology, the development team would work in sprints that are a short burst of work over 2, 3, or 4 weeks. The goal in a sprint is to complete some minimal viable product by the end of that sprint that can be deliv-

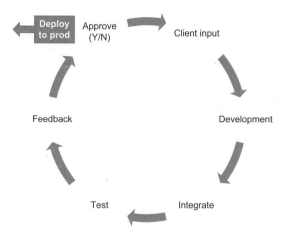

Figure 4.3 Agile process diagram

ered to a client. In most cases, a 2-week time period for code release will not provide enough time to release a large change, but a small viable proof of concept on a feature is possible. This can then be delivered to an environment for clients to "touch and feel" and provide their feedback.

The development team that works in an Agile methodology is typically small, and tends to be cross-functional, or full-stack, where the team has ownership of all components of the application development and deployment. This means that the team will own the user interface, the business logic development, the database schema and development, the configuration management, the deployment, and the operational aspects of the application. A team that strictly follows Agile will follow the 12 principles in the Manifesto of Agile Software Development:

- Customer satisfaction by early and continuous delivery of valuable software.
- Welcome changing requirements, even in late development.
- Deliver working software frequently (weeks rather than months).
- Close, daily cooperation between businesspeople and developers.
- Projects are built around motivated individuals, who should be trusted.
- Face-to-face conversation is the best form of communication (co-location).
- Working software is the primary measure of progress.
- Sustainable development, able to maintain a constant pace.
- Continuous attention to technical excellence and good design.
- Simplicity—the art of maximizing the amount of work not done—is essential.
- Best architectures, requirements, and designs emerge from self-organizing teams.
- Regularly, the team reflects on how to become more effective, and adjusts accordingly.

Agile focuses more on individuals contributing to the greater good than relying on technology and processes to bring software to a reality. This leads to quicker, and sometimes more impactful, decisions being made at the lowest level within the development team. The teams are empowered but also reap the consequences should something go wrong. For instance, a poor design decision made by one developer could impact the rest of the team when it comes to support.

How does security integrate in the Agile methodology? Similar to the DevOps methodology, Agile allows for quick development and deployment of fixes for security vulnerabilities. These found vulnerabilities can be triaged by the application security team, presented to the Scrum team for prioritization, and worked in a future sprint. This means that, in theory, a fix for a security issue could be in production within a few weeks; shorter if the issue is severe enough. Where there are some potential issues is getting security vulnerabilities prioritized and understood by the development team and the product owners. There will almost always be pushback, especially when time frames are short and client features need to go out. However, similar to Waterfall, the Agile team may have a separate Scrum team that is responsible for resolving defects found in production and potentially picking up security issues as well. When there is a separate work stream like this, it allows the development to continue unimpeded while support and security work would be merged into the development branch or released as its own fix pack.

4.2.3   *Lean*

Lean has been in practice for decades, going back to the early automobile assembly lines in order to streamline processes, optimize people and resources, and more importantly eliminate waste. When the Lean concept was introduced to the world of software development, its purpose was to focus on reducing waste and maximizing value to deliver quality products quicker. Thereafter, it was not surprising to see development practices leveraging both Lean and Agile to optimize software development practices in what is commonly called Lean Agile. There are five key principles that lay the foundations of Lean:

- *Defining value*—This is what the customer is looking for and is willing to part with their money to get.
- *Map the value stream*—Identifying the tasks and components that make that value a reality. Those that do not add value are wasted motions.
- *Creating flow*—This is where impediments are removed, and the process is defined well enough to ensure that the value stream is smooth.
- *Establish pull*—This is where the work in progress is reduced while ensuring that just enough is being done for a smooth flow of work. The goal here is to eliminate context switching, which is ineffective.
- *Pursue perfection*—This is reducing overall waste and always looking for process improvement by asking questions around the efficiency of the current process.

These key principles can be applied in various fields and practices, including software development. It may not be surprising that many people adopt Lean practices even in their daily lives for nontechnical practices.

Since the introduction of Lean Agile, the software development practice has been able to reduce rework and waste by replacing Waterfall development in many organizations. This would increase the ability to deliver marketable features quicker and continue to improve the development practice along the way. The Lean culture not only allows teams to continue to improve but also creates a culture where discovering ways to become more valuable for the collective team becomes an acceptable practice.

Today, most mature software development teams are practicing Lean Agile as an inherent by-product of the two methodologies combined. Lean software development principles incorporate the original Lean and Agile principles by

- Identifying and eliminating wasteful steps and practices
- Building in quality through paired programming and test automation
- Encouraging knowledge sharing practices with other team members
- Deferring commitments and plans without having full knowledge of scope/plan/work
- Delivering faster with targeted scope and features
- Embracing and respecting people's opinions/input/feedback for continuous improvement
- Optimizing the whole by seeing the bigger reward and not focusing solely on one function or one practice

In software development, reducing waste means focusing on the most needed requirements that are the most marketable and consumable for the users, as shown in figure 4.4. In addition, leveraging Lean also supports the concept of having a *full-stack team*, where the team includes not only the core developers, testers, and project managers but also the environments, network, and security resources. These specialized roles are also included to ensure delivery of the product at the highest value.

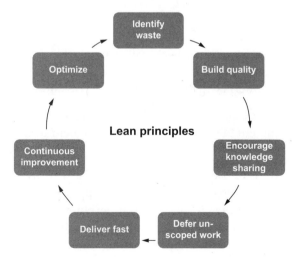

Figure 4.4   Lean process diagram

How does application security work inside of a Lean methodology? Security involves many different aspects, including application, infrastructure, and business risk. Because these aspects are so vast, identifying and prioritizing the security risks have become more complex and manual. In the Lean world, this may amount to potential waste and rework. Lean in application security should be used to unblock security processes and procedures and insert security into the software development life cycle. This is accomplished by aligning security practices into software development that will increase participation and reduce rework by incorporating security requirements and practices during requirements, analysis, and design phases. In addition, Lean in security includes establishing security monitoring and continuous improvements as the product evolves and matures through the software development life cycle.

One important callout related to Lean in application security is that it works well with other software development methodologies such as DevOps and Agile, considering that Lean is an approach that looks for continuous process improvement. As mentioned with other methodologies, the tools that are used elsewhere to provide security are still applicable here. Threat modeling, code reviews, test automation, and monitoring are all still needed to provide assurance that security is baked into the product when it is delivered to the customer. The major difference is the focus on a "test and learn" approach that attempts to continuously review the security processes in each stage in order to understand where improvements should be made. An example of this would be in the case of threat modeling. When performing a threat model, regardless of the methodology, it's important to validate that the model is accurate. After a recently completed threat model for an application, it may be found that through validation, a control that was assumed to be present was not. In this case, the security team and the development team will review their threat modeling process and develop better process documentation, as well as ensure that the appropriate stakeholders are included in the threat modeling process.

4.2.4 *DevOps supports security better*

DevSecOps, SecDevOps, DevOps with security, it's been called many things. I've mostly heard it referred to as *DevSecOps*, so that is the term I will use here. Like the parent term of *DevOps*, the *DevSecOps* definition can depend on the process and technology.

> **DEFINITION**   IBM defines *DevSecOps* as automatically baking in security at every phase of the software development life cycle, enabling development of secure software at the speed of Agile and DevOps.

The methodologies I covered previously each provide a means for security to be integrated; however, the DevOps methodology provides a unique opportunity for security to be more rapidly combined with other features in the development pipeline. As described, DevOps, and by extension DevSecOps, allows for development teams to have security fixes deployed to a production environment as quickly as the CI/CD pipeline can support.

In today's environments, where your applications are running, security issues are ever present. In early 2021, Redscan released a report that reviewed the trends in vulnerabilities that were added to the National Vulnerability Database (NVD) from 1989 to 2020. This report highlighted how much has changed over that time and specifically how 2020 was a banner year for new vulnerabilities. The report found

- More security vulnerabilities were disclosed in 2020 (18,103) than in any other year to date, at an average rate of 50 CVEs per day.
- 57% of vulnerabilities in 2020 were classified as being "critical" or "high severity" (10,342).
- There were more high and critical severity vulnerabilities in 2020 than the total number of all vulnerabilities recorded in 2010 (4,639, including low, medium, high, and critical).
- Nearly 4,000 vulnerabilities disclosed in 2020 described as "worst of the worst," meeting the worst criteria in all NVD filter categories.
- Low-complexity CVEs on the rise, representing 63% of vulnerabilities disclosed in 2020.

What does this tell us about what we are up against in application security? Vulnerabilities are being released at a rapid pace, and they are becoming easier to exploit. This means that in order to stay ahead of significant issues, application security needs to be able to move swiftly as well. With this in mind, the methodology that the engineering organization has decided to use matters. For instance, in the Waterfall methodology, waiting possibly weeks or even months to release a resolution to a found vulnerability would leave the organization exposed much longer than necessary. Even in an Agile organization, a fix might be weeks away. Pretty fast, but not fast enough for an attacker who might already have code that exploits a CVE that was just publicly released. Attackers today can take information from a CVE and turn it into an exploit within hours.

This is where a methodology like DevSecOps can support the rapid deployment of security fixes (figure 4.5). A well-tuned pipeline should allow, depending on the vulnerability, for a fix to a security issue to be deployed within hours assuming that the application security team has a well-defined process for triaging and assigning found vulnerabilities, and the DevSecOps team has the ability to pull in code changes, test, and deploy in a rapid manner.

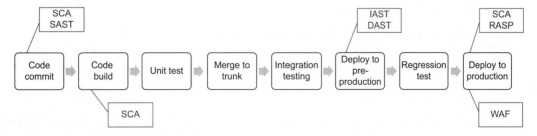

Figure 4.5 DevSecOps process diagram

There are several key practices to keep in mind when building security into a DevOps pipeline:

- *Security issues are no different than any other software defects.* In fact, they should be indistinguishable from software defects, considering that vulnerabilities are essentially a software defect that has security implications. Consider a defect like a memory leak in a software program. This can be leveraged by an attacker to consume the resources on the server and make the application unavailable. However, even without the security considerations, this is still an application issue that impacts the performance.

- *Automation of security should be a priority.* Just like there are automated tasks within the CI/CD that run tests, perform deployment, and run checks, security should be no different. In this case, the running of SAST, DAST, SCA, infrastructure code configuration checks, and the like should be made part of the CI/CD with feedback to the development team.

- *Present tools to the development team.* Once the previous step is integrated in order to ensure that security is an automated part of the CI/CD, the findings in those tools need to be presented to the development team as early as possible and enabled to block the build from completing successfully and deploying vulnerable code. This last point is critical. Code should not be allowed to continue to a production environment with known vulnerabilities—just like the failure of a regression test would stop the build from progressing.

- *Once the application is deployed to a production environment, it is important to continue to monitor it for security related issues.* As I mentioned previously, things like insecure third-party libraries are a constant concern and can be introduced after the code is deployed to production. If everything goes well in the CI/CD and there were no found vulnerabilities with the developed code, that still doesn't mean that a third-party library that is used by the application would always be secure. Additionally, as infrastructure is today being set up and configured as code, called infrastructure as code (IaC), there is a unique opportunity to apply a consistent approach to secure infrastructure, but in order to do this, the organization needs to have a method of monitoring for configuration drift. This is where a single change is made in a production environment, often through manual means, which varies from the IaC templates that the organization normally uses.

Considering these practices when developing the pipeline will give the organization the better protection against the deluge of vulnerabilities. Practices aren't always enough. Having the right tools integrated at the right time matters as well.

4.2.5   *DevSecOps example*

Taking the example of Superior Products, they have been using the DevOps methodology for some time and their development teams consist of developers, testers, operational people, and, of course, Dashing Danielle. She has worked tirelessly over the past few months building in the following tools and processes:

- SAST has been integrated into the developer's IDE where the developer has the opportunity to scan their code for security issues early.
- SCA is integrated into the IDE as well as in each developer's browser as a plug-in. The IDE integration allows for the developer to identify issues in the third-party libraries that they are using in the building of their software. The browser plug-in allows the developer to research new libraries with confidence that there are no known security vulnerabilities impacting the library they are reviewing.
- When the developer issues a pull request to submit code, the code repository tool requires the developer to submit the results of their SCA and SAST in the pull request.
- The Continuous Integration tools have SAST and SCA tools enabled that incrementally scan the code changed when the developers code is integrated with additional code changes from other developers.
- DAST is integrated into the testing environment to ensure that once the code is integrated and deployed to the testing environment, security tests used to scan while the application is running are triggered. This also includes the use of automated penetration testing tools to augment the DAST scan.
- Dashing Danielle integrated the ticketing system that is used in Superior Products so that any tools that identify a security issue will generate a defect, assign it to the appropriate development team, and alert them of a new finding on their collaboration channels. The defect is opened with recommendations from the scanning tools on how to resolve the found issue.

This setup allows Superior Products to rapidly identify security issues, get them to the right team, provide resources on how to resolve the issue, as well as develop a criticality and timeline for issue resolution based on the organizations resolution policy. This well-oiled machine is capable of finding and resolving security issues rapidly before the code is deployed to production.

What about Acme Services? They're not as up to speed as Superior Products, and although they are using an Agile methodology, their releases are only deployed to production once every 4 weeks. They are still relying on a SAST tool that only runs once the code has been checked into their code repository and the continuous integration engine picks up the changes. Furthermore, the development team has decided not to trigger a failed build when vulnerabilities are found due to the timeline commitments to get code deployed at the end of the 4-week sprint. This means that code is built with vulnerabilities identified and is then deployed to a testing environment with the known vulnerabilities. Acme Services has decided to partner with their internal penetration testing team to run a penetration test prior to the final build package being completed. This ultimately means that vulnerabilities are discovered late with the intention of queuing up the vulnerabilities that are found into the next sprint and subsequent release. This leaves them potentially exposed for weeks and shows the power of having tools integrated throughout the process.

4.3   *Application security tooling in the pipeline*

As I mentioned, most of the tools that have been discussed previously in this book are still valid in a DevSecOps pipeline with subtle differences. There are also platforms and tools that are built specifically for the rapid release cycle of DevSecOps that can aid in the development and delivery of code in a secure manner, as shown in figure 4.6.

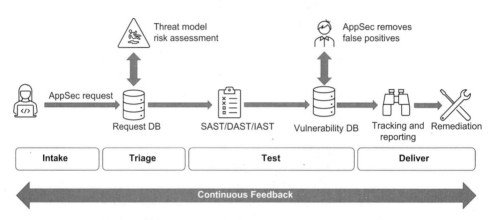

Figure 4.6   DevSecOps according to OWASP

In the rugged DevOps pipeline, your initial entry is through intake where there are still manual and people-led activities such as threat modeling and a secure design assessment. From here, a well-tuned pipeline lets the tools do the work of identifying and coordinating the vulnerabilities that may have been uncovered. I'll cover these next.

4.3.1   *Threat modeling in DevSecOps*

I covered threat modeling in earlier chapters where I described the process of identifying threats that impact a given design or architecture with the goal of identifying threats that can impact an architecture as early as possible. One key difference with threat modeling in the DevSecOps methodology is the need to address operational threats early as well. This means finding threats that impact the code once it is deployed to a running environment. Some example threats that impact the operational environment are

- Lateral movement in an operational environment where a compromise allows the attacker to pivot to another system.
- Changes to configuration after the application has been deployed that open the environment up to potential attacks—for instance, turning off security controls during a troubleshooting session.

- Improper segmentation between production and nonproduction environments that lead to the ability of an attacker to compromise a nonproduction environment in order to pivot to a production one.
- An attack on any of the key resources for application security, such as hardware security modules (HSMs), and secrets used by the application that potentially lead to an availability issue.

Threat modeling is still a valid input into the development of requirements in DevSecOps by simply asking "What can go wrong?" and "What can we do about it?" One of the key benefits of having operational resources assist with the exercise of threat modeling is that they are in the unique position of seeing firsthand how the application can be abused. If you ever listen in on a conversation between a developer of an application and a person responsible for the deployment and operation of that application, you will hear two different voices on how the application actually works. The operational resource will have a much different perspective on how the application is actually used by end users. Chances are, they will see the application being used in creative ways that were not considered by the developer or even the application security team. This is the power of threat modeling in DevSecOps. Identifying potential flaws with those that understand how the product works, and can be broken, will improve the quality and security of the application when the design decisions are being made.

One of the hurdles with threat modeling in the DevSecOps methodology is that it does not react well to slow processes. As I described in previous chapters, threat modeling can be done through a manual process with a whiteboard and subject matter experts or through a tool such as Microsoft's Threat Modeling Tool. Neither of these can feasibly be used in an environment where releases are happening multiple times a day. This means that threat modeling has to occur at a higher level during design and architecture decisions when requirements can be outlined and integrated.

To complete a threat model in the DevSecOps methodology, the team will engage in the same threat modeling process as in any other methodology. This means that during the design phase, while requirements are being determined, the subject matter experts will gather to perform a more formal threat model that takes into consideration the design choices being made and the impacts to the application based on those choices. The threat model should be well documented and included in the requirements tracking tool or the code repository tool that the development team is using so that it is available for review and for updates as new alterations are made.

However, in the DevSecOps model, some critical decisions are made at impromptu meetings in the team room or in virtual meetings. In this case, threat modeling is less of a formal activity and instead relies on security-minded resources being able to think on their feet about the different issues that may impact the design choice that they are making. This requires security to be tightly integrated with the DevSecOps team. A successful approach to this is to have application security resources embedded in the actual DevSecOps team that can raise questions about the various threats that may impact a given decision. This security-minded team should understand the following:

- What are the current threats to the application based on the design choices and architecture?
- How do these threats impact the application, and are there known weak points?
- What current countermeasures are in place or need to be implemented to eliminate the threat or reduce the risk?

Even taking a moment to stop and ask these questions will help the team determine what the basic risk is on the decisions that they may be making during discussions that fall outside the more formal threat modeling process. Getting to this point will require a culture change within the organization since it requires people rather than tools like the ones we'll cover next.

4.3.2   *SAST in DevSecOps*

Static application security testing is not known for its blinding speed. In fact, as security tools go, SAST typically gets a bad rap. I've done my fair share of complaining about SAST tools, their speed, and their abundance of false positives. I've seen others liken it to the shotgun approach. Not very precise, but effective if you are looking for results. This can become exacerbated if the organization has not taken the time to properly tune the SAST tool. This can be a recipe for disaster. It produces a lot of results that then need to be triaged and processed. What's more, it adds a lot of time to the build process, further upsetting the development team.

As I mentioned, DevSecOps only works well when there is actionable information that can be utilized by the development team in a timely manner. Although SAST tools can be noisy with potential for a lot of false positives, it's actually an extremely useful tool for detecting issues early in the development pipeline, especially when the application security team and the products they support use SAST in their IDEs and tune the SAST tool per application with specific invariant enforcement, antipattern detection, and specific issue detection, as depicted in figure 4.7.

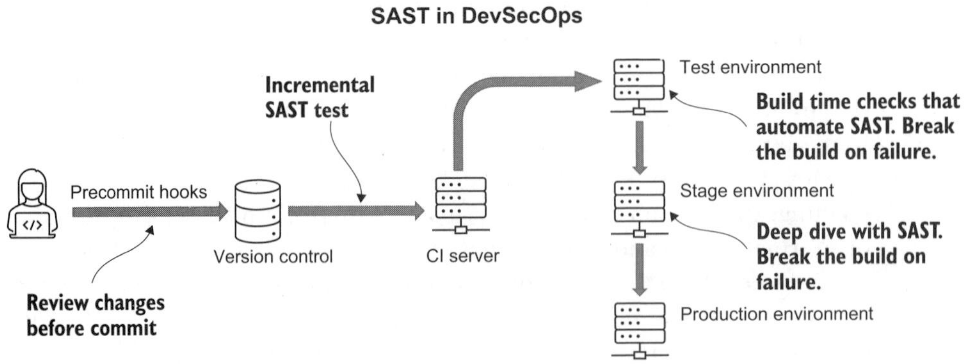

SAST in DevSecOps

Figure 4.7   SAST in DevSecOps

As you can see, integrating SAST with the intention of getting feedback to the developer as soon as possible provides the ability for the development team to respond and resolve issues quickly. As an example, one of the developers at Superior Products is working on a new feature and is ready to check in their code. Prior to doing so, the developer runs the SAST tool that is integrated into their IDE and scans the code for potential vulnerabilities. During the scan, it is discovered that the developer has a potential cross-site scripting vulnerability that was coded since the code takes input from the user through a form but does not validate that the input does not include script. The integrated SAST tool provides recommendations on how to resolve the issue, and the developer confirms with Dashing Danielle that the recommended remediation will resolve the issue. The developer codes the fix, rebuilds, and rescans with a clean output from the SAST tool.

Once the developer commits their code to the code branch, additional static analysis scans are performed where the entire application is taken into consideration as opposed to the targeted and incremental scan at the IDE level. The branch scan detects a possible buffer overflow that was introduced when the developer's code was merged with another developer's code. The buffer overflow is reviewed by Dashing Danielle and the team, and a remediation plan is devised. With the code resolution in place, the local and branch builds both successfully complete with no further findings from the static analysis scans.

4.3.3   *DAST and IAST in DevSecOps*

Once the code has proceeded through the pipeline, from the developer's environment through the build process and is deployed to a test environment, it is ready for further security testing. One of the methods I spoke of previously is dynamic application security testing (DAST). This provides a look inward at the application and attempts to discover security issues as it runs in an environment. Likewise, interactive application security testing (IAST) can be run inside the application and see attacks as they happen, allowing the tool to observe and report on vulnerabilities. As you can assume, you may not want to run DAST or IAST in a production environment, as shown in figure 4.8, as it has the potential of disrupting normal, legitimate traffic and creating a production outage. However, there are some DevSecOps models that organizations use that allow for at least DAST to be run in both the preproduction and production environments.

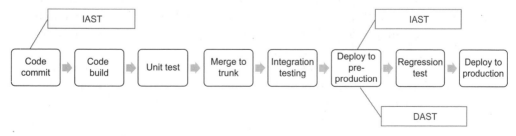

Figure 4.8   IAST and DAST in DevSecOps

Ideally DAST and IAST would be run in the same testing environments that are being used for other testing, like regression and integration testing, as these environments should already be set up and configured for testing. One of the benefits of this setup is that IAST tools need to see activity in order to report on a finding. In other words, to uncover a vulnerability in the code, the application is instrumented with an agent that continuously monitors the application for incoming attacks and reports on the findings. Having a suite of regression tests will help the IAST instrumentation detect potential attacks.

Fortunately, many IAST tools can be run even earlier in the process. Developers will have running application environments that are local on their machine or will at least have an environment where early testing can be done prior to pushing code to a branch. If the organization has decided to make IAST available to the developers in their local environment, the developer will be able run the chosen IAST tool in that initial environment to uncover issues prior to pushing code to a branch. If the organization has made the commitment to integrate IAST in the developer's environment, then the developer will be able to run unit tests that will intentionally execute workflows that should trigger alerts in the IAST tool. When something is found, the developer will be able to react quickly to resolve the issue.

The preproduction environment is where more functionality has been integrated with the application, and the IAST tool will be able to discover broader issues that can only be located once the code has been integrated in an environment that moves beyond the unit tests and begins to run integration and system tests. It will take additional time for the developer to resolve the issue since it would be found later in the process, but it is still preferable to finding an issue in the production environment.

Complementary to IAST, DAST can be pointed to an environment and run as a security test against that environment. Although it can be used in the development environment, same as IAST, it is more effective as a point-and-shoot tool in preproduction environments where all the code and features are integrated. Ideally, the DAST tool will only test what has changed in an application, perhaps a new feature, UI, or API. This can be accomplished using parameters for a targeted DAST. This type of incremental scan fits well into the DevSecOps model.

DAST can be run in a production environment, but in most cases the risk of hindering production traffic is too high. Additionally, if the tools have been properly integrated in the lower environments and the developer's environment, then the need for production environment testing is less critical, as shown in figure 4.9. I prefer to avoid running testing style tools in the production environments and instead focus on the run-time protection tools in production.

One additional point of DAST and IAST in the DevSecOps model is that it is necessary to have a feedback loop back into the developer's collaboration and defect tracking tool. When this is working well, the findings in either of these tools will be able to alert the developer of a finding. This is more critical the farther right in the pipeline

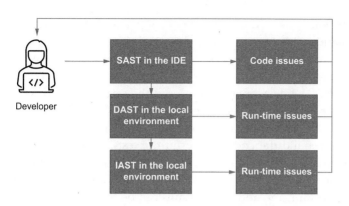

Figure 4.9   IAST and DAST in developer's environment

the issue is found, like the preproduction or even the production environment. Table 4.1 shows the pros and cons of SAST, DAST, and IAST.

Table 4.1   The pros and cons of three different application security scanning tools

Tool	Pros	Cons
SAST (static application security testing)	Can find line number where issue exists Applied early in the life cycle Can make remediation recommendations	May not support all languages in the organization Can produce many false positives Does not see the code while it's running
DAST (dynamic application security testing)	Not language or technology dependent Not as many false positives as SAST Can test software you don't own	Can't always locate the impacted line of code Can't find code specific issues Found later in the SDLC
IAST (interactive application security testing)	Agents or library that is continuously monitoring Lower cases of false positives Works well in DevSecOps	More difficult to deploy and maintain Potential development work in order to integrate it Can usually only see something as it's tested

At Superior Products, the developers have the appropriate static analysis tools running in their environment, as mentioned previously. To take their scanning tools and techniques a step further, they integrate both DAST and IAST to ensure they are able to get additional security issues identified and resolved in a timely manner. Dashing Danielle has helped them devise a process to leverage the IAST tool in combination with unit tests, and other testing suites. This has been integrated into the developer's local environment, which provides them the advantage of seeing only the vulnerabilities that impact the code changes that they made, before the code is checked into a code branch. The tool can identify issues during the running of the tests and point to specific lines of code so that the developer has the ability to make the needed changes.

Prior to code check-in, one of the developers at Superior Products leverages their IAST tool in combination with their unit test to determine whether any vulnerabilities are present with the new code that has been written. The IAST tool discovers that there are a few SQL injection flaws in the new UI. After consulting with Dashing Danielle, it's discovered that the developer has not used the scrubbing function that has been built to take user input and detect whether there is a possible injection attack being attempted. Once the developer adds this additional function to reject possible injection attacks, they rebuild the code and rerun the tests. This time the IAST tool determines that no issue has been found and the team is satisfied with continuing to integrate the new code and deploying it to a lower test environment. Here the system and integration tests are run, and additional results can be found from the integrated IAST tool. During this additional testing, it is found that an XSS attack is possible in code from a developer who skipped the IAST scan. A defect is opened, the team is alerted on their collaboration tool, and the developer is visited by Dashing Danielle, who spends time outlining the purpose of the IAST tool and the benefits to the organization, which is not only more secure but also has saved potential costs related to detecting and resolving the vulnerability in production.

In this preproduction environment, Superior Products has integrated their DAST tool as well to uncover additional issues. The DAST tool will complement the IAST tool nicely, where findings from IAST rely on indirect testing of the application to provoke a finding, and the DAST tool will crawl the entire application and send attack patterns to weak areas of the site to test whether an attack would be successful. The results from the DAST tool will be less precise than the IAST tool, leading the development team to work with Dashing Danielle to triage and discover duplicates from the IAST tool. In this instance, the DAST tool identified a potential buffer overflow issue when the DAST tool overwhelmed one of the inputs through fuzzing. The development team worked with Dashing Danielle to identify whether this issue was discovered in the IAST or other tools in the DevSecOps pipeline. However, once the duplication review and triaging of the issue is complete, the development team has determined that the finding is true and will be able to resolve it prior to it getting released to a production environment.

As I previously mentioned, DAST can be run in a production environment, but this is not recommended, as it can have unforeseen impacts, such as availability issues or corruption of data. There are options to have DAST run less destructive testing, but the organization needs to weigh the cost and benefit. Another alternative reason for running DAST in production would be for testing the security tooling and alerting for the security organization. Perhaps the organization would like to learn whether the security operations center (SOC) is able to detect incoming attacks. Otherwise, so long as the organization has confidence that its preproduction environment mirrors its production environment (and it really should), then running DAST in the preproduction environment should suffice.

NOTE In reality, most organizations will only choose one lower environment to run these types of tools. License cost can quickly explode if you are being charged "per environment." It depends on the vendor and their license structure.

4.3.4 SCA in DevSecOps

As I covered in previous chapters, software composition analysis is used to detect issues with libraries used to build the application that are from a source outside of the organization. These are typically libraries that are from third-party sources or within the frameworks used to build and run the application. An example would be Log4j used by Apache as a logging framework. Frequently, these third-party libraries will be found to have vulnerabilities in their code that require patching. Nothing different than what any organization would do if they found a security issue within their own code that required a patch. In order for an organization to resolve an issue that was found in the third-party library, they will need to package the latest, nonvulnerable version of the library in their own application.

NOTE There are cases where the vulnerable library may not have a nonvulnerable version to upgrade to. Every organization will treat this situation differently. In general, the organization should review its mitigation tools, techniques, and processes to ensure that it is able to address the risk until the vulnerable library can be upgraded.

SCA tools are used to match the third-party libraries that are used in the application against a list of known vulnerable libraries that are publicly disclosed; usually on a well-managed repository like the National Vulnerability Database (NVD). It should be no surprise that the earlier in the process this can be completed, the better for the organization, as a change in a library could mean a redesign of the application depending on the library, as shown in figure 4.10.

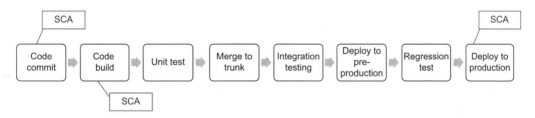

Figure 4.10   SCA in DevSecOps

What this means in the DevSecOps pipeline is that the developer needs access to information regarding the safety of the libraries that they are considering and packaging within their application. This can be accomplished in a few ways. Most vendors today have IDE plug-ins or even browser plug-ins that will let the developer know that the library they are reviewing or about to leverage in their application has a known vulnerability associated with it. Keep in mind that with SCA, the library must have a known weakness, usually in the form of a published CVE that is reported in the NVD. Some SCA vendors will have their own process for detecting weak libraries, but all of them will leverage a public repository like the NVD to locate known CVEs that are associated with the library.

With this early access to CVE information, the developer can make the decision to use a nonvulnerable version of the software prior to even writing the first line of code that integrates that library into the application. However, new CVEs are being released daily. This constant flood means that the day after a developer has chosen a secure library to use, it could become vulnerable to a newly discovered issue. Or worse, this can and usually does happen when the library is already packaged and deployed to an environment. This is where the rest of the DevSecOps pipeline needs to pick up the burden. As with the other tools in the DevSecOps pipeline, the earlier in the process, the better. Once the code has been committed to a branch, the integration server that performs the build and test tasks needs to perform the task of calling the integrated SCA tool, usually through an API, to determine if any of the libraries in the software bill of material (SBOM) are considered vulnerable. During this build process, any finding can be resolved by breaking the build and requiring a change to the library.

This sounds great, but you're probably already thinking about the implications of finding a vulnerability at this stage in the development pipeline. If you checked in the code and you have a library that has been identified as vulnerable, it will be difficult to package and test a new library in a short period of time. Additionally, there may not be an immediate path to a secure library. In other words, there may be a library with no secure version released yet. This is where a robust risk management process needs to be in place. Knowing what the application risk appetite is and the organization's overall risk appetite means that the team can prioritize a resolution that matches their risk. For instance, consider a found vulnerability in a library that is used by one of the applications at Superior Products. The library is used to provide a graphing function in the UI to display charts. The particular vulnerability is related to how the graph is rendered. After the build is broken due to this finding by the SCA tool, Dashing Danielle reviews it and recognizes that this particular rendering function is not actually being used in the application, as they are using the library for a different purpose. With this in mind, the risk is identified as being low and the build is allowed to proceed after the application security provides a *waiver*, meaning that the build can proceed for a set period of time. When the waiver expires, the build will be broken again, but this buys the development team time to provide a secure library once it is available.

4.3.5 *Run-time protection in DevSecOps*

Run-time application self-protection (RASP) and web application firewalls (WAF) play an important part in the protection of the application once it is running in a production environment, as depicted in figure 4.11. Throughout the DevSecOps pipeline, the goal is minimizing the risk to the organization as code is deployed at a rapid pace. When the organization either cannot catch an issue before it is released to production, or an issue is found after the code has been released, the organization then needs to rely on run-time protection to limit the risk.

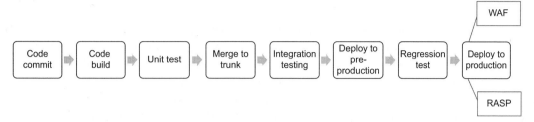

Figure 4.11   Run-time protection in DevSecOps

As mentioned, the best approach in the DevSecOps pipeline is to perform incremental scans using the security tools as early in the process as possible in order to locate and resolve issues as close to when the code is being developed as possible. As the code progresses, the security scanning becomes more aggressive to locate any issues that require more overall application visibility.

However, at some point the code needs to make its way to a production environment where it will face the test of real-world attacks. This is where protection mechanisms are required to provide defenses against attacks that were not found earlier in the development life cycle. Not all of these attacks could even be found during the earlier stages of the life cycle. Novel means of attack are constantly being developed by attackers, which means that the scanning of the application is simply not enough. A prime example is the fact that many attackers will leverage multiple vulnerabilities chained together to compromise a system. This means that it's more than just a single critical, but instead it could be a few lows that turn out to be the culprit in an organization's compromise.

One of the key features of run-time protection tools like a WAF is that many are offered as software as a service (SaaS). This means that the management of the tool is transferred to a third party that hosts the software. The organization can also choose to host their own WAF within their network, but there is an increased cost of managing the internal WAF. This SaaS-based WAF has its benefits and drawbacks. When a new attack method or vulnerability is identified, the third party is generally responsible for delivering a ruleset in the WAF to protect the application going forward. If the WAF is internally maintained, then the security or the operations team will be responsible for delivering the new ruleset from the vendor. One way is no better or worse than the other in the DevSecOps model; it's just important to know that the management and the timing of when the rulesets are delivered to the WAF need to be considered.

With RASP, by its nature, it is integrated with the application and runs alongside of it. This means that there is no SaaS offering, and the DevSecOps team is required to ensure that it is functioning and up-to-date. New rulesets may come in from the vendor of the RASP tool, but similar to the WAF, the team will need to ensure that the rulesets are deployed and do not create a performance or availability issue. Additionally, as new attacks are discovered, it is up to the organization to integrate those signatures into the RASP or WAF. For example, the organization may see a specific type of attack that is not related to the generic rules that are applied by the vendor of either a RASP or a WAF. This specific attack might only impact the organization or the industry they are in, as in the case of a coordinated attack against something like a sports-betting application that shares a common technology stack with other sports-betting applications. In this case, if there is a coordinated attack against sports betting with a specific exploit that is being leveraged only against this industry, then the organizations will want the ability to deploy custom rules that can quickly block these incoming attacks. This assumes that the vendor does not have a generic rule to block the exploit.

For both WAF and RASP, one of the key considerations is the testing of any new rulesets that are deployed. As I mentioned previously, most organizations will not use multiple licenses in their protection tools to test multiple lower environments. Especially for run-time protection tools, you are only getting the benefit from them when you are running them in an environment that has the potential to see and block active attacks. These lower environments are not likely to see external attacks unless they are open to the internet to allow customers to test in them, or they are used in penetration testing. One recommendation is to have these run-time tools in a preproduction environment where broad testing is done to ensure that a new ruleset that is enabled in the tools does not create a regression issue. The most common issues are where the new rules block legitimate traffic or otherwise cause the application to no longer function as expected. With these tools deployed and providing protection for the application, the DevSecOps team will have more confidence in delivering new features to production.

4.3.6 *Security orchestration*

Application security orchestration and correlation (ASOC) was introduced as a concept in 2019 by Gartner (http://mng.bz/neJd).

> **DEFINITION** Gartner defines *ASOC tools* as those that "streamline software vulnerability testing and remediation by automating workflows. They automate security testing by ingesting data from multiple sources (static, dynamic, and interactive [SAST/ DAST/IAST]; software composition analysis [SCA]; vulnerability assessments; and others) into a database. ASOC tools correlate and analyze findings to centralize and prioritize remediation efforts. They act as a management layer between application development and security testing tools."

ASOC is a combination of two different tools that both assist in the DevSecOps pipeline, as shown in figure 4.12. One is the application vulnerability correlation (AVC) and the other is the application security testing orchestrations (ASTO). AVC tools ingest vulnerability information from multiple sources so that the vulnerabilities can be de-duplicated automatically, therefore reducing the amount of time and effort that the team has to spend in doing this work manually. ASTO tools can orchestrate and automate multiple commercial security tools in the DevOps pipeline in order to ensure that security testing is not only happening but also that it is integrated with the continuous integration platform that the organization is using.

ASOC in a DevSecOps pipeline

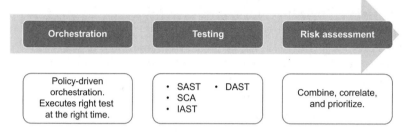

Figure 4.12   ASOC in the DevSecOps pipeline

ASOC tools are becoming more prevalent as vendors are recognizing the need to provide this capability to the organizations that are looking to integrate the following capabilities in the DevSecOps pipeline:

- Correlation and analysis of vulnerability information from multiple application security testing tools like SAST, DAST, IAST and others.
- Integration with defect-tracking tools that are used by the development organization to address defects and vulnerabilities.
- Integration with CI/CD tools and platforms used by the development organization to build and deploy their applications.
- Rapid speed and accuracy of results to reduce the noise. Ideally, the vendor will leverage some level of artificial intelligence or machine learning to help reduce false positives and provide more actionable results.
- Reporting that can be used to measure an organization's success with reducing new vulnerabilities.

ASOC can simplify the prioritization process by discovering whether the vulnerability is applicable and then assigning a criticality to it so that it can be prioritized. If the ASOC tool is using machine learning (ML), it may look to see how past responses to vulnerabilities may influence future behavior. Additionally, when the ASOC is integrated with the defect tracking tool used by the development team, they can be sure that the results they receive are actionable. This also allows the application security team to see vulnerabilities across the organization and build reports that are valuable to leadership. As described, an ASOC fits well in the DevSecOps methodology, given its ability to automate, deliver quality results, and provide a single pane of glass across the organization.

4.3.7 *Security education*

Security education is near and dear to my heart. It's the underdog when it comes to security process, tools, and technology. Why is this important for DevSecOps? Simple. Having security-minded developers and operational people when decisions are being made rapidly reduces the burden on the application security team and helps to deliver more secure code from the start.

When most people hear "security education," they think about the video or slide material with a quiz at the end. This is still widely used across probably all organizations at some level. Although there is a time and place for this type of training, it's not effective for raising the security IQ of the organization in a sustained manner. This only occurs when the organization has invested in a training platform that can deliver training on demand, or even better, at the time when an issue is discovered. Some technology solutions can integrate with defect tracking tools in order to provide a link to application security training modules for the specific vulnerability that was found. For instance, perhaps an SQL injection vulnerability was found in a penetration test. When the application security team opens the vulnerability in the defect tracking tool, the application security training module can detect that the ticket was opened and add a link to the training platform so that the developer has access to information on how to resolve the found SQL injection.

One of the key conditions of training is it must be quick and to the point. Most of us get pretty aggravated when we have to sit through not just boring, but also long, training. The most effective training is timely, brief, and often if necessary. As we've been talking about DevSecOps, it's important to point out that many SAST tools have IDE plug-ins that allow for coordination of vulnerability discovery with some quick hit training module. This allows the developer to immediately see why the line of code may lead to a vulnerability. These don't need to be long either; otherwise, what keeps the developer from simply going to the internet for help? These quick hit modules should be just a few minutes long and in the language of the developer. No corny videos, please.

To augment this quick hit training, it's important to ensure that more traditional training is still available. However, not all security education needs to be death by PowerPoint. Many training platforms today are engaging and approachable by a potentially hostile audience. However, the organization has other options for delivering security training. Some application security training platforms offer the option to host tournaments that will provide a training ground for a large group of developers where they can test their skills in something like a hack-a-thon. Other platforms offer gamified training that intends on providing training where the learner has the ability to test their skills right there and then through training that provides real-world, hands-on scenarios.

Some large organizations will host internal developer conferences that include a security component. This provides a platform for the security organization to showcase some of the new technology and processes that are working around the organization.

This is even more effective when development teams bring their experiences with security and show how it has better enabled them while making them more secure. It's worth mentioning that the organization doesn't have to draw on their internal resources exclusively. Bringing in security speakers from the outside is also helpful in showing what some of the organization's peers are doing. This is a great example of where you can generally get free, or near free, security awareness.

The biggest payoff with developer training is that it reduces the burden on the rest of the organization and application security team. Anyone who has run an application security function will tell you that there is no way your team can scale to cover all the various applications and areas of concern. The team must rely on the organization to build security in when they are developing code and the tools that are layered into the development life cycle can only do so much. Secure code starts with security-minded developers.

4.4 Feedback loop

One of the unique features of DevSecOps is that it is a constantly moving pipeline. This means that in a mature DevSecOps pipeline, there will always be code moving through the various parts of the assembly line until it is deployed to production. The security gates are gone from the process. So how do we make sure that developers are getting the feedback like in figure 4.13, the code is secure, and the organization is safe from increased risk?

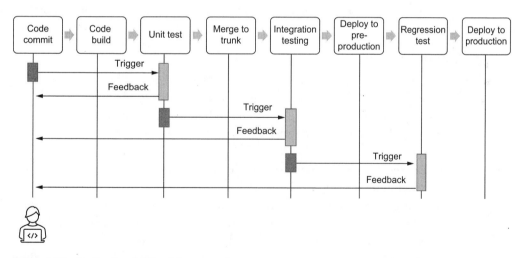

Figure 4.13 DevSecOps feedback loop

To do this, the pipeline needs to have hooks throughout that provide constant feedback to the developer, regardless of where in the process the issue is found. The SAST tool running during code check-in may append the output of that analysis to the code check-in. The integration server will run tasks that execute security scans such as IAST and DAST once the code has been deployed to a workable environment. The output from those tools may trigger a message in the development team's collaboration tool, as well as automatically open a ticket in the defect tracking tool. It's also possible that the organization has a policy to block a build on vulnerabilities of a certain type or of a certain criticality level, like a criticality of high or above or if it's an SQL injection vulnerability, in which case the build would break and the developer would be notified through email or their collaboration tools that the build has been broken due to a change that was made during their check-in.

This type of feedback loop allows for the pipeline to continue moving while performing an event-driven approach to the security feedback loop. This means that it is occurring asynchronously and does not create the more state-machine style pipeline where each stage is waiting on the next to complete cleanly before proceeding. This still needs to rely on a "go/no-go" decision before deploying to production. The organization may take the position that they will allow certain vulnerabilities of a particular level into production as long as there is a path to resolution in a short period of time, say, a few days. However, the more mature organization will not allow any discovered vulnerabilities to be delivered to a production environment and will require a clean production build in order for deployment to occur.

As you can see, the DevSecOps pipeline serves the same purpose for two different work streams. On the one hand, being able to deliver value to the customer in a matter of hours is immensely desirable. Likewise, every security person should want that same capability to deliver security resolutions to the organization in a rapid manner. It's a win-win.

Summary

- DevSecOps plays a critical role in enabling the development team to deliver software with confidence that security is built into their pipeline.
- There are other development methodologies that can still deliver security but struggle to do so at the speed that is required in the modern development life cycle.
- DevSecOps breaks down the segmentation between the security team and the development team and integrates security throughout the pipeline.
- The common tools used in application security still apply (threat modeling, SAST, DAST, IAST, RASP, and WAF). In fact, they are able to be applied earlier with a faster feedback loop to the development team.
- Feedback loops are critical to the success of resolving found vulnerabilities by getting the information to the development team where they collaborate the most.

5

Security belongs to everyone

This chapter covers

- Expanding application security through various methods
- Building a culture of security that includes education
- Exploring the maturity models that can be used in an application security program
- Explaining decentralized AppSec in software development

Stop me if you heard this before, but security is everyone's problem. We've all heard this many times, but what does it really mean? In my experience, the ability to scale an application security team to meet the need of a large organization is difficult, if not impossible. Many of the organizations that I have worked with have had hundreds or even thousands of developers. In these organizations, even what I would consider a large application security team was no match for the sheer volume of work in the organization. This means that organizations must find other, more creative ways to bring security to the overall development of software.

As I mentioned in previous chapters, the best defense against attackers is to ensure that all members of the organization are able to understand the security risks that the organization faces and work together to address them. This does not mean that everyone needs to be a security specialist, but having at least basic security knowledge goes a long way. Nothing makes me happier than someone reaching out to me asking about the security impacts to a design choice. This means that they are at least thinking about security and how their choices can affect it. And I'll admit, I don't always have the answers, but being able to work through an issue with someone else teaches both of us. I can't imagine that I'm the only security person who feels that way. Not because we're actually wanted, but because when more people think this way, the security folks have the right advocates in the organization. Getting to this little bit of heaven requires an organization that has put the effort into building a culture that not only takes security seriously but also thinks about it as much as the security teams do.

5.1 Security is everyone's problem

I try to draw parallels when I am thinking about security, and one that comes to mind here is your common household. One person in the house is not generally the security person who goes around the house every day making sure that the doors and windows are locked, that the alarm is on, the stove is off, that the cars are locked, and that everything in the house is secure. I suppose that might happen in some households, but the point is that this is not an efficient way to approach the security of the house. In reality, it is the responsibility of everyone in the house to ensure that they are considering the security and safety of the house and those inside. If the smoke detector is out of batteries and begins to beep, yes, maybe the tallest person in the house has to change the battery, but others in the house can hear it beeping and can let the tall person know so they can change the battery.

In an organization, the security team should not be the only ones aware of or looking out for security issues. Yes, they are the ones who typically manage the tools and processes that manage the security risk of the organization, but they don't always have 100% visibility into all the areas of the organization. More importantly, organizations are releasing new features and functionality all the time. It is unlikely that the application security team has insight into those new features until they are about to be released. That is often too late for the application security team to react, and it becomes more of an exercise in reducing or accepting the identified risk than building security into the design early in the process.

When the organization takes the steps to build a security culture, they will be able to augment the application security team and create more secure code. However, this requires an application security team that has built the frameworks, processes, tools, and education that is needed to enable the development organization to achieve that level of security.

5.1.1 *Structure of an application security team*

It is extremely difficult to hire enough resources in the application security team that will fit all the needs of the organization. Although every application security team is structured differently and has different needs, most application security teams provide the following core functions:

- Threat modeling and risk assessment
- Penetration testing
- Implementing scanning tools
- Triaging discovered vulnerabilities
- Code and architecture review
- DevSecOps and automation support
- Secure education and evangelism
- Documentation, whitepapers, standards, and requirements development

On a daily basis, the application security team members perform these tasks as their core function, but there is other ad hoc work that happens, such as general consulting on design and strategy across the organization. It is often hard to find the "unicorn" application security person who can do all or even multiple items from the core functions. This requires the application security team to hire multiple people with more focused skill in the core areas. For instance, in order to meet the needs of the functions, the team may hire the following roles:

Security architect   Penetration tester   AppSec engineer   DevSecOps engineer

Security roles in an application security team

Each organization has a different description for common roles. Here are a few of the common application security roles and a brief description:

Security architect—Represent the application security team on strategy in the organization and develop secure architecture, standards, and documentation

Penetration tester—Provide testing of applications for security-related issues and develop summary reports on findings

Application security engineer—Work closely with the application development team to ensure that security is integrated in the development process for the development team

DevSecOps engineer—Take the responsibility of the application security engineer with the added responsibility of automating the processes in the development pipeline

NOTE This is a very unpopular opinion, but one that a lot of my application security peers share: penetration testers are not application security engineers. Many organizations work hard to build a team that can perform penetration tests against applications. Don't get me wrong, this is needed. However, a mature application security team will incorporate staff with a multitude of different skills and talents in order to have rounded capabilities.

The organization will also have to sprinkle in the obligatory support around the team like leadership and project management. As you can see, this team can focus on delivering security to the organization through the tools, processes, and people. However, scaling the team to meet the organization's needs is next to impossible. The recommended size of the application security team varies, depending on the size of the organization and the budget they have dedicated to security. In large organizations, this ratio is difficult to meet and depends on how seriously it takes building security into their applications. However, in most cases, the application security team is roughly 1% of the development headcount. Again, this is not a recommendation, but rather what is typically seen in the industry. I have been a part of teams that are oversized and undersized based on that measurement. This is why creating a culture that supports the security of the applications that are being developed is critical to reducing the overall risk of organization.

> **Exercise 5.1**
> Take a look at your own organization's application security team and understand what functions they perform. If your organization doesn't have one, research some popular organizations and their application security team structure. Each organization I have worked for has had a different set of goals and staffing model to support application security. You will never find the same model in every organization.

5.1.2 *Just hire more application security people*

In most engineering organizations, when you have a new project or push to meet a deadline, the organization will just hire more engineers, testers, architects, and others to meet the need. This is not only impractical for application security but is also often cost-prohibitive. Security teams in an organization are often working on a smaller budget compared with the overall IT spend. Although the spend varies by organization and industry—and there was a significant increase in security spend during the global pandemic in 2020—most organizations spend 5% to 15% of their IT budget on security. The bulk of this spend goes to security operations and perimeter defense tools like a security information and event management (SIEM), network detection and protection, firewalls, and others. The application security team typically gets a small portion of that budget that is mostly dedicated to personnel.

Despite spending most of their budget on personnel, the application security team can never scale to the size needed. However, this is not the biggest problem facing the application security team. It's actually very difficult to hire the people you need. There has been a term that has been used a lot in the industry called *negative unemployment*. This means that there are more jobs open than qualified people to fill them. To be clear, this is not just application security, but across the board in security like analyst, network security, information security specialist, and others. This means there are millions of jobs left unfilled in security. Those of you reading this book who work in security know exactly what I'm talking about.

The reality is that application security resources are even more difficult to locate than other personnel in their peer groups. Generally, you are looking for someone who has not only security expertise but also development experience. Your best bet is to find someone who has been a developer and gained an interest in security. The importance of finding someone who has development experience cannot be overstated. Someone with this background brings the following to the team when they join:

- Understands the development pipeline
- Can interpret code and perform code reviews
- Understands the overall development process
- Can speak the language of the development team

Having these qualities as well as an understanding of security will be an asset to any application security team. This allows them to take vulnerabilities that impact an application and be able to interpret this issue in a way that is understood by the development team. For instance, a prototype pollution issue may have been discovered through a DAST tool and assigned to be triaged by the application security team. These issues can be complex to describe and walk through with the engineering team if the application security member cannot describe how prototypes works in JavaScript. Having a background in development means that the application security person can at least describe the issue, know how it impacts the application, and help develop mitigations. More importantly, when the development team makes the claim that the vulnerability does not impact them, which they will do, then an application security person who knows development will be able to determine whether the impact is real.

You can see how these types of hires can be hard to find. With a constrained budget, and a small pool of resources to hire from, the application security team will struggle to find the right people who can deliver security to a development organization.

Organizations can also make it difficult on themselves when they don't have a good job description or even job title for what they are looking for. An application security architect is different than a solution architect. A security engineer is different than a security analyst. Even worse, some organizations will have their own internal titles that may map to industry standard job titles, but only muddy the waters. This means that well-qualified individuals may pass on a role due to a misunderstanding of the title.

One last point I will make regarding hiring in application security. Sometimes the right person for the team has no clue about security. The application security team is usually operating parallel to the engineering teams they work with, which means that having members of the team who understand the engineering process is as important and, depending on the role, sometimes more important than understanding security. The team will need people who can integrate tools, develop and understand code, speak intelligently about the software development process, and operate and tune tools. To achieve this, the team does not always need to hire the best and brightest security people, as these gaps need to be filled with a team that is diverse in thought and background.

5.1.3   How to close the gap

So, what does this mean for an organization that wants to raise their security posture without having to hire a massive army of penetration testers, security engineers, and security architects? When you can't afford a car, but you need to drive to the store, find a friend who has one and borrow theirs.

> *Look for the helpers. You will always find people who are helping.*

> —Fred Rogers

Getting anything done in application security usually means that you will be borrowing time from the resources in engineering or at least working with the product and engineering teams to jostle for space in their releases. In most cases you will want to make this as transparent and open as possible. Nothing drives a manager more crazy, me included, than their team getting pulled into tasks that are unrelated to the work they should be doing. However, security is everyone's responsibility, right? It's also the responsibility of the application security team to make sure that the engineering team understands what needs to be done and provides the most amount of support they can.

One approach to making this work is by engaging with the engineering leadership on a regular basis to ensure that priorities are aligned. This isn't just application security priorities, but also the priorities of the product. You will not advance security if you are bringing only your problems and needs to the table. Listening to the product team and the engineering team about their concerns with security and their pain points when it comes to balancing security with feature releases will go a long way. To effectively spread security in the engineering organization, you need to build a relationship that is developed with mutual trust and support in mind.

5.2   Security education

I admit that I believe in the power of training and education. I have taught undergraduate and graduate computer science students and have led training programs at organizations on application security. Training is a cheap and effective way to raise the security IQ of the development organization. But this goes beyond the annual training and handful of courses throughout the year that is usually obligatory and ineffective. In fact, although the vast majority of organizations have your standard security education in the form of phishing and social engineering training, most organizations do not focus on engineering security training. This is a huge gap.

There are a multitude of approaches to bringing security education to the engineering teams (figure 5.1). Each approach has its benefits and are delivered in different manners in order to be most effective. Online training, just-in-time training, and micro-learning can be delivered pretty quickly and efficiently to the engineer to address an immediate need. Alternatively, conferences, lunch-and-learn, and in-person training can be long but much more in depth.

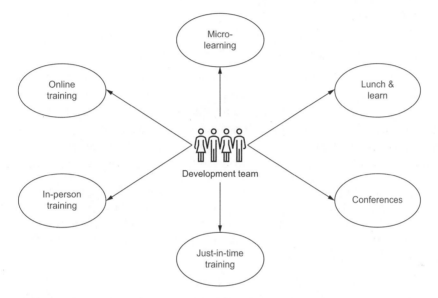

Figure 5.1   Security training options for a development team

With a well-rounded approach to security education, the organization begins to build the ecosystem that supports a more security-minded engineer. This is a cost-effective and scalable approach to reducing the burden on an often-small application security team and ultimately raising the awareness of security in those who are responsible for writing code.

5.2.1   *Raising the security IQ*

Creating a culture of secure engineering is a multipronged effort, but it starts with effective training. Some examples of training that can be done on a periodic basis in the organization are shown in the following table.

Each of these are effective means of delivering security education to the engineering organization. There are varying costs in terms of budget as well as time. For example, online training through a third-party platform can be expensive, especially if you are paying per user. But you're able to quickly roll it out to a large audience simply by assigning it to engineers. In-person training led by a third party can be expensive per

Self-paced training online	There are a lot of options for online training platforms. Some are more general training platforms that offer courses in various disciplines. Others are specific for security, like awareness or secure engineering.
Instructor-led training	Depending on the organization, there may be a learning and development team that can run training. However, much of this will be training that is specific to the organization, and most of the time will not be security related. If the organization is looking specifically for security training, they will need to leverage a third-party company that can come on-site to perform the training.
Application security–led training	The application security team can also provide training to the engineering organization both online and in-person. One of the benefits of this is that the application security team can focus on known issues within the organization to focus on. However, this requires the application security team to maintain the training and keep it relevant.

person and doesn't scale well. When you compare it to the costs of an online platform, in-person training is highly focused and the opportunity to ask questions and follow up with the instructor adds a benefit that is often not there for online training. Many organizations will take the approach of having training where the targeted in-person training is done infrequently and specific to a core group, and the online training is open and available to the wider organization to take advantage of on-demand.

> **NOTE** Many training platforms offer integration into the development environment that will allow for the developer to take a short training module that explains the issue with assistance on how to resolve it. Often these can be integrated into the analysis tools that the organization is using, specifically with SAST tools that are part of the IDE.

One additional method of in-person training that can be effective, and more cost-effective, is when it is led by the application security team. Organizations that take this approach will designate, or even certify, several members of the application security team to be trainers. This allows the organization to hold several training sessions per year at a reduced cost. There is also the added benefit that the application security team can provide specific use cases that apply to the organization and also present recommendations that align with the organization's requirements, goals, and standards.

The application security team has a unique opportunity to augment the training approach of the organization. This is the team that is seeing the daily activity across the organization and knows where the organization is most vulnerable. This gives the application security team the ability to take the information they have to formulate more specific training for the engineering organization. Take for example if the organization is seeing SQL injection vulnerabilities consistently appearing in scans and penetration testing. The application security team can provide training for the engineering organization that focuses on SQL injection. Taking it a step further, if the vulnerabilities are frequently coming from one development team, they can provide specific training just for that team. This doesn't have to be a significant investment of effort. An hour or two with the development team led by one of the application security team members would suffice. The benefit of working with a team that has a history of releasing the same vulnerabilities is that the application security team can provide examples of the issue and remediation using the code base that the engineering team is working in.

5.2.2   *Microlearning and just-in-time training*

Microlearning is by no means a new concept, but it has been taking off in the past few years. The goal is to break down larger training sessions into quick, bite-sized training that is easily consumed by the intended audience. Although there is no real measuring stick on time and size of the microlearning, it is commonly less than 5 minutes long. This allows the learner to understand a distilled concept and take away the key points in a short period of time.

This type of learning works well in the DevSecOps model that I covered previously. The fundamental goal of microlearning is to provide quick learning while the learner is performing their job. A great example would be if a developer has coded an SQL injection vulnerability identified through their SAST tool that is integrated into their IDE. In this case they can take a quick microlearning module that describes the impact and remediation of SQL injection vulnerabilities. This provides enough information to the developer to understand the issue and provide a remediation that resolves the vulnerability.

Microlearning doesn't have to be video based; it can be delivered in other mediums like blogs, e-learning, games, podcasts, and infographics. How this works in your organization really depends on the culture and the learning habits of the engineering teams. It also depends on the content that is being taught. Something that is complex in nature may require a hands-on activity like a game or interactive learning, whereas something a bit simpler might be well received with just a short read or infographic.

Microlearning also works well when it is used as a refresher or a reinforcement of concepts that were taught in longer form training. The organization may have more formal annual training that is used to teach core concepts, but microlearning that is targeted to specific topics that were covered in the formal training can be sprinkled throughout the year to help reinforce those topics. This is especially helpful when it ties in resources that the organization maintains, like documentation. When considering an approach to microlearning the organization should consider the following:

- *Find the optimum length and delivery mechanism.* As mentioned, microlearning can be delivered in more than just a video format.
- *Ensure that the approach has support from the organization and the leadership.* This will ensure that it is not considered as an optional training but is instead considered part of the overall education of the audience.
- *Make sure that the training has clear objectives and that there is an approach to measuring success.* This could be setting an objective to reduce a certain type of vulnerability in a particular development team. This can be measured by tracking net new vulnerabilities of that type.

- *Consider mixing up the delivery methods so that the training doesn't become repetitive and stale.* This means that not every microlearning on a topic like cross-site scripting needs to be an infographic. Have several options, including a hands-on option.
- *Keep metrics on the microlearning like frequency, most visited, and who is accessing.* This will help with making improvements over time.

One of the most critical aspects of microlearning is that it is delivered and available at the right time. As I mentioned previously, you want to be able to reinforce good habits when the bad habits are being identified. If you cannot integrate with your developers' IDE to link out to a microlearning module, then look to your organization's learning management system (LMS) or collaboration environment to host the content. The important thing is to make sure that when an issue is found, the developer has access to resources that will provide them guidance.

As an example, I'll turn back to Superior Products. The organization has decided to incorporate microlearning to target two specific vulnerabilities that have been showing up frequently in their scanning tools and penetration test. One is SQL injection, and the other is cross-site scripting. In order to take advantage of microlearning to combat these two issues, Superior Products has incorporated two methods of delivery:

- Two infographics that reinforce the basic security methods to combat both SQL injection and cross-site scripting (XSS). The infographics will point out that scrubbing and sandboxing user input, using an allowlist of known good values to pattern match, and using parameterized queries instead of concatenated SQL statements will help control these vulnerabilities, as shown in figure 5.2.
- Two separate videos for each vulnerability that are 5 to 6 minutes long. They briefly show how SQL injection and XSS are used by attackers followed by more specific code examples that show how to resolve the vulnerabilities.

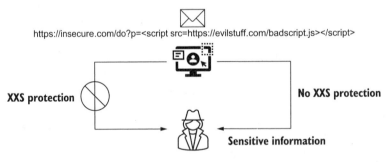

Figure 5.2   Simple example of a XSS infographic used in microlearning

Dashing Danielle has discovered that she can use the SAST tool in the IDE to link to content that the organization hosts. In this case, she has configured any found SQL injection or XSS issues to include the stock remediation recommendations from the

SAST vendor with a link to the internal collaboration tool that hosts the infographics. This is a simple solution, and one that Dashing Danielle is able to use to add content to the infographics over time.

> **NOTE** Jira is one of the more popular issue tracking tools on the market. It allows for the tracking of defects and agile project management. Since it is an issue tracking tool, it is often used by security teams to track security vulnerabilities as well.

Additionally, Dashing Danielle was able to build a task in the continuous integration tools that opens an issue in the issue tracking tool for the organization, like Jira ticket, and assigns it as a task to the team member who submitted the code when an SQL injection or XSS vulnerability is discovered. The task can do the following:

- Leverage the scan results from the SAST and DAST tools that are used in the CI.
- Pull out the SQL injection and XSS issues from the scans.
- Determine the pull request or code check-in that introduced the vulnerability.
- Open a Jira in the team's project and assign it to the submitting developer.
- Add a link to the opened Jira ticket to the microlearning on the specific vulnerability that was introduced.

In this case, the microlearning is hosted in the organization's LMS and is accessible to all developers at Superior Products. This allows access on demand and outside the workflow described. More importantly, the microlearning is assigned to the developer who needs to make the change, and the details of the change are bundled with the opened ticket. Dashing Danielle can also use this process to track how well the team is doing in resolving both the SQL injection and the XSS issues. Using Jira, Dashing Danielle is able to see the opened and closed issues related to each vulnerability. If the training and other process in place are working, these should be reduced over time.

5.2.3 *It's more than just training*

Training doesn't have to be boring. Something as simple as an hour presentation on a security topic once a month goes a long way. Some organizations call this a lunch-and-learn or a brown-bag session. These can provide a quick and interactive method of discussing security topics that are relevant to the organization. What is most effective with these types of sessions is when they are led by people from the engineering organization who are working on something that has security implications, like the following:

- New authentication or session management framework being developed in an application
- A technology change that requires a different security model
- Applying encryption using a new database technology
- Secure messaging for clients

The engineering team can be nudged by the application security team, but it's an even bigger win when the engineers bring topics to one of these talks. The goal is to bring topics that the rest of the organization can learn from. What did they encounter when developing the new feature that might cut down on the churn for others? What makes the new feature a better security model than previously? When it comes from a peer team in engineering, the other teams are more likely to welcome the conversation and take advantage of the retrospective, especially if the technology stack is the same or similar.

When such an event cannot be coordinated with the engineering organization, the application security team should take advantage of the time to bring in new topics that are important to the security of the organization. For example, a change in the industry that requires support from engineering, like the retirement of insecure standards, is a prime topic to be discussed in this forum. The application security team can also use this time to present what other similar organizations are doing to provide better security. For instance, if the organization is in the health care space, the application security team can bring in topics related to new regulations that impact the security and privacy of the data that the organization collects.

The application security team should also look to bring in speakers who are external to the organization if appropriate. It's one thing to have an engineering team or the application security team discuss certain security topics, but an entirely different thing if a speaker from the industry presents a topic that is relevant to the organization.

Conferences, meetups, and other forums are also a good source of security information for the engineering organization. As security leaders, we should be encouraging members of the organization who are outside of security to attend security conferences. However, many engineering-oriented conferences usually run a security track. These tracks are great, considering that they are normally on topic for the specific conference. For example, if the conference is specific to deployment technology and methodologies, you'll see the security track cover the security of infrastructure code and the running environment.

5.3 *Standards, requirements, and reference architecture*

Tools and training can provide some reasonably good security controls by alerting, defending, and teaching. However, building a house requires a good blueprint first. That blueprint needs to be built on solid guidance, historical evidence, heuristics, and best practices. Translated to the software development business, this means having a solid foundation built on standards, requirements, and architectures. These should come from

- Input from the industry that the organization is in, like health care or finance
- Input from the broader security industry that applies to the organization's services
- Input from within the organization based on previous discoveries and learnings

However, writing standards, requirements, and architecture is only the first step. Getting buy-in requires structure.

5.3.1 Creating and driving standards

In many organizations, you will find a group that is dedicated to ensuring that the organization is following a body of standards. This often is driven from an enterprise function, like the enterprise architecture team if it exists, but can also be from a center of excellence (CoE) or a community of practice (CoP). Regardless of where the direction comes from, having a central group that defines standards for the organization helps establish the foundations needed to build security in early. Often organizations will take the approach of running what's called an *architecture review board* (ARB) to drive standards and best practices across the organization. This team is commonly decentralized and spans several domains with experts in each domain, as shown in figure 5.3. Every organization is structured differently so the domains may vary by name and practice; however, the guiding principle here is to see that representatives have a vested interest in ensuring that the organization has a common approach to building solutions and provide the appropriate leadership and oversight at the domain level while using domain expertise to create and validate architecture.

Sample Architecture Review Board (ARB) with domains

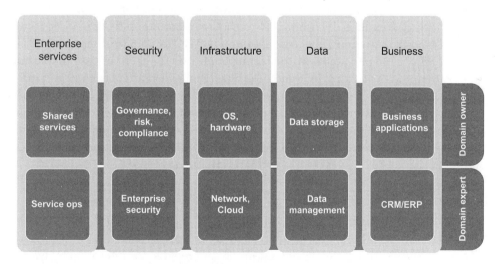

Figure 5.3   Overview of an architecture review board

The ARB will be tasked with creating a consistent method to how architecture problems are solved and setting guidelines on technology that is to be used in architecture. This is often a consensus board, meaning that representatives from the various stakeholders in the organization will participate and have a voting interest in the decisions and the setting of standards. There are a few things that are gained by an ARB in an organization:

- Better visibility of the solutions across the organization
- More consistency in an architectural approach
- Reduced complexity of systems by potentially reusing patterns
- Potential consolidation through visibility
- Awareness and education through shared knowledge

So, what is security's role in the ARB? It's clear that if you want to drive good security standards and patterns, this is the place to be. A prime example of levering the ARB to drive a security standard is to standardize on the version of Transport Layer Security (TLS) that is used in the organization. It is not uncommon for organizations that have several business units or multiple products with different customers aligned to the products to have varying versions of TLS running in their environments. The security representative in the ARB, who is usually a senior architect within the security organization or the security architect in the enterprise architecture team, will be able to bring forward a requirement to standardize the organization on a particular TLS version.

To illustrate this, I'll turn to Superior Products again. Dashing Danielle, due to her exceptional security leadership and trust among her peers, has been brought in as the formal security representative in the ARB after the previous security representative on the ARB left to pursue a career in asparagus farming. For her first task on the ARB, Dashing Danielle is determined to move the organization to a more secure version of TLS. As of this writing, the most common and secure TLS version is TLS 1.2. Although TLS 1.3 is out and available, the technical hurdles for client migration to using 1.3 are substantial. With this in mind, Dashing Danielle crafts a short presentation that describes why they need to standardize on the version of TLS, including the security implications, as well as the increase in requests from customers regarding their Superior Products stance on the supported TLS version. Along with the presentation, Dashing Danielle creates a brief written standard on TLS that looks something like this:

> TLS is a protocol created to provide authentication, confidentiality, and data integrity protection between two communicating applications. Applications in Superior Products shall support TLS 1.2 by January 1, 2022. After this date, servers shall support TLS 1.2 for client-facing applications. Lower versions of TLS such as 1.1 and 1.0 shall be disabled on servers that support TLS 1.2 if it has been determined that the lower versions are not needed for interoperability.

This is a simple statement that addresses the what, when, and who the standard applies to. Armed with the standard and the presentation, Dashing Danielle joins the next ARB meeting that occurs on a biweekly basis where she presents the case for standardizing across the organization on TLS version 1.2. She receives backing from some of the members of the ARB, but others are skeptical of the customer impact. Dashing Danielle promises to come back to the next meeting with more concrete evidence of the client impact so that the standard can be put to a vote and integrated into the approved standards, as depicted in figure 5.4.

Architecture review process

Figure 5.4   Approval of an architecture in a review board

Dashing Danielle works with several stakeholders in the operational organization as well as client services to test a nonproduction environment in order to gather metrics on the impact of the change. Additionally, she gathers metrics from the network team to understand which customers may still be using the lower versions of TLS so that the team understands the size of the change needed. With this information, Dashing Danielle is able to put the ARB at ease on the required change and the impact to customers. With this hurdle overcome, Dashing Danielle brings the standard to review and approval in the ARB where it becomes a formal standard that is now required to be adhered to by January 1, 2022, by the products within the organization.

However, Dashing Danielle is not able to rest on her laurels at this point; it's now time to do the hard work of driving the change across the organization. Although the ARB has approved this standard, it's up to Dashing Danielle to help drive the change across the organization. With the data that she gathered as part of the development of the standard, she begins to work with the customer service teams to develop a communication plan to the customers. She works with the operational teams to establish timelines and processes to initiate the enablement of TLS 1.2 and the disablement of the lower versions. Throughout the rollout in the preproduction environments, she works with the operational and development teams to resolve any discovered issues as part of the change. Additionally, she works with other members of the ARB and leadership in the organization to make sure that it remains a priority in the organization.

Although this is a simple illustration, the reality is that this would most likely be a much larger project in most organizations led by a project manager with all the stakeholders involved. The purpose of this illustration is to show how external pressure from the industry can lead to the creation of a standard, and the process to get that standard approved and eventually realized by the organization.

Exercise 5.2

Take a look at your organization and think about an area that lacks standardization. Some of the easy ones are around encryption, technical debt, versions of protocols, or even use of certain software. Draft a standard that would address the gap. If your organization is ready for it, take it to the ARB or equivalent. If your organization does not have an ARB, bring it to your engineering leadership for review.

5.3.2 Creating reference architecture

The ARB described in the previous section has another function as well. This is to review and approve architecture that should be implemented across the organization. This doesn't mean that all architecture designs need to go through and be approved by the ARB; it means that architectures that have broad impact or can bring savings to the organization should be reviewed and built with consensus. A well-devised ARB addresses architecture decisions to provide the following benefits to the organization:

- Scalable education to stakeholders and architects on new standards, architecture, and strategic direction
- Communication channel to deliver documentation, including the board's decisions, metrics, and current projects
- Review of high-impact projects that are business critical, and impact architectural quality and alignment

With these benefits in mind, the organization leverages the ARB to approve of cross-business critical architecture that has a business impact. This is often called *reference architecture.*

> **DEFINITION** *Reference architecture* is used to provide a template and common taxonomy for a solution in a given domain. It aims to create commonality for developing a solution. Additionally, the purpose of creating reference architecture is to align the organization's strategy around a specific set of tools, standards, guidance, and implementation. This helps drive lower costs in not just licensing but also in development time and effort.

Similar to creating standards, reference architecture is a prime opportunity for security to be injected into a process whose goal it is to develop and design a common approach to solving a problem. There are several opportunities to inject security into reference architecture. Some examples are

- Federated identity management
- Secrets management when encrypting client data
- Authorization model using OAuth

These examples provide an opportunity to bring together architecture that meets the organization's need to solve a problem, like an authorization model, but does so with the intention of building security in. Once this reference architecture is developed and approved by the ARB, it is ready to be used by the organization when various applications are looking to develop a solution. Leaning on the example of the authorization model, building this reference architecture means that each application will have the same approach to designing authorization into their application. When the reference architecture is built with security in mind, and it is reused, this cuts down on the security concerns of that application going forward. It also means that if issues are discovered or changes need to be made to the reference architecture, that those changes can be easily communicated to the impacted applications through the ARB.

It's clear to see why this is important from a security perspective. Being able to design securely once and reuse everywhere is powerful. However, in reality there will be nuance to the adoption of that reference architecture. Not every application will be able to leverage the reference architecture verbatim, and it is impractical to build a reference architecture that covers all possible scenarios. This is where local architects will need to interpret the architecture in a way that meets the spirit of the design, especially the security aspects, while applying it in the context of the application.

I'll use our favorite organization Superior Products to illustrate this further. Superior Products has several applications that are accessed through an API gateway. The user logs in through a mobile device or other user agent to the API gateway, which then provides the access to the services through an API provider. This is a less-than-ideal scenario since Superior Products has to manage the user credentials in a datastore. The organization would like to move to a solution that allows for decentralized authentication through a third-party identity provider.

> **DEFINITION** An *identity provider* (IdP) is used to create, maintain, and manage identity information through a decentralized network. This distributed network provides authentication information and services.

Dashing Danielle has heard the pain points from several different applications on the management of credentials and ensuring that users are able to gain access to the API services they offer. With this in mind, she sets off on some research to determine what opportunities there are to develop a pattern and reference architecture that can be used by the applications in Superior Products. She comes across several different options but lands on a solution that leverages a third-party IdP solution that is popular in the industry.

> **NOTE** There are many IdP solutions on the market. One of the leaders is Okta, but there are others like Ping Identity, RSA, Microsoft, and Oracle.

Dashing Danielle works with the third party to develop a basic architecture that can be used to bring to the ARB to get buy-in. The architecture consists of a simple diagram (shown in figure 5.5) that includes an unnamed IdP, the API gateway, and the back-end services.

Simple reference architecture for API access

Figure 5.5 API architecture to be used as reference architecture

Dashing Danielle documents the following workflow to help establish the basic understanding of how the IdP will be used in accessing Superior Products APIs:

- A user will log in through the mobile or web application, where the IdP will then be used to check the credentials and issue a token.
- Another token is created for that user and app through the API gateway's OAuth token-generation service. This is used to access the application going forward.
- The API gateway and the IdP ensure that the request is within the boundaries of the user's permissions and returns a token to the end-user application that is used to call the actual API.
- The API gateway verifies the token before serving up the requested API.

Dashing Danielle brings this architecture pattern to the ARB, where, after several iterations and clarifications, it is approved as a reference architecture in the ARB. Dashing Danielle is then able to take this approved architecture to the various applications that are currently experiencing issues with managing users of their APIs. She coordinates with the chosen third-party IdP to bring the solution across the board at Superior Products.

> **NOTE** To learn more about APIs and security, check out *API Security in Action* by Neil Madden (www.manning.com/books/api-security-in-action).

At Acme Services, things are not going as well. There is no ARB, which means that there is little opportunity to coalesce around a common architecture or standard. Each product development team finds themselves often developing a design that resembles their peer applications but using different solutions. This drives up the cost for the organization. Because there is no ARB, two of the teams came to the same conclusion that they wanted to leverage a third party to manage identities for them but ended up pursuing two different third parties, leading to additional complexities in the organization's architecture. Eventually, their API economy is accessed in a disjointed way that increases cost, reduces supportability, and becomes a nightmare to manage.

5.3.3 *Bringing requirements into the organization*

One of the benefits of creating the reference architecture and standards is that these will lead to the development of requirements that can be easily consumed by development teams. Where standards and reference architecture focus primarily on the strategic level, requirements bring it down to the level where the code is actually being developed. As a reminder, requirements are part of the initial steps of software development. These are used to describe how the software should behave and the various goals it is being designed to achieve.

As I have been laying out in this section, the ARB is used to approve and manage the various architecture and standards, but it does not deal with requirements, as that is in the hands of the local development team, including the product owners and architects. However, the reference architecture, standards, and industry practices are used as guidelines for developing those requirements. For instance, in the case of the reference architecture described previously, there would be several requirements around the access of the API gateway, the token generation, the IdP, and others. From a security standpoint, these requirements would focus more on ensuring that the architecture is applied in a way that does not compromise the confidentiality, integrity, and availability of the application and the data. That means that, as an example, the requirements will be written to state that tokens will be sent over a secure channel (e.g., TLS); that the tokens will be short-lived, which reduces the potential exposure and that the design is able to handle potential disruptions with the IdP.

> **Exercise 5.3**
> Using the reference architecture earlier, write a requirement that can be used to implement a portion of that architecture. Even better, if your organization already has a reference architecture in place, access it and write a requirement that meets a portion of that architecture. If the team you work in is required to meet that architecture, introduce the requirement in your team.

When creating requirements, it's important to ensure that they provide sufficient guidance on what is being asked and that, especially when they are tied to an architecture or industry standards, they meet the spirit of the overall guidance. Being able to create requirements that meet the overall framework means that the architecture can be met by the development team through prescriptive statements. There are other guiding means that can assist in generating requirements. I'll talk about those next.

5.4   *Maturity models*

Where reference architecture and standards are primarily developed within the organization to give specific guidance on what the organization believes is best practices for developing software, frameworks and maturity models are used to help organizations measure themselves against the industry.

> **DEFINITION**   A *maturity model* looks at the people, processes, and technology in an organization and measures that against a numbers-based maturity level. It is a measure of the organization's current position in a given disciple and provides steps on how to raise the maturity to a higher level. Although in our case we are curious to know the security maturity of an organization, maturity models are used broadly in other technology domains.

There are two well-known maturity models that are used for developing security. One is OWASP's Software Assurance Maturity Model (SAMM), and the other is Building Security in Maturity Model (BSIMM).

- OWASP SAMM: https://owaspsamm.org/
- BSIMM: www.bsimm.com/

Both are useful ways for an organization to understand where they need to put their focus when it comes to developing security practices. However, as you will see, each of their approaches are different.

5.4.1 OWASP SAMM

OWASP's SAMM is a maturity model that follows a more traditional approach to raising the security maturity of an organization, as depicted in figure 5.6. SAMM focuses on the secure software development life cycle while being designed to be technology agnostic. There are three levels of maturity in SAMM, with 1 being the lowest and 3 being the highest. It is not important for every organization to put together a roadmap that gets them to level 3, as every organization has a different risk appetite. If the organization does not process or manage any sensitive data and does not have any critical products, level 1 or 2 might suffice. The current version of SAMM contains five functions:

- Governance
- Design
- Implementation
- Verification
- Operations

OWASP Software Assurance Maturity Model (SAMM)

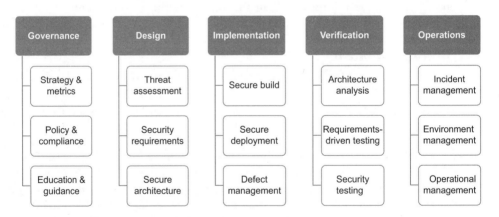

Figure 5.6   Overview of the SAMM version 2

If this looks familiar, it's because this tracks well with the SDLC and enables the organization to assess and then build a plan to address gaps in each stage of the SDLC. Within the five business functions, there are 15 security practices that align to those functions. Each practice dives into the specific items that are used to meet that practice and has a set of activities that align to three maturity levels, with each level becoming increasingly more difficult to achieve.

For example, table 5.1 shows the security practice of threat assessment under the Design function in SAMM. The focus is around an application risk profile and threat modeling, so each of the questions is related to the organization's practices in order to identify the current maturity level.

Table 5.1 **Example questions in SAMM related to the threat assessment practice**

Maturity Level	Question
1	Do you identify and manage architectural design flaws with threat modeling? You perform threat modeling for high-risk applications. You use simple threat checklists, such as STRIDE. You persist the outcome of a threat model for later use.
2	Do you use a standard methodology, aligned on your application risk levels? You train your architects, security champions, and other stakeholders on how to do practical threat modeling. Your threat modeling methodology includes at least diagramming, threat identification, design flaw mitigations, and how to validate your threat model artifacts. Changes in the application or business context trigger a review of the relevant threat models. You capture the threat modeling artifacts with tools that are used by your application teams.
3	Do you regularly review and update the threat modeling methodology for your applications? The threat model methodology considers historical feedback for improvement. You regularly (e.g., yearly) review the existing threat models to verify that no new threats are relevant for your applications. You automate parts of your threat modeling process with threat modeling tools.

Each of these questions is designed to highlight processes that the organization should follow to provide better overall security in its SDLC, with each process becoming more difficult to obtain. In this case, simply performing a threat model is a foundational step. Having a process that revisits that threat model and methodology on a regular basis is a more mature approach to identifying application business risk.

With the assess and build process, the organization can leverage SAMM on existing products and life cycles. Should the organization purchase another company or product, SAMM can be used to measure the security of newly acquired software. There are four basic steps to SAMM that assist the organization into assessing its current level and implementing a roadmap to a more secure level (figure 5.7).

Similar to other maturity models, the first step is to obtain the organization's current maturity. In this stage, the organization will evaluate its current posture and practices by identifying and interviewing stakeholders.

Software assurance maturity model structure

The organization defines the desired target maturity level.

The organization begins the implementation path with prescriptive steps to achieve the desired level.

During the assessment, the organization defines the organization's current posture as it relates to SAMM.

The organization develops the implementation path to getting to the desired maturity level.

Figure 5.7 Structure of the SAMM

OWASP has developed a handy toolbox that provides interview questions that should be used during the assessment: https://owaspsamm.org/assessment/. Here are some example questions:

- Do you understand the enterprise-wide risk appetite for your applications?
- Do you regularly review and update the strategic plan for application security?
- Do you publish the organization's policies as test scripts or run books for easy interpretation by development teams?
- Do you require employees involved with application development to take SDLC training?

The goal of these questions and the responses is to build a rating that is used to ultimately provide the maturity level of the organization. Although not all questions have yes/no answers, the SAMM toolbox allows the responder to provide some nuance to the answers, such as yes with a caveat. In other words, "Yes, we review x annually," or "Yes, we review x before significant decisions." Once the interviews have been completed, a score will be associated with each of the functions and security practices that shows how the organization meets the maturity in that given function. This score is then combined with the other areas to create an overall maturity score for the organization. In order to successfully perform an interview, you'll want to ensure consistency with the interview process with the interviewer and be flexible with the process. Look at different formats for performing the interview, like anonymous questionnaires, workshops, or in-person interviews. The organization's culture should be taken into consideration during this activity to ensure the organization gets the most benefit.

Now that the organization understands it current posture, it's time to set a target and define a plan. As was mentioned before, the target does not necessarily need to be level 3 across the board. In some cases, the organization may take the approach that they will accept a certain level of risk due to not being at the highest level, or the application is not sensitive enough to warrant the overhead of the higher maturity level. Although each effort varies, when setting the target, it's critical to understand what the effort might be for the application team. This also means that the team must include the dependencies that might be on each of the activities with other teams and external sources.

With the assessment complete, and the targets defined, the team can follow a general roadmap planning exercise that outlines how the organization will gradually build the maturity to the desired level over time. Although there is no prescriptive time frame related to SAMM, the organization may be under internal or external pressure to obtain a particular level by a certain time. For instance, the organization may be asked by clients to adopt a formal process around something like threat modeling by year-end. If the organization does not currently have a threat model process, they would want to prioritize the threat modeling activities in the roadmap and work backward from the year-end date in order to define the milestones.

Lastly, the fun part: implementing the path to a more mature, secure SDLC. With the roadmap in hand, the application security team will work with the organization to help adopt the new processes. It is important for the stakeholders to be aware of the changes, the purpose, and the milestones all throughout this phase. The application security team will need to collect metrics and track progress along the way to ensure that the organization is on target for the desired level.

The SAMM provides an organization a well-defined approach to discovering their current security posture as it relates to software security. It is a prescriptive approach to building maturity. But wouldn't it be nice to see what other organizations are doing to build security into their development process?

5.4.2 Building Security in Maturity Model

Where SAMM allows the organization to look at its current security posture in the secure software development process and build a roadmap that reflects OWASP's guidance maturing, BSIMM looks at the industry peers of the organization to help build that roadmap (figure 5.8). BSIMM is built on interviews with 128 organizations over nine industries. Like SAMM, BSIMM is organized into four domains with 12 software security practices and 122 activities.

As of this writing, the current version of BSIMM is version 12, which included 9,000 software security members in both the security groups as well as security champions in the organization. The industries that were included in BSIMM 12 were

- Financial
- Fintech
- Independent software vendors
- Tech
- Retail
- Insurance
- Health care
- Cloud
- IoT

Building security in maturity model (BSIMM)

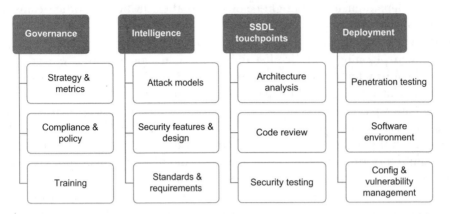

Figure 5.8   BSIMM structure and organization

BSIMM includes three levels of maturity that relate to the observed frequency of the given activity, with level 1 being frequently observed and level 3 being infrequently observed.

> **DEFINITION**   *Activities* are actions carried out or facilitated by a software security group (SSG) as part of a practice. Activities are divided into three levels in the BSIMM based on observation rates. Frequently observed activities are designated level 1, with less frequent and infrequently observed activities designated as levels 2 and 3, respectively.

For each of these activities, the organization can measure their posture against others in their particular industry. Although this is not the prescriptive approach that OWASP takes with SAMM, it helps the measuring organization know how it compares to its peers. One of the considerations with BSIMM is that the best practices that are outlined may not be a great fit for your organization, but it is hard to argue if you come across activities that are being completed by many organizations in your industry. One example of this is identifying your personally identifiable information (PII) obligations, which means knowing the requirements related to the capture and retention of PII in your system, as well as building an inventory of PII across the organization. When the vast majority of the organizations that participate in BSIMM are doing this activity, it's a safe bet that your organization should be as well.

To this point, the BSIMM provides five of the top activities that most organizations should pursue regardless of their industry. These are activities that are being integrated in almost all of the organizations that are part of the BSIMM. Table 5.2 shows an example of several activities in the BSIMM. Once again, peer pressure is a strong motivator and these activities have consistently ranked at the top five for several years.

Table 5.2   Example questions in BSIMM related to the threat assessment practice

Activity name	Domain and practice	Description
Implement life cycle instrumentation and use to define governance.	Governance: strategy and metrics	This can be best defined as applying application security tools into the SDLC process in order to gather metrics as it relates to the security policies in the organization.
Ensure host and network security basics are in place.	Deployment: software environment	Before running your developed software, ensure that the environment it will be deployed to is secure. That means having the systems and network that it's deployed to properly secured.
Identify PII obligations.	Governance: compliance and policy	No surprise, but this is related to the data that an organization accumulates. More importantly, it's about knowing what type of data is being stored and where it is being stored.
Perform security feature review.	SSDL touchpoints: architecture analysis	When architecture changes that impact the security level or model, an architecture review should occur to understand the risk.
Use external penetration testers to find problems.	Deployment: penetration testing	Your internal testers and tools are great at finding certain issues, but nothing brings a security issue to the forefront quicker than an issue uncovered by an external tester.

While these activities are the most common across the organizations that are part of BSIMM, it's important to see the trends of where organizations are showing the most growth over the past versions. For instance, the top three activities that have seen the biggest growth in the past several versions are

- Use orchestration for containers and virtualized environments
- Ensure cloud security basics
- Use application containers to support security goals

Each of these have seen several hundred percent increases from the past versions, meaning that more organizations are beginning to adopt these activities over the past few years. This is no surprise given the increase in adoption of cloud and container technology. As these technologies expand, the need to increase the security around them grows.

What do these metrics show about an organization's software security initiative? It shows not only how an organization measures up to its peers, but also how the industry in general is moving and how the organizations are addressing the new concerns. Armed with this knowledge, it's time to build a plan around how to attack any known deficiencies in the organization with Synopsis's Maturity Action Plan (MAP). This helps the organization address the open challenges and objectives by building an action plan that raises the maturity. Currently, Synopsis offers services that help the organization determine what steps need to be taken to build the MAP. This includes first looking at the organization's current posture with an assessment of the security program. From there, a future state is defined and the gaps are highlighted to build the roadmap. The last step is to develop the action plan to achieve the desired state.

As I mentioned, BSIMM is a great measure against peers in your respective industries. One of the key aspects to understand with BSIMM is that if most of your peers are tackling software security with the same or similar activities, then this is a good indicator that you should be doing it as well. This is the power of BSIMM.

5.4.3   *Addressing your security immaturity*

Both BSIMM and SAMM take two different approaches to building secure software. So, which makes the most sense? Of course, it depends. If you absolutely need to see how you measure up against the other organizations in and out of your organization, then conducting a BSIMM engagement makes sense. However, if you are looking to do a basic self-assessment that shows your current software security posture, then SAMM is the better option, as it is open, and assessments are conducted by the organization.

The most important factor in following a maturity model is to understand what your organization can bear. Getting a BSIMM assessment and a MAP that shows where you should be in the next 12 to 24 months will be worthless if your organization is not prepared to do the work of increasing the maturity. This means that the leadership must be brought into the strategy, and the engineering organization must be aligned with the application security function. More importantly, the right resources must be dedicated to the initiative. Take for example that in both the SAMM and BSIMM, architecture analysis is an activity. This activity requires knowledgeable resources both in the engineering team and in the application security team to be able to review the architecture for security control effectiveness and mitigation of threats. Not all of the organization's resources will be able to effectively perform this level of activity.

The last comparison points to make about the BSIMM and SAMM is to know whether you require or need an external assessment. Since BSIMM is proprietary to Synopsis, the BSIMM assessment is by default external. The SAMM allows you to perform a self-assessment; however, like I stated previously, you will need expertise in your organization to conduct that assessment. However, you can have a third party perform a SAMM assessment if that is the preference.

There is no right answer with a maturity model, but it is an important factor in what I will talk about next. With a maturity model, especially BSIMM, it makes it easier to sell an overall software security initiative to the stakeholders in an organization and build a better path toward a democratized and decentralized security program that builds security into software early.

5.5   *Decentralized application security*

As I have mentioned numerous times at this point, securing software requires a village of security-minded individuals and teams. Application security resources cannot be in every coding decision, every design review, and every assessment. The current approach of a centralized team that applies software security tools that create an output of security vulnerabilities that need to be resolved in a certain time period creates friction, frustration, and drag on the development of software. Moreover, this centralized application security function becomes a team of ankle biters who are attempting to provide security by telling the development teams that they are awful at writing secure code. Decentralized application security focuses on spreading the security burden around. Figure 5.9 shows how the centralized approach differs from the decentralized approach.

Centralized vs. decentralized AppSec

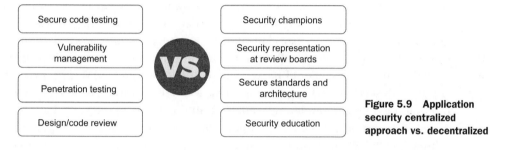

Figure 5.9   Application security centralized approach vs. decentralized

In the decentralized approach, the application security team focuses their efforts on building the structure of secure software development as opposed to the daily operational aspects of managing tools and driving closure of vulnerabilities. These are still important and needed in all organizations, but application security teams cannot scale to the level needed in order to be ever present.

Building the structure to support the secure development of software, the application security team will create the reference architecture, the standards, and the requirements to be used by the engineering organization. Additionally, it is critical that they become a part of the fabric of developing software. This means that they should sit on review boards and other architecture or leadership groups to ensure that security is made part of the process. Lastly, the application security team should focus on building an education structure that helps create champions or, at the very least, raises the security education of the development organization. I will cover this more in depth in the next chapter, but the critical takeaway here is that security needs to become part of the culture of the organization in order for the software to be developed in a secure manner. One popular method of building or expanding the security culture is with a security champions program.

5.5.1   *Security champions program*

I've talked about them a bit in previous chapters. They're called many things, mostly *champions* or *coaches*, but the goal of security champions is to spread the wealth of security across the organization. Starting a program that builds security champions will rely on a change of culture in the organization and includes buy-in from the engineering leadership and the organization as a whole.

The general definition of a security champion is a nonsecurity employee who is part of the organization, usually in some type of development or development support role. They can be from one of the following roles:

- Developer
- Quality assurance
- Architect
- Designer
- DevOps

To start the security champions program, the application security team will first need to identify what teams and applications are part of the program. Not every team or application may take part, especially if they are a small team or low risk to the organization. Obviously, the focus will be on the highest risk applications in the organization to begin with. This list should be well vetted and approved by the appropriate leadership in both security and engineering. This will help ensure that no team was missed and that the ones that are intentionally left off the list are agreed upon.

Once the list of teams is agreed upon, the role of the security champion should be defined (table 5.3). The most critical qualification is that they should want to be there and have a passion for security. Forcing employees into the champion program will lead to a failed program. These champions will be required to spend a certain amount of their time on driving security. In some cases, this can be as low as 5% of their time dedicated to driving security in the product area that they are a part of. However, the organization needs to set the time effort expectation early so that there is no confusion around priority and activity. The expectations of a security champion vary from organization to organization, and it depends on their goals.

Table 5.3   **Expectations of a security champion**

Share security knowledge	Help make key security decisions	Create and drive security best practices
Build threat models	Perform security reviews	Participate in research and development initiatives
Participate in bug bounties	Attend security conferences	Prioritize security work in the backlog
Monitor for vulnerabilities in the application	Write security test cases as part of the overall application testing	

Now that the expectations have been set and the teams identified, it's time to nominate champions. This process is as simple as working with the leadership in engineering to identify potential candidates. Once identified, a formal nomination is made of the candidates. This includes communication to leadership, the rest of the champions team, and the engineering team that they are a part of. The organization may also put the nominated security champions through formal training to achieve a level of security knowledge. This is not an uncommon approach in most organizations and can be achieved with either internal or external training. Training can be assigned with target levels to attain or certifications to complete. Some security training platforms include education paths designed specifically for training champions. The organization can also take the approach of leveraging internally developed education from the application security team if it exists.

Communication and the storage of information also need to be defined. Depending on the collaboration tools that are used in the organization, it could be as simple as setting up a channel just for champions in a collaboration tool like Microsoft Teams, Slack, or Discord. Additionally, the champions team will periodically develop content that needs to be stored for easy retrieval. Again, depending on the organization, this could be tools like Confluence, Hive, SharePoint, or the like. This content should be used as the knowledge base for all activities for the champions team and the development teams that they are part of and should include

- The champions team charter
- The members of the team and the teams/applications they serve
- Activities and meeting minutes
- Processes for threat modeling, vulnerability management, and performing security reviews
- Training program and opportunities
- External resources

Although nobody likes more meetings, periodic touch points with the group of champions is a required activity. This can be just a simple biweekly or monthly meeting that is used to discuss upcoming activities, ongoing projects, and current vulnerabilities. This also aids in keeping the participants engaged in the champions team and raising the visibility across the organization. One way to reduce the effectiveness of the champions team is to allow it to lapse or reduce the engagement of the team members.

With a team defined, it's time to leverage it to take advantage of this increase in security footprint. Now the application security team has advocates for building secure software. And these advocates are embedded in the applications. But that's not the end of the decentralized model.

5.5.2 Leveraging the decentralized model

Our favorite security champion Dashing Danielle has been asked to join the application security team more formally, as she has been demonstrating a keen ability to deliver security in Superior Products' flagship application. Before she can formally join the application security team, she needs to help find a successor to her role as security champion in the team. She announces her future move to application security to the team and asks whether anyone else would be interested in taking her champion role. Brilliant Brian has been working in the team for several years and has strong knowledge of the product. He has also been in many of the same meetings as Dashing Danielle, where security has been the prime topic. He has become increasingly interested in the security space and gladly raises his hand when the opportunity comes up to be part of the security functions in Superior Products.

Dashing Danielle first works with Brilliant Brian to develop a training path that will get him to the champion level. At Superior Products, they are using a leading provider of secure engineering training that includes several education modules that are built to create security champions. Brilliant Brian is onboarded in the training program with the first module slated to start immediately. This will get him to the first level of three levels in the platform. Once he completes all three levels and passes an assessment for each one, he will be considered a security champion. Based on the current pace, Brilliant Brian will complete the training in 4 months.

While training is underway, Dashing Danielle introduces Brilliant Brian to the various documentation and processes that each security champion must be familiar with. She invites him to the biweekly champions meeting, where he is able to get a sense of the expectations for him and the other champions in the team. He acquaints himself with the ongoing projects and topics in the champions team.

Fast-forward a few months after Brilliant Brian has completed the training and assessment. He is now the active participant in the security champions biweekly meeting for the product as Dashing Danielle begins to pick up responsibility in the application security team. Brilliant Brian has been working diligently with the development team to help integrate and maintain the security scanning tools set forth by the application security team. He has joined in on code reviews to identify problematic code patterns that fall outside of the documented practices and reference architecture that has been developed by application security. He has raised the level of security education in the team by encouraging other members to attend the security training offered in the organization. He even submitted a talk to a local conference on some of the techniques he has been using in the team to bring security to the developed code. With Dashing Danielle and the leadership team comfortable with Brilliant Brian's handling of the security of the team's code, Dashing Danielle is able to take the next step in her security career and become a formal member of application security. Brilliant Brian is able to leverage the work that Dashing Danielle has already done, as well as the continuous efforts by the application security team to build the development security ecosystem. From this effort, the development team has seen a reduction in new vulnerabilities being introduced in their code. A win-win for all parties involved.

Summary

- Security is not just an activity that security teams are responsible for. Each team has a responsibility to ensure that they are considering the security implications of the design choices they make.

- Security teams are not able to scale to meet the demands of security in any sufficiently large organization. This raises the need for more security-minded individuals in the organization.

- Security education is not just for security teams; developers and those who support the development process can and should take advantage of security training. This raises the security IQ of the organization and helps spread the knowledge.

- Training comes in many different forms and can include microlearning, traditional classroom training, conferences, brownbag sessions, and others. A mix of some or all of these will help the organization raise the security awareness.

- Standards, requirements, and reference architecture are methods to create content that can be leveraged by the development teams, which helps to decentralize the application security function.

- Maturity models can be used to determine where your organization is today and where you want to take it. For maturity models like BSIMM, you can measure your organization against similar organizations in the same industry. This is helpful when you need to understand where others are placing their efforts.

- A decentralized application security model depends on having well-trained individuals who are prepared to address security concerns for their area. This is commonly solved through a security champion's style program that builds security-minded individuals into the development teams.

6
Application security as a service

This chapter covers

- Changing the application security model from gated activities to enablement
- Creating an environment of application security as a service
- Learning the services that should be part of the application security as a service ecosystem
- Closing the divide between security and engineering

What is a great way to stop getting invited to the engineering holiday party? Block an application release or hold up a build due to a found vulnerability. Historically, application security has been the team that comes in at the end of a productive coding release to show various issues with the code, deployment, libraries used, and other ways of showing how the software is not ready for prime time. This gated approach is something that has been pushed for by security for various reasons. The prime one being that the security organization is tasked with identifying, helping to reduce, and measuring the risk of the organization. In this capacity, the security team obviously wants to ensure that there are no vulnerabilities that put the organization at risk going out to production. A better approach is to create an ecosystem of security that enables the development teams to access security services along the path to production.

However, many organizations look at the security gates as a level of development to strive for despite the difficulties. The clear concern is that this approach will require changes to the application in order to apply stronger security that could delay the release of the application. So, what many organizations end up doing is having a release valve that allows them to still push their code to production and assume some level of risk due to the open security issues. This risk is often owned by the business owner of the impacted application or by a senior leader in engineering. Although this works to ensure that value is still being delivered to the customers, this also means that risk is being created for the organization.

Although every organization needs to find a balance between releasing features and minimizing risk, many opt to release features and accept the risk—often without understanding the real impact and without real consequences to the acceptance. To be honest, very few organizations actually hold the risk accepter accountable for a risk that materializes into a breach. In other words, not many organizations will withhold compensation or levy other penalties like termination in the case of a breach that was perpetrated by an accepted risk. It is important for the security organization to properly identify the risk, put it into the context of the application and business, and ensure that if it is accepted that the risk owner knows what they are accepting.

6.1 *Managing risk during development*

In earlier chapters, *risk* was defined as the potential for loss of an asset or damage to an asset. This comes in every shape and size, from intentional or unintentional actions, natural disasters, human error, and system failure. While these risks can occur at any time with little or no warning, it doesn't mean that the organization has no ability to address them.

Although risk is a broad topic on its own, in the context of software development there is still risk that can be addressed by the organization and the engineering team. There are four generally accepted ways of managing risk:

- *Avoid*—This is where the organization attempts to remediate or find an alternative solution that removes the risk. This is often costly compared to the other options, as it means additional work or a change in technology.
- *Accept*—Here the organization understands that the risk is low or the effort to remove the risk is higher than what the actual risk is. This will lead them to take the risk on with the anticipation that at some point the risk will be removed. An example is when the organization has a product that is being sunset in the future. Until that time, any noncritical risk may be accepted.
- *Mitigate*—When an organization mitigates a risk, they are looking to implement some service or control that will essentially reduce the risk of occurrence or

severity of the risk. For example, an organization that has a critical vulnerability due to a third-party component that they chose to use and that does not have the ability to upgrade to the latest version may look to a web application firewall (WAF) or run-time application security protection (RASP) to provide run-time protection until the component can be upgraded.

- *Transfer*—Transferring risk is typically thought of as purchasing cybersecurity insurance where the organization will pay to have some other entity own the risk. An example of this is when an organization purchases disaster insurance on property that houses their infrastructure or employees.

Which one the organization chooses largely depends on their risk appetite. In some cases, the organization may be forced into one path over the other. As I mentioned, if a critical risk is discovered and there is no clear path to resolution, the organization may be forced to accept the risk and accelerate the decommissioning of the technology that poses the risk to begin with. In this case, the organization will accept the risk and accelerate the migration to the newer technology so that the risk can be ultimately remediated through avoidance. Another example would be if the organization builds its critical infrastructure that supports their software in a flood-prone area. In this case they may be forced to purchase flood insurance, thereby transferring the risk to the insurance company.

6.1.1   *Defining and reducing risk*

In previous chapters, you learned how risk can be identified. Just as a reminder, risk is determined in the OWASP Risk Rating as the likelihood combined with the impact. This means that if a risk such as unauthorized access to sensitive information through the exposure of administrator credentials is identified, then the organization needs to review how likely the issue is to occur and what happens if an attacker gains access to the sensitive data. In this case the likelihood might be low, but the impact could be high.

How does this risk identification impact the development team? As mentioned, the organization has several options to address risk at the high level, but actually prioritizing and addressing the risk in a development team is different. Not all risks are created equal, and even the same risk will impact different teams in the organization differently. For example, if the organization has chosen to mitigate a discovered risk, then the development team will be an integral part of that effort by integrating the mitigation controls like a RASP. The development team will need to work with the application security team to get the organization's RASP product packaged with their code, deployed with the application to production, and provide maintenance and reporting.

6.1.2   *Define the application risk*

One of the most critical parts of understanding the risk to the organization is knowing the actual risk level of a given application. For example, the organization may have several applications that they develop internally. Each of them will have a different risk impact to the organization based on the data they collect, the audience it's exposed to, and the financial impact to the organization. Although it is difficult to put together an actual calculation that defines what the risk is to an organization, there are several steps that can be taken to identify what risk an application poses to the organization.

In chapter 2, I covered the OWASP risk rating methodology, which is a simple calculation that takes the likelihood of attack and the impact in order to calculate the overall risk. This becomes an issue because determining the likelihood of an attack is difficult since much of this depends on the opportunity and the lack of controls in place. But some organizations may have critical applications with known vulnerabilities that are never attacked. It's not that the possibility is not there; it's that the opportunity or the exposure is not. Another way to view the risk of an application to the organization is to instead look at it from the application standpoint instead of the vulnerability. You can approach this by first categorizing the applications by their level of importance in the organization (table 6.1).

Table 6.1 Application importance in an organization

Application category	Definition
Critical	Critical applications are vital to the operations of the organization. These are applications that require the highest level of uptime and would result in significant financial loss or critical damage should the application become unavailable or should its data be breached. A critical application could be a clinical application used to administer doses of medication to patients.
Important	Important applications are ones where uptime is expected, and the data maintained by the application would pose a severe impact to the organization should it become exposed or unavailable. An important application could be one that provides supply chain management services within an enterprise.
Support	These applications are used widely in the organization to provide some service that relates to the operation of the organization. Downtime and breach of data would have a mild impact to the organization. For example, an application that provides client support functions would not pose a significant risk to the organization.
Internal	Internal applications, as the name specifies, are applications that are only used internally within the organization. These applications are used to assist with the internal operations of the organization such as customer relationship management tools. Although they may seem important, these types of applications usually have workaround methods, and their uptime and data pose a mild risk to the organization.

Once the application importance has been identified, the organization can then begin to determine what the cost of a potential breach of data or disruption of the application would be. This, of course, varies by application, organization, and the breach itself. However, the organization can put the breach into perspective of other historical and contemporary breaches in their industry. One great example of leveraging contemporary data is the Verizon "Data Breach Investigation Report" (DBIR).

This annual report provides insight into the breaches that have been reported during the year. The report quantifies the overall loss beyond the direct impact; for example, payment to a ransomware group that goes above the business disruption costs. It also identifies several factors:

- Direct loss as a result of the attack
- Cost of digital forensics and incident response
- Legal counsel

Because it is difficult to put a number on an actual breach without the details, the Verizon DBIR helps with getting a range that can be used to understand what a potential breach of data would mean for an organization. There are two things to consider per Verizon's DBIR:

- Organizations that go through a data breach underperform the NASDAQ by 5% in the 6 months following a breach.
- Some incidents have little to no financial impact, where the majority can run between $1,000 and $600,000 per incident.

That is a wide swing in cost, but it at least gives an organization some numbers to think about when considering the cost of a possible breach. One of the most common types of attacks that cost the organization is ransomware. These have a clear financial impact where the organization not only has to pay the ransom, but also the downtime while restoring data from backups or negotiating with the attacker. According to Sophos's 2021 "State of Ransomware" report, the average payment was $170,000 in 2020 with the highest payment being $3.2 million.

What often happens with both the ransomware and data breach costs is that the attackers will charge what the organization is likely to accept. In these cases, if the attacker overcharges, the organization is likely to rebuff the attempt and find an alternative path to resolution. This means for smaller organizations, a smaller amount would be requested. For larger organizations, the attackers may attempt a larger payday.

How does this factor into the organization's overall risk associated with the applications they have? Consider that for your average application, it can be assumed that there will be several vulnerabilities per every so many lines of code. These can be identified through the scanning tools that I have covered throughout this book while others can go undetected through the lack of tooling or the inability of the tools to find issues.

Now that we know that there are vulnerabilities in our code, and the cost of a security incident can run a wide range of costs, the organization can begin to put together what their overall exposure to a security issue is and the potential cost. But this doesn't mean that the organization has no recourse against these issues. In chapter 3, I covered some of the protection tools that can be used to mitigate vulnerabilities. These tools or processes are considered countermeasures against a given vulnerability. However, not each countermeasure will be effective against every vulnerability. Take, for example, the use of a WAF as a countermeasure. It is often extremely effective against such vulnerabilities as SQL injection or cross-site scripting (XSS) but will be ineffective against hardcoded secrets in code.

The organizations would need to consider each of the countermeasures that they have at their disposal and quantify their effectiveness against the vulnerabilities that have been identified. A sample of this is in table 6.2. These countermeasures can be overlaid over a vulnerability to determine an effectiveness. The organization can use a simple rating scale and get as granular as they choose in order to determine the effectiveness. For instance, they can use a scale of 1 to 5 to designate how effective the countermeasure is for a given vulnerability type.

Table 6.2 Effectiveness of countermeasures

Countermeasure	Vulnerability	Effectiveness
WAF	XXS	5
WAF	SQL injection	5
WAF	Path traversal	3
RASP	XXS	3
RASP	SQL injection	5
RASP	Path traversal	5

As an example, the WAF could be rated a 5 against SQL injection and XSS, and a 3 against path traversal. This is an important concept as we look at a code release and the risk it poses to the organization as it goes to a production environment.

6.1.3 Release-by-risk

What would be better than detecting vulnerabilities and blocking the progress of the code when a vulnerability is found? Allowing the release to continue based on a risk calculation and aligning that to the overall risk tolerance of the organization.

> **DEFINITION** *Risk tolerance* is the amount of risk that the organization and, more importantly, the business is willing to accept to meet its objectives. This allows the organization to employ the appropriate amount of security that reduces overspend while applying the most amount of security. It is important to understand that the security organization does not own risk. They can only highlight the risk to the organization and put it in the appropriate context for the business to eventually accept or own.

What this looks like in practice will depend on the organization and several factors. The biggest factor is what their code release pipeline looks like (see chapter 4). Where this works best and where you get the biggest bang for your buck is when the organization is using a DevSecOps pipeline with releases that occur frequently since this allows for a rapid release. In figure 6.1, code is developed and eventually deployed

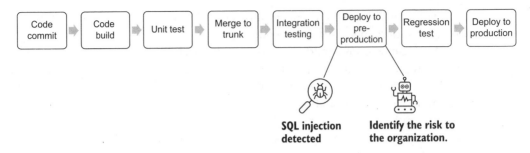

Figure 6.1 Identifying the risk of a found vulnerability

to a preproduction environment where DAST and IAST tools are used to uncover potential vulnerabilities. In this case, an SQL injection attack is discovered by the DAST tool.

In the pipelines I discussed earlier, the issue would be presented back to the developer as well as the application security team through a defect ticket like Jira. This defect ticket would be used for tracking the issue to resolution. The code would, most likely, not be allowed to be sent to production, depending on the severity of the issue.

In the model where the organization has taken the approach to manage the risk as code is deployed, the found SQL injection takes a different path as depicted in figure 6.2. Automation in the integration tool will match the criticality of the vulnerability that is pulled from the tool that it was identified in and match that against the risk

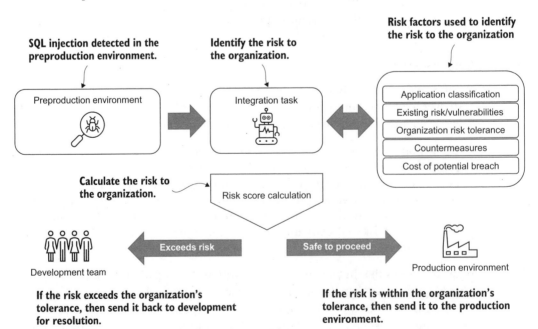

Figure 6.2 Determining the risk during integration

appetite for that application. This means that if the SQL injection issue was identified as a medium severity, the integration tool will apply that rating against the application classification, the existing amount and severity of the known vulnerabilities in the application, the organization's risk tolerance, the existing countermeasures, and the potential breach cost.

Looking at an example at Superior Products, the newly minted application security architect, Dashing Danielle, has been given her first assignment. She is being tasked with taking the approach of building the release-by-risk process in Superior Products. Her first goal is to find an application to pilot this effort with. She decides to work with her old team to define this process with the application she once helped code. This provides her some good assistance from her old team and gives her an application that she is familiar with.

For much of the work that needs to be completed, Dashing Danielle works with the information security team in the enterprise security organization. With this team's help, she comes up with an application classification that is "important." She and the information security team make that determination due to the fact that the application, Stuff-For-You, an e-commerce application that allows for the purchasing of goods online, accounts for more than half of Superior Products' revenue. This is substantially more than any other application at Superior Products.

Dashing Danielle further works with the information security team to understand the risk tolerance of the organization as it relates to Stuff-For-You. Organizations will have different approaches to how they quantify their risk tolerance. Some will approach it by determining that they will not allow for certain types of threats to materialize or certain data to be compromised. More mature organizations will measure their risk tolerance in what business impact the organization is willing to accept. In discussions with the information security team and Dashing Danielle, they devise a method of identifying both the risk tolerance and the cost of a potential breach. There are several risks that are identified for Stuff-For-You, but the four main ones with their associated cost of potential breach are outlined by Dashing Danielle and the information security team (table 6.3).

Table 6.3 Four main risks identified for the Stuff-For-You e-commerce site (costs are not real)

Risk	Definition	Cost of breach
Privacy breach	The intentional or unintentional release of customer personal or financial data	$50 per stolen record
Stolen intellectual property	The release of internal Superior Products' intellectual property to a competitor or attacker	$2 million per incident
Reliability and availability of the system	When the application becomes unavailable to authorized users	$10,000 per hour down
Data integrity issues	Corruption of data that leads to errors in processing legitimate transactions	$100 per incident

Exercise 6.1

What risks would you include that are specific to your organization or application? It could be specific to your industry or application. Take one and complete table 6.3 for that risk. You can then keep that one in mind as we go through the rest of this chapter.

Superior Products is able to define that any security vulnerability that leads to one of the main risks may be blocked from being released to production or would need to be measured against the overall risk tolerance prior to release. Otherwise, the organization can take the approach of limiting the financial exposure by capping the amount of money associated with any of the risks. This means that they could specify that they are only willing to accept up to $3 million of risk in each application. This is the risk budget of the organization. Superior Products has decided that for an application classified as important, they are willing to tolerate up to $5 million in risk for Stuff-For-You.

At this point, Dashing Danielle has identified the following items about the release-by-risk process she is building for Stuff-For-You:

- The application classification is labeled important.
- Four risks have been identified, along with their associated costs.
- Superior Products' risk tolerance is $5 million.

Now Dashing Danielle needs to identify the countermeasures as well as the existing risks and vulnerabilities in Stuff-For-You in order to complete the process. For this she can look internally within the team to document the current countermeasures:

- WAF to provide DDoS protection and basic protection against SQL injection, XSS, and path traversal attacks.
- Endpoint detection and response tools on the database and application server to identify potential data exfiltration.
- Reputation and risk monitoring to detect whether a privacy breach has occurred, and proprietary data is found on social media or the dark web.
- Secure SDLC to ensure that vulnerabilities are detected early and often with processes in place to remediate them based on risk.

With the countermeasures identified, Dashing Danielle is able to align them to the identified risks, similar to what is identified in table 6.4.

Table 6.4 Four main risks with countermeasures

Risk	Definition	Cost of breach	Potential countermeasure
Privacy breach	The intentional or unintentional release of customer personal or financial data	$50 per stolen record	Reputation and risk monitoring
Stolen intellectual property	The release of internal Superior Products intellectual property to a competitor or attacker	$2 million per incident	Reputation and risk monitoring Secure SDLC

Table 6.4 Four main risks with countermeasures *(continued)*

Risk	Definition	Cost of breach	Potential countermeasure
Reliability and availability of the system	When the application becomes unavailable to authorized users	$10,000 per hour down	WAF Secure SDLC
Data integrity issues	Corruption of data that leads to error in processing legitimate transactions	$100 per incident	WAF Secure SDLC

NOTE These costs, risks, and countermeasures are by no means a complete list, but I point these out to provide some context around the process. In reality, the risks and countermeasures per vulnerability would be much more nuanced.

The last step that Dashing Danielle works to complete is to apply the risks and countermeasures to the currently known vulnerabilities in Stuff-For-You. She reviews the ten open vulnerabilities that apply to the development team and works to apply the associated risks and countermeasures (table 6.5).

Table 6.5 Open vulnerabilities impacting Stuff-For-You

Count	Type	Risk	Potential Countermeasure
3	Reflected XSS	Privacy breach Data integrity	WAF Secure SDLC Reputation and risk monitoring
2	SQL injection	Privacy breach Data integrity Reliability and availability	WAF Secure SDLC Reputation and risk monitoring
2	Broken authentication	Privacy breach	Secure SDLC Reputation and risk monitoring
3	Weak TLS	Privacy breach Data integrity	Secure SDLC Reputation and risk monitoring

Now that Dashing Danielle has what she needs, she is able to align the current vulnerabilities that are known in the Stuff-For-You application and know what the delta is between that and the organization's risk tolerance for the application. Even better, she now knows how to measure new risks against the current backlog of risk debt that the application has. This risk debt is the amount of potential risk there is in terms of cost to the organization. After further review with the product and engineering team, Dashing Danielle is able to establish that the Stuff-For-You application is currently carrying roughly $1 million in risk debt. This leaves $2 million of potential spend that the application can take on. The organization can now prioritize new issues that come in and focus their attention on reducing vulnerabilities that have the largest impact to the risk debt.

Most importantly, the information that Dashing Danielle has gathered allows her to use these data points so that she can ensure that the organization never exceeds its risk budget, as figure 6.3 shows. Dashing Danielle works with the development team for Stuff-For-You to create an integration task that pulls the data points on

- *Application classification*—Important
- *Existing risk debt for Stuff-For-You*—$1 million
- *Organization risk tolerance*—Loss of $3 million
- *Mapping of countermeasures to risk items*—WAF
- *Cost per each possible risk*—$50,000

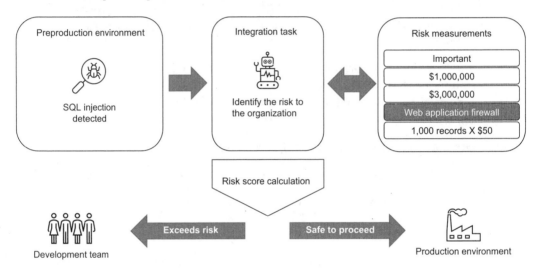

Figure 6.3   Cost and risk balance for an SQL injection

In this example, when the SQL injection is identified, Dashing Danielle has all the information needed to make the decision whether this found issue should block a code release or whether it is within the boundaries of the organization's risk tolerance. This process is great, so how could it get any better? Like anything worth doing, add some automation.

6.2   *Enablement instead of gates*

The common approach to vulnerabilities is to block critical and high findings from going into a production environment. This is a ham-fisted approach that doesn't really reduce the organization's risk. Many of the lower vulnerabilities that are found, like medium and low ones, can still be leveraged in an attack on the organization. In fact, most attackers will use a series of vulnerabilities chained together to compromise an application. Take for example the vulnerabilities shown in table 6.6.

Table 6.6 Example vulnerabilities that can be chained in an attack

Type of vulnerability	Criticality
SQL injection in an administrative form	High
Lack of multifactor authentication (MFA) on administrator accounts	Low
Credentials logged in plain text	Medium
Privilege escalation in main site	Medium

The organization may conclude that each of these alone, while troubling, should be taken individually, and the focus would be to resolve the highest one first, which would be the SQL injection. However, it is plain to see here how this would play out if an attacker was able to identify and take advantage of these issues together. Let's assume that the attacker was able to gain access to the logs. Yes, that's not easy, but attackers are smart. Often these logs can be transferred by email or even sent to other parties. Essentially, it is not a stretch that the logs could be discovered by an attacker.

Depending on the type of credentials logged, the attacker may be able to log in to the system with either privilege credentials or use the privilege escalation vulnerability to gain administrative access. Considering that there is no MFA on administrator accounts, the attacker would be able to access the functionality with just the credentials. Once logged in as an administrator, the attacker can then take advantage of the SQL injection vulnerability to steal or corrupt data.

Given this example, most organizations that take the approach to simply block releases to production when a critical or high is found will only stop the last step in the example I gave. Truth be told, if an attacker is logged in to your application with elevated privileges, an SQL injection vulnerability might be the least of your worries. Don't get me wrong, critical and high vulnerabilities are dangerous. But when the organization is facing dozens, or more, vulnerabilities, a measured approach is needed.

6.2.1 Automate the release-by-risk

When the organization has put in place a process that reviews each found vulnerability against the risk tolerance in order to understand how the vulnerability will impact the overall risk, they have taken the first steps in intelligently addressing their overall risk. This process can be improved by automating the integration to remove any of the manual steps done by the application security team or the team's security champion. As described previously, during the release process, once an issue is found, the integration will have a separate task that takes the inputs that the organization has already outlined regarding its risk tolerance. Blocking or allowing a release to continue is now no longer subjective or based on coarse-grain decisions like blocking all critical and highs.

Dashing Danielle has been able to use her relationship with the development team to create an automation task that is triggered when a vulnerability is found in any of the scanning tools used by the DevSecOps pipeline, as shown in figure 6.4. This task

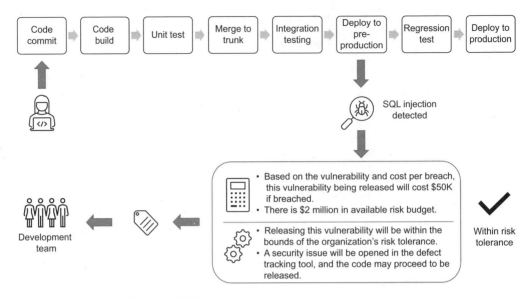

Figure 6.4   Software release-based risk

calls a small program that she wrote that calculates the finding against an organization's risk tolerance. The leadership with Superior Products is in favor of this approach, as it takes much of the manual effort out of risk and vulnerability management. They are willing to accept that some vulnerabilities will be released to production, but at the same time, they know that found vulnerabilities will be assigned back to the team where the normal processes will be implemented in order to remediate or mitigate them as appropriate. This means that even if a vulnerability is released to production, the ability to resolve it quickly is still available while keeping the organization within its risk tolerance.

Not all organizations will be willing to leave risk decisions up to an automated process, but each organization can modify this automation to ensure that there are opportunities to override or block releases when the risk, even when it's within tolerance, is still objectionable.

6.2.2   *Removing the barriers by adding guardrails*

In many organizations, there is a process to stop a release. This is often done through something like a change release where the organization uses a board to review pending and proposed changes to a system and the board either approves or postpones those changes based on the priorities and risk of system stability. In other organizations, the development team will enable blocks on certain conditions such as a failed test, security or otherwise. In either of these cases, the purpose is to ensure that something does not go to production that poses a potential risk to the security, availability, or operation of the application.

As I mentioned earlier, the approach of safe enablement instead of gating provides a means for the development team to release software in a way that is within the boundaries of the risk tolerance of the organization. Figure 6.5 shows where these guardrails can be implemented. However, there is more to providing a secure environment for developers to release to that enables them to have confidence in the security. This begins with setting the objectives that the organization is attempting to achieve in a secure release:

- The build process must follow organizational standard tooling and processes.
- The deployment process must follow organizational standard tooling and processes.
- The build and deployment processes must be modular and allow the addition and removal of tasks.
- Security scanning tools are integrated and block builds that fall outside of the organization's risk tolerance.
- Container images are pulled from an organization-approved image registry that maintains the integrity of the containers.
- Infrastructure management and deployment is defined as infrastructure as code (IaC) and is tested against organizational standards.
- Only pipelines with the organization's controls in place are allowed to deploy to a production environment.
- Controls in the production environment ensure that no production data can be removed from the environment to any other environment.
- All environments are monitored for malicious activity, data exfiltration.

The previously mentioned objectives are a good starting point, and many organizations may add or remove others to ensure that they have the appropriate objectives for their organization. However, the primary goal of these objectives is to create a pipeline that allows developers to deploy code to a production environment while reducing the burden on individuals on the team to identify and block potentially hazardous releases. Each of these objectives do need to be automated and follow the feedback loop that has been discussed previously so that the right people get the right information at the right time.

In figure 6.5, for each stage, feedback should be provided to the relevant teams on the outcomes in the stage. For instance, in the build phase, a critical security vulnerability found through a scanning tool should open a ticket in the defect tracking tool, such as Jira. It should contain all the relevant information related to the vulnerability, including any microtraining or additional security documentation to assist the developer in resolving the issue. In the run phase, any abnormal access to production data, whether reading or writing, should send an alert to the security operations center (SOC) for triage and resolution. The goal here is to have an automation and alerting framework in place that allows the development team to continue to move forward without concern over the security of the code being delivered. There is one more step

Guardrail objectives in an organization

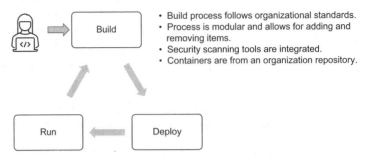

- Build process follows organizational standards.
- Process is modular and allows for adding and removing items.
- Security scanning tools are integrated.
- Containers are from an organization repository.

- Deploy process follows organizational standards.
- Process is modular and allows for adding and removing items.
- Security scanning tools are integrated.
- No production data can be moved from production environment.
- Monitor for malicious activity and data exfiltration.

- Deploy process follows organizational standards.
- Process is modular and allows for adding and removing items.
- Security scanning tools are integrated.
- IaC is measured against organization standards.
- Only approved pipelines deploy to production.

Figure 6.5   Protecting the SDLC through guardrails

in application security as a service, and that is through an ecosystem of services that bring engineering enablement to a new level.

6.3   *Bridging engineering and security through services*

Today, you can get pretty much anything as a service. Software, platforms, infrastructure, and databases are probably the most common as-a-service offerings out there. However, even ransomware is offered as a service today, which is telling on how far we've come.

> **DEFINITION**   Generally, *as-a-service* (aaS) means a service that is offered to customers through an interface. Most of the inner workings of the service are abstracted from the customer and managed by the service provider.

SaaS is probably the most common and well-known aaS. *SaaS* is where an organization produces an interface that can be used by clients to operate software. Way back in the day, like 10 years ago, software was often delivered through physical media and disseminated to customers for them to install on physical machines. The software was available only on the machine that the software was installed to unless there were other copies installed on other machines. Licenses were often tied to a data file that needed to be installed on the same machine as the software or on a networked license server. Although the technology and concept of SaaS has existed for decades, it really caught on in the late 1990s during the early stages of the World Wide Web. Companies like Salesforce began to offer software as a service to customers where instead of installing massive software packages on end-user devices, they could simply open a browser and access the same software. Although things like network speed and graphics rendering were limiting factors for a lot of software being offered this way, there were plenty of opportunities to bring software to employees of enterprises.

Fast-forward to 2022 and the SaaS market has exploded. Can you remember the last time you put a CD or other disk into your laptop or desktop to install software? Do you still even have a CD or disk drive in your laptop or desktop? If you are really young, do you even know what a CD or disk drive is? The world we live in today is largely driven by accessing software through a browser. In fact, browsers have almost become the new operating system for the online world. One of the most critical parts of this model of SaaS is that much of the functionality is delivered through application programming interfaces (APIs) that provide discrete building blocks that are used to create a complete experience.

> **DEFINITION**   An *API* cannot really be summed up neatly. It can be defined as a way for a program to access functionality in the operating system, a method for two applications to converse with each other, or a way for a browser or other user agent to retrieve data from a server. The simplistic view is that an API is a method to retrieve data or functionality from a system or application.

Given that organizations are building software that fits this model of SaaS and these services are leveraging APIs to enable that SaaS environment, it is only natural that developers are looking for that same opportunity at their fingertips. Much of the software that they are using in their day-to-day activities are SaaS. Whether it's the ticketing system, the project tracking tool, the build and integration tools, the code repository, or the various scanning tools, each one is hosted either on-premises or in a cloud environment. Furthermore, each of these tools has a method of access and integration that is most likely through APIs. One of the most common questions that are asked of vendors is, "What APIs do you have, and how can you integrate with my current toolset?"

6.3.1   *The application security-as-a-service ecosystem*

There are APIs for almost everything in engineering, so why should application security be any different? Call me a dreamer, but I envision an environment where application security services can be called through an API or through other services that the engineering team can take advantage of. I touched on some of these throughout this book, such as the ability to embed microlearning into the workstreams or add detailed information regarding vulnerability remediation in defect tickets. What if we took that a step further and allowed these application-security services to be called at any point in the development process?

For any organization to approach this, they first need to identify the services of value that should be made into APIs. Not everything can or should be called through an API, but there are some basic ones that most organizations should turn into a service that can be called (table 6.7).

Table 6.7   Example services that can be created for application security

Application security service	Definition
Certificate and secrets management	This service should abstract away any backend service that the organization uses to request new certificates, keys, or secrets. Ideally this service would allow the caller to request a key pair or a public certificate, or generate a secure password and store the sensitive items in a centralized vault.
Code signing	This service would allow for the caller to provide a code artifact, like an executable or script, which can be digitally signed with the organization's private key.
Automated penetration testing	This service should abstract away a suite of tools for automated penetration testing by simply passing a URL for unauthenticated scans, or a URL with credentials for an authenticated scan. Many organizations will have more than one tool used for application penetration testing, including DAST and fuzzing tools. The goal with this service is to create one entry point to run multiple tools and return a result set.
Data masking	This service allows for data to be scrubbed of sensitive information before it is used. The service would take a data set, remove the sensitive information by replacing or using format preserving encryption that allows for applications to still use the data as if it were the original values.

Using these basic services as a starting point, the organization has opened the door to allow for the engineering teams to raise the security of the product at any point during the development life cycle. Figure 6.6 shows the where the application security team has created several of these services that can then be called through an API by the engineering team during any stage of the development life cycle.

Application security as a service

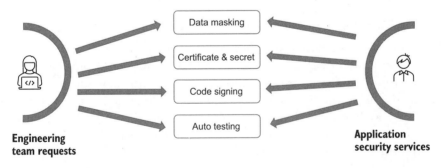

Engineering team requests

Application security services

Figure 6.6   Application security as a service example

The beauty of this model is that because they are APIs, they can be called during most stages of the development pipeline. For example, at Superior Products, developers on the team can make a request to the certificate and secret management API to request an internally created certificate from the Superior Products certificate authority. This gives them the opportunity to test various workflows with a valid certificate issued from the approved organizational certificate authority. If you are familiar with how most development teams operate, you will know that self-signed certificates are typically used at this stage in order to keep the development progress moving. This is not necessarily a bad practice if they are used locally, but it is not uncommon for self-signed certificates to be perpetuated throughout the environments.

> **DEFINITION** A *self-signed certificate* is a public-key certificate that is signed by an internal, nonpublicly trusted entity. In the example of an HTTPS connection, a self-signed certificate can be issued by and installed on the web server in order to provide integrity and encryption, but the authenticity of the issuer cannot be determined because it has been signed by the web server and not a trusted party.

This certificate service can be called during the build process in order to make a request to the organization's third-party, external certificate authority in order to acquire a legitimate certificate that can be deployed to the production environment. This service call allows for the team to request certificates on demand and be able to deploy them to an environment. Additionally, the certificate service should include the ability to track the expiration and provide the ability to rotate or revoke the certificate if needed.

At Superior Products, the development team is also able to take advantage of the automated security testing throughout the life cycle. The application security team has decided to incorporate several tools that can be used to get a basic security posture of the application. This is not designed to replace the current tools in the secure SDLC, but rather to augment and provide a quick read. The service simply requires a URL that is passed to the API and can be run authenticated, or unauthenticated depending on the use case. The services that Superior Products has made part of the automated security testing are shown in table 6.8.

Table 6.8 Example application security services used for automated security testing

Application security service	Definition
TLS test	This test will review the basic attributes of the TLS connection to ensure that the TLS version used, and the cipher suites, are secure. It will also validate the certificate to confirm that it is valid and does not pose a security risk.
Fuzz test	Fuzz testing can be thought of as a testing technique that brute forces its way around your application. It will attempt to send random, and often large, sets of data to your inputs and parameters to attempt to uncover coding errors that can lead to security issues.
DAST	I've covered DAST previously, and in the case of this service, the DAST component will be a simple point-and-shoot test that runs a scan against the URL it is provided.

This security testing API is exposed to the development team and will take in a URL and credentials, if configured that way. Once the call to the API is made, a series of coded services that have been developed by the application security team will be kicked off to run the TLS test, the fuzz test, and the DAST scan. When all three are completed, a report will be returned to the calling function that provides the basic output from the tools. Given the power of this single API it is important for the development team to encourage the developers to run this scan early and often prior to code check-in. Additionally, this service can be called during the build process prior to a nonproduction environment or production deployment. One consideration with this type of service is the length of time it will take to run. Given the tasks that it is attempting to complete and based on the size of the application, there is potential for this service to run for a long time. This again demonstrates that this does not replace the other tools in the SDLC but is there to augment and provide better insight into the security of the developed application.

Exercise 6.2

If you work in an engineering or application security team, what other services can you think of that would make sense in this service model? The sky is the limit here, and each organization will have different needs or capacity to deliver these services. Think of at least three that would make sense in your own organization.

Often you will see these services accessible through APIs that are included as part of the overall application security web ecosystem. A landing page may already exist as part of the organization's documentation library, or it could be a standalone website that the application security team hosts. Regardless, the application security team can host and manage an API set through any number of ways and should leverage the overall engineering organization for support to create that where needed. However, there are other services that the application security team can create and manage that are not accessed through an API.

6.3.2   *Services requested through tickets*

APIs are a great means of getting relatively quick security service in an automated fashion. There are, however, some things that cannot be automated or that require a bit more effort from the application security team to provide sufficient assistance. Take, for instance, a secure code review. Although there are tools that can be used to do code reviews, and often you can do this in the source code management (SCM) tool that is run by the organization, this is a manual effort by a security SME; at least until the robot overlords take over.

It should be no surprise that in order for this to work, the application security team should already be working out of a ticketing system like Jira or Bugzilla. Ideally, the ticketing system that is used by the application security team aligns with the overall organization's tool. This provides the team the support in the organization and allows them to take advantage of the ability to hook their tickets to tickets in other teams.

Some of the common services that an application security team can make available through a ticket request are shown in table 6.9.

Table 6.9   Example application security services that require a manual review from the team

Application security service	Definition
Code review	This allows for the engineering team to make a request to the application security team to perform a code review. Each organization could take a different approach on when and how these code reviews happen. For instance, the organization may decide that only critical components or ones that impact sensitive data require a code review.
Threat modeling	I covered threat modeling previously, so you should be familiar with what goes into performing one. This ticket request should include the necessary inputs to complete the threat model by the application security team. For example, the data flow diagram and an architecture diagram at a minimum.
Design review	A design review request would ask the application security team to perform a review of a particular design decision. Similar to the code review request, this may only be done when there is a significant change to the architecture, or when there are impacts on data and security.

For this service request model to work appropriately, there needs to be a process in place in the application security team to take in new requests and ensure that they are assigned, tracked, and worked to completion. Many application security teams work in an Agile type of environment where the ticketing model will work well. For instance, at Superior Products, they are working on a change to the current authentication model so that they can integrate with a federated identity provider. This will be a code change and impacts several key components and capabilities in the Stuff-For-You application. Brilliant Brian, the security champion for Stuff-For-You, recognizes the importance of the change and the impacts to the critical components. He provides the best guidance he can to the team but understands that he will need further support from the application security team. He gathers the appropriate information and opens a Jira ticket in the application security team's project to request a design review to first understand whether the current path the team is on makes sense and is incorporating all the best practices that the organization has. Because this ticket is opened in Jira, both the engineering team and the application security team can track progress. Within a week, the application security team has a team member assigned and has provided their guidance back to the engineering team.

With the appropriate design considerations made, the engineering team is able to begin implementing the design and finalizing architecture based on the application security team's direction from the design review. They will submit their final architecture through another ticket to the application security team that is used to perform a threat model. This will trigger a preliminary review by application security, but once again a resource will be assigned, and a work session will be required to perform the threat model with bit application security and engineering resources.

Once the threat model and design review are completed, the engineering team for Stuff-For-You is able to focus on completing the code. Prior to releasing the feature in an upcoming release, Brilliant Brian asks that the code go through a formal application security code review before it is allowed to proceed to a production environment. Since the Stuff-For-You team is using a SaaS-based SCM where their code is hosted, the team is able to open a ticket and request that the application security team review the code in the repository. As part of the review, the application security team requires that any relevant scans are made available as well as the corresponding ticket that was used for both the design review and the threat model as depicted in figure 6.7. This will provide proper context of the application and other findings that were made in those earlier stages.

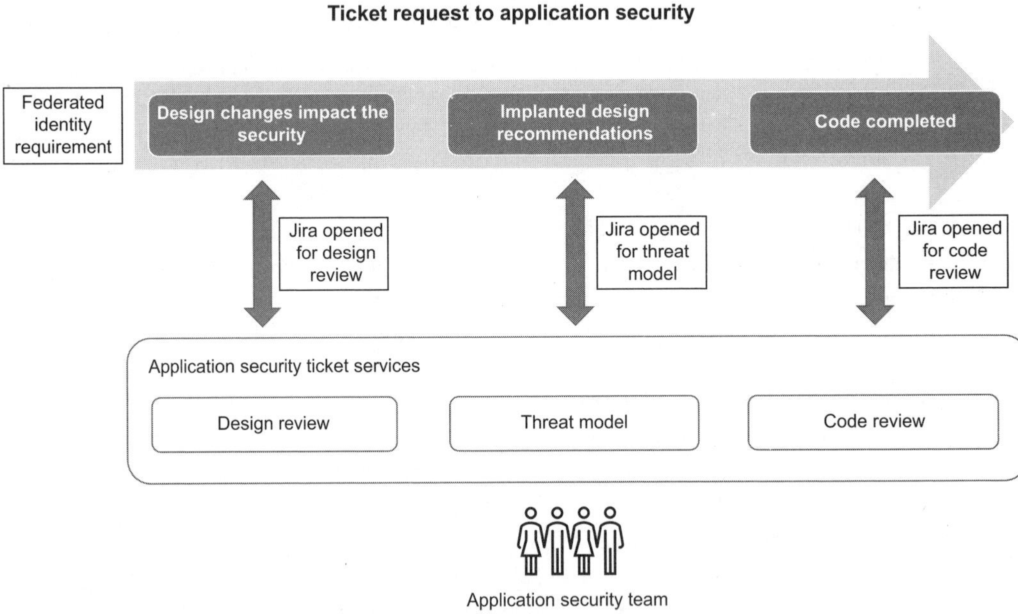

Figure 6.7   Ticket request to application security for a federated identity requirement

Keep in mind that because everything is being tracked through Jira tickets, the artifacts, outputs, and other tracking details are available to those who have access to the Jira project. This is both good and bad. Some of this information may be sensitive and could highlight weaknesses in the application. Due to the sensitive nature of some of the artifacts like the threat model, it may be appropriate to put these in a location that is not as wide open as the ticketing system, and instead store them in a location with more suitable security controls in place that ensure that access to this data is limited to the least privilege model. I've covered some options for accessing services through ticketing and APIs, but one last point is to build an environment or ecosystem that has application security available at the developer's fingertips.

6.3.3 Ambient application security

There is one more opportunity in the application security ecosystem that can be thought of as *ambient application security*. What this means is that the application security team will build and provide tools, processes, and people that will allow for application security to always be available throughout the development life cycle. Once again, every organization will be different and have different needs in their application security journey, but table 6.10 shows a few items that would be part of the ambient application security.

Table 6.10 Example application security services that are part of an ecosystem of security

Application security service	Definition
Chatbot	Chatbot technology is pretty ubiquitous today. When you go to a site and click on an icon that allows you to chat with someone, in most cases, the first level communication is with an automated service like a chatbot. These are developed to handle the low-hanging fruit. For the application security team, this is a great tool to head off any calls or emails that might instead come directly to the team.
Threat intelligence	Security is not static and the vulnerabilities and risks that organizations face change almost daily. The application security team should be leveraging either a third-party source or develop their own threat intelligence program that essentially monitors for changes in the landscape and alerts the organization.
Secure engineering training	As I covered in previous chapters, security training is a huge part of making the overall organization more secure. The applications security team should develop and promote the education security options to the organization and make the training accessible on demand so that engineers have the ability to raise their security awareness.
Newsletters and events	Simple and mostly free, newsletters, communications, and even organization-wide events around security will keep security in the front of the minds of the organization. Running a monthly newsletter that tells the organization what the application security team has been up to and what changes are ongoing in the industry will provide context and needed information to the engineering teams. As mentioned in previous chapters, the events can be simple lunch-and-learns or full-blown security conferences.

With these types of activity in place, the organization has shown that security is a critical component and that it is taken seriously. Although these are not services that can be called during the development life cycle, they still play a prominent role in ensuring that engineering teams are getting the relevant security information to build secure software.

Since Dashing Danielle has been moved to the application security team, she has been tasked with building the culture of security around the organization. She has decided that she would focus her initial efforts on developing a chatbot that is available to the engineering organization as well as running a secure engineering event to coincide with Cybersecurity Awareness Month. She approaches the CISO (chief information security officer) with the recommendation to purchase an off-the-shelf chatbot technology that she is able to integrate into the landing page that is managed by application security.

As part of the integration, the chatbot will learn from and leverage the existing documentation that the application security team has in place. Additionally, the chatbot will integrate with the existing services and communication channels that exist in the organization so that when an engineer interacts with the chatbot, the chatbot will be able to interact with the backend systems to open tickets or otherwise communicate with the rest of the security organization. For example, an engineer who interacts with the chatbot may be looking for steps to remediate an SQL injection vulnerability that was found in their code. The engineer will go to the application security landing page and access the chatbot. They will request more information on remediating the SQL injection. The chatbot will provide the guidance that is documented in the application security best practices and offer the ability to open a ticket to the application security team for more support (figure 6.8).

Application security chatbot interaction

"Welcome to the application security chatbot. How may I help you?"

"I found an SQL injection in my code."

"SQL injection information can be found at the application security best-practices and remediation site."

"Would you like to open a ticket to the application security team for more help?"

"Yes."

"Great. I am placing a request to the application security team. You will receive an email confirmation soon."

"Can I help with anything else?"

"No."

Figure 6.8   Sample application security chatbot interaction

This is a pretty basic example of chatbot technology, and it absolutely depends on the technology being used and how it is trained. However, you can hopefully see potential for this technology. As Dashing Danielle is attempting to roll this chatbot technology out to the organization, she takes the opportunity to give a talk and demonstration at a lunch-and-learn that she coordinated with the engineering organization. During this session, she was able to demonstrate how the chatbot technology will reduce the simple questions that the application security team generally sees as well as show how it is able to work with existing services in the organization to assist with general request management. The goal of ambient application security is to have not just services that can be called or available through ticketing, but to make it part of the fabric of the engineering organization so that security is always available and part of the engineering ecosystem.

Summary

- Defining the risk of an application is required in order to have the appropriate context when addressing the impact that vulnerabilities and new risks have on the application.
- The organization should take the approach that removes gates and blocking activity in favor of a release-by-risk approach that enables the organization to continue to release code that has risk so long as the risk is within the organization's tolerance.
- Automation enables the organization to remove the barriers to release and instead provide guardrails that allow code to be deployed to a production environment with confidence that the risk is properly managed.
- Moving to an application SaaS model provides the organization the ability to create an overall ecosystem for engineering to receive the security support they need to develop secure software.
- Ambient application security creates the environment where security is ever present. This can be achieved through inexpensive yet broad initiatives such as security events and newsletters.

Part 3

Deliver and measure

This last part will focus on ways that you can build on what has been discussed in the first two parts and pivot to developing a roadmap that aligns with the development organization. That roadmap then needs to be measured and tracked in order to measure the success of the program.

In chapter 7, you'll start putting the pieces together on a roadmap by looking at the current security posture of the organization and understanding what the security and nonsecurity goals are of the organization. The roadmap will need to ensure that the security goals align with the business goals of the organization; otherwise, the security goals may run into failures. Additionally, the application security team needs to consider the gaps that exist in the organization that create a security concern and use a gap analysis to identify where their efforts need to be placed.

Chapter 8 will provide guidance on how to measure the effectiveness of the security tools and processes that are being used by the organization. You'll see how using key performance indicators (KPI) and feedback from your partners in the development organization will better enhance your metrics and help you get a better measurement of the progress your program is making.

The last chapter in the book looks at some advanced topics in application security that will help you understand how attackers get into systems and how to provide protection against those attackers. However, the application security team doesn't just have to be ahead of the attackers—they need to also be ahead of the engineering teams they work with. These engineering teams are often on the cutting edge of new technology, which requires the application security team to react and upskill.

Building a roadmap

7

This chapter covers

- Determining an organization's current application security posture
- Identifying the gaps and the immediate needs of the organization
- Developing a roadmap that addresses the short- and long-term goals

Congratulations! You've been put in charge of the application security program at an organization. Your mission, should you choose to accept it, is to bring secure software development to the organization with minimal budget and a small team. Where do you begin? A lot of this depends on whether you are starting from scratch or whether there's a program that already exists. For the remainder of this chapter, I will assume that you are starting from scratch. Many of the concepts hold regardless.

Often, if you find yourself in this position, you will have a lot of great ideas that you are coming into the role with. You want to implement the latest trends, ideas, and tools that are available to you. However, security is not like engineering where you can solve problems with general impunity in how you solve them. You will have constraints and practices that you will have to adhere to that will limit your ability.

You will find out that everyone in the organization is doing things at least slightly, if not vastly, different. You will find a lot of "this is the way we've always done things" from your team and from the people in the organization that you are there to help. You will need to get a lay of the land before you can put together a plan to tackle the most burning questions and security issues in the organization.

> **NOTE**   While the first two parts of this book focus more on the tactical steps of implementing tools, processes, and techniques that are used to deliver software security, this third part will begin to cover more strategic topics around metrics, maturity, and looking for ways to continuously improve.

7.1   *Getting the current security posture*

There is nothing unique or specific to the job of an application security leader in regard to understanding what your team and organization look like. The simple things like learning tools and processes are something that we all have to do regardless of the job. However, in this chapter we are talking about you coming into a role to run the application security program. There are some key things you will want to know quickly when you come in. I will break this down into a few sections. Figure out

- The organization structure and find your friends
- What tools are implemented
- What vulnerabilities exist
- What policies exist
- What roadmaps exist (application security and product)
- What boards, committees, or community groups exist that application security should be a part of
- What communication channels and distribution lists exist
- What reoccurring meetings you should be on

All of these are perfect starting points to understanding the organization and how you will interact with it. It'll give you the data points you need, and more importantly who to work with. I typically approach this effort by thinking and asking others about what would happen in the case of a breach or attack. Do I have enough information or know where to get the information in order to get to a resolution? I'll cover getting this information in more detail here in this chapter.

7.1.1   *Going on tour*

One of the first things most leaders will do when they get into a leadership role is to start looking for your peers and partners. Your peers are the ones who will help you navigate the coming adventure. Your partners are the ones you will be working with to solve the problems facing the organization. Although every situation and organization is unique, there are some common questions that you will want your peers and manager to answer to help you understand your team and roadmap:

- Where do I find the organization chart and my team organization?
- What open positions are there on my team? Who might be leaving?
- What is the budget for the team, and how does the budget cycle work?
- What ongoing projects should I be aware of and what state are they in?
- What open, known vulnerabilities are there in the organization?
- What security tools are already deployed or in the process of being deployed in the organization?
- Where are the policies, standards, and other documentation related to application security?
- What is application security's relationship to the rest of the organization?
- What penetration test reports exist for the products in the organization?

These questions will help the incoming leader understand what the current posture of the organization and the application security team is. However, the incoming leader will still need to talk to their partners in the organization. These partners will be found in the following places:

- Engineering and software development
- Site reliability engineering and operations
- Client relations
- Product ownership

Getting in front of this audience will help the application security leader begin to forge relationships with their partners across the organization. In the past I have set up time with several leaders in these functions to ask basic questions about their interaction with security in general, and application security specifically. I will listen to what their role is, ask about their background and items on their immediate horizon. However, there is one question that I'm always chomping at the bit to ask:

"What is your biggest security concern?"

Don't underestimate the power of this question. One thing I find from this is that when you come into the role of operating an application security team, you will have ideas in your head about what it is you want to do with the team and how you want to solve problems. But when you ask others what their top security concerns are, you find more about the real issues facing the organization. I've been surprised by responses to this question in the past where something that I was not thinking about, or had not heard about, quickly became a priority for me after talking to a partner in the organization. Without giving details, there have been cases where the engineering teams are seeing issues that they know are a security concern, but they have become accustomed to resolving it on their own and therefore have not bubbled it up to the security organization or application security team. These are opportunities for the application security team to work to resolve a pain point that is present in the organization and get a win.

The last effort that should be made on this grand tour is finding the best ways to communicate with your peers and partners. Some prefer email, while some like collaboration tools like Microsoft Teams or Slack. Some might prefer a face-to-face conversation or an old-fashion telephone call. You should also understand what reoccurring meetings or gatherings that your peers and partners are in that you should be a part of as well. For the application security leader, this often means technical conversations on architecture decisions as well as leadership and client meetings. These are all opportunities for you, as the leader of application security, to build your network, become visible, and begin to provide input. Knowing how to communicate with peers and partners will provide you with the appropriate channels to take in and provide input and guidance from others.

7.1.2   *What tools exist?*

In this book I covered a lot of the possible tools that are available to an organization. Just to recap, the most common ones that fall under the application security team's purview are

- Static application security testing (SAST)
- Dynamic application security testing (DAST)
- Interactive application security testing (IAST)
- Software composition analysis (SCA)
- Web application firewall (WAF)
- Run-time application security protection (RASP)
- Threat modeling tools

There may be others, but these are the primary ones that you will see in most organizations. One of the most misleading answers you will hear in the application security team is that you have tool X deployed across the organization. If you hear that and become apprehensive, congratulations, you're on your way to application security greatness. The truth is that many application security teams struggle to get complete coverage for several reasons:

- License constraints
- Lack of an inventory of products across the organization
- Incomplete configuration of the current tools
- Tools that have been turned off for support reasons

What this means is that many organizations may have something like a SAST tool deployed, but it is likely not deployed in every development team, it may be turned off for certain builds due to the number of false positives, or it may have been installed but never configured. This leads to a false sense of security, or worse, a situation where the application security team can claim that the tool has been deployed, but in reality, it is not being effectively used.

To solve this, the application security team should first ensure that they build out a matrix that lists the products in the organization with the software security tools that are managed by the team, as shown in table 7.1. This is the simple first pass that can then be built upon over time.

Table 7.1   Products and their application security tool coverage in Superior Products

Product	SAST	DAST	SCA	WAF
Stuff-For-You	X		X	
Stuff-For-Me		X	X	X
Things-You-Need		X	X	

This is a very rudimentary table of the products and the application security tool coverage they may have, but it's a start. In reality, each product may have many subproducts that each have their own development team and development pipelines. Over time, you will want to build this table to break down the component pipelines and their adherence to the software security tools. In addition, as your program grows, you will want to include the various controls and tools that you have at your disposal. The purpose of this is to have as much situation awareness as possible in the event of an active attack or breach. That is not the time that you want to hunt and peck for information.

> **DEFINITION**   *Situation* (or *situational*) *awareness* is the ability to have knowledge of the various elements around you and being able to determine their meaning, impact, and potential future state.

Having this situational awareness allows the team to answer one of the most difficult questions you will face: "What is the impact of on ongoing attack?" It is true that as an application security team, you are often not on the front line of a cyberattack. That is normally up to the security operations team that monitors and blocks active attacks and scans. However, the application security team plays a critical role in an ongoing attack. In many situations the attack may require an upgrade or other change to the software that the organization uses to build their applications.

In late 2021, a vulnerability was found in the popular software component developed by Apache, called Log4j. This vulnerability allowed for an attacker to perform a remote code execution on a vulnerable system that could allow for the complete takeover of the system. The vulnerability was ranked 10/10 for a CVSS score, meaning that this was as bad as it gets (https://logging.apache.org/log4j/2.x/).

> **DEFINITION**   *Apache Log4j* is used to provide logging services within an application. This component is used in many of the largest corporations and systems around the world, including Apple's cloud computing and the popular video game Minecraft.

This vulnerability sent a shock wave across the software industry as organizations scrambled to identify the exposure and close the gaps. At the time of the discovery of the vulnerability, there were three different remediations that could close the gap.

Two of the techniques were related to configuration changes that could be made in the running component that simply removed the ability to make calls to a remote server where the malicious code would reside. The third remediation was to upgrade to the latest version of Log4j.

However, the patch that was released by Apache actually introduced another less severe vulnerability. Also, it was discovered that one of the configuration changes did not completely remove the exposure. During this time, the situation was extremely fluid and information was ever changing. Security folks, from the operations team to the application security team, were scrambling to understand the impacts of the vulnerability and, most importantly, how their organization was impacted. This is where situation awareness provides an immense amount of support, and there are a few questions in this scenario that need to be answered:

- Where is Log4j used in the organization?
- Who is responsible for making the updates to Log4j?
- What are the compensating controls in place?
- How long until the fix can be applied across the known locations?
- What is the residual risk of the vulnerability once the compensating controls are in place?

In this example, some of the compensating controls were to block external access to known malicious servers that were hosting exploits specific to this vulnerability. Additionally, WAF and load balancer rules could be used to determine whether an incoming payload looked malicious and therefore drop the request. Placing detection tools on the endpoints to detect whether a system has been compromised was an additional control. However, the ultimate fix was to patch or remove the ability for this code to operate. A vulnerability like the Log4j one cannot be resolved through tools and instead needs to go through the SDLC process of code change, build, test, deploy, and monitor. There is no easy or quick way to do this. So, it largely relies on the organization having pipelines that can deliver code to their environments in a rapid manner.

This is a prime example of having to know what you are running in your organization and perhaps more importantly, what components are used to build your software. In the Log4j example, one further complication was that there were many flavors of Log4j and some third parties actually took the Log4j component and renamed it to something else when they packaged it with their software, which made it even more difficult to detect where it was being used.

To solve the Log4j issue, the application security team and the engineering teams had to use the tools they had available to them, like the SCA tools that can determine whether the build contains vulnerable libraries. There was also a lot of manual effort by doing simple searches in code bases and code repositories for the vulnerable component. Trust me when I say that there were a lot of people working tirelessly to locate Log4j in their environments. However, this was one vulnerability in a sea of others.

7.1.3 What vulnerabilities do you have?

While high-profile vulnerabilities become all the craze largely due to the public pro-file, many forget that there is usually a large backlog of vulnerabilities in an organiza-tion. The security tools that are integrated in the SDLC and penetration tests that occur throughout the year will produce a good amount of security vulnerabilities. These are often tracked to resolution by the application security team and the engi-neering organization. However, as ones are closed, others are opened, leaving a con-tinuous backlog of security issues. Couple this with the fact that things like technical debt really become security debt.

> **DEFINITION** *Technical debt* is the result of taking the easy and faster route now rather than the correct route. This leads to the accumulation of poor deci-sions, which can lead to more difficult architecture maintenance down the road. Think about having to upgrade a component one major version for-ward. Now think about upgrading that component several major versions for-ward. The easier path is to upgrade one major version since multiple versions will most likely mean that there will be additional design changes needed. The organization that tackles their technical debt appropriately builds in the end-of-life and upgrades during the normal course of development in order to keep technical debt from growing.

When you are a new application security leader, you will want to know quickly what vulnerabilities you and your team need to tackle within the organization. One of the first steps in any vulnerability management program is to make sure your data is accu-rate and that there is a clear path to resolution for the engineering team. You will need to know several things in order to effectively manage the closure of these known vulnerabilities (table 7.2).

Table 7.2 Task required to manage known vulnerabilities

Task	Task activities
De-duplicate the known issues.	Make sure that the open vulnerabilities that you are tracking are not multiples. In other words, an SQL injection could be opened in several tracking systems and they all could be the same one.
Validate older issues.	Sometimes vulnerabilities are left open for a long time because it requires a rather large design/architecture change. In these cases, the vulnerability may actually have already been resolved from an upgrade, change in design, or even a decommissioning of the impacted application.
Categorize and associ-ate timelines to the open issues.	Having the list of vulnerabilities is great, but you need targets for resolution times. This means that you will need to have documented times to resolution based on criticality. I have provided guidance on this in chapter 3, but you will need to set a deadline for resolution on all the open vulnerabilities you have.
Ensure that the issues have assigned owners.	This is more difficult than it sounds, but you need to know who owns the reso-lution of a vulnerability. That is usually a member of the engineering team who is responsible for coding the fix.

Table 7.2 Task required to manage known vulnerabilities *(continued)*

Task	Task activities
Ensure that the issues have clear instructions on resolution.	In order for the engineering teams to be able to resolve the vulnerability, the application security team should ensure that enough information is available in the resolution steps for the engineer who codes the fix.
Have a single location for all your open vulnerabilities	You will definitely want to be able to get all your vulnerability information into one location. That is often in a dashboard, but it can be in the defect tracking tool that is being used to track vulnerabilities. The bottom line is that you want to be able to see what vulnerabilities impact the organization at a quick glance.

Now that you have the information you need in hand, you will want to come to a common goal together with your peers and partners. What vulnerabilities are most important to the organization and pose the biggest risks? It may be simple targets like the organization will eliminate all open critical and high vulnerabilities within two quarters. Or the organization will eliminate all vulnerabilities on their publicly exposed applications. Knowing what the organization's goals are around vulnerability management will help determine the best approach to keeping stakeholders informed with the progress.

Proper ownership, and solid instructions on resolution, are inputs into a remediation process. As the application security leader, you will want to put together or review the current remediation process that might be in place. This often means simply communicating with the stakeholders and performing follow-ups to ensure that the resolution of issues is on track. The application security team should provide a simple set of charts that show the overall organization exposure to the known vulnerabilities. An example of this would be at Superior Products, where the application security team has defined a standard that has the following timelines for resolution (table 7.3).

Table 7.3 Timelines to closing open vulnerabilities

Vulnerability criticality	Time to close
Critical	Less than 30 days
High	Less than 60 days
Medium	Less than 90 days
Low	Less than 365 days

With these timelines standardized across the organization, the application security team at Superior Products can then create a chart that shows the open vulnerabilities in the organization with the associated timelines as well, and most importantly, the number of vulnerabilities that are outside of the standard timelines.

In table 7.4, the darker items are the ones that are outside of the organization's timelines. The table should provide, at a quick glance, where Superior Products has the highest risk. The next lightest color ones are approaching their deadline, and the ones in the lightest color are still within the timeline. To be clear, this does not mean that the ones outside of the timelines are any better or worse than the ones within the timeline. It is entirely feasible that a vulnerability within timelines could lead to a compromise of Superior Products before any others.

Table 7.4 Basic chart showing open vulnerabilities with criticality and time to close

Time to remediate	Critical	High	Medium	Low
>365	0	3	5	3
60–90	0	0	3	7
30–60	1	5	4	15
0–30	1	7	6	12

The quick-glance chart is good to show the overall organization's exposure, but what about the specific products in the organization? That is where a separate chart should be used that breaks down the products and their open vulnerabilities by criticality (table 7.5).

Table 7.5 Chart showing the open vulnerabilities by criticality

Product	Critical	High	Medium	Low
Stuff-For-You	1	5	4	13
Stuff-For-Me	0	5	12	13
Things-You-Need	1	5	2	14

Here, the Superior Products application security team can work with each engineering team that owns the given product to focus on closing out the vulnerabilities specific to that product. The data in the table also helps on reporting to senior leadership when priorities need to shift on products that may have a high vulnerability count or many critical or high vulnerabilities.

7.1.4 What additional information is available?

When leading an application security function, information and friends are your two most powerful resources. Locating the policies that impact security architecture and standards will help you define your program going forward. Although organizations will implement their policy mapping differently, the general flow of a policy being created at the highest level down to its implementation in a procedure often follows a basic structure where policy is created at the strategic level by the leadership and focuses on a goal (figure 7.1). In relation to a strategic goal like encryption, a general encryption policy may be created that states that the organization will ensure that encryption is used at rest and in transit. This is a prime example of the *what* related to the organization's security goal. However, this doesn't tell us the *how*. Here is where standards, guidelines, and procedures come into play. As an example, the standards would specify what level of encryption is required for symmetric and asymmetric encryption—what type of certificate authority should be used and how certificate signing requests should be completed. Additionally, the guidelines and procedures will provide additional information and steps on how to complete the end state. For example, a procedure could outline the step-by-step instructions on creating an asymmetric key pair on a Linux machine using OpenSSL.

Mapping standards and policy

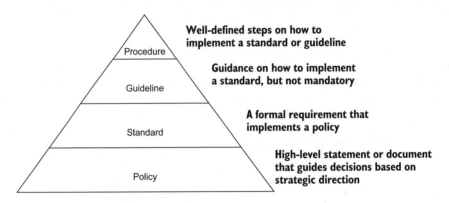

Figure 7.1   Policy relationship in an organization

Often the policies will be owned by the governance, risk, and compliance (GRC) or information security teams in the organization. It's important as the application security leader to know where the policies are and how they are used and approved in the organization. Knowing what the policies are will help the application security team craft standards, guidelines, and procedures in the organization that adhere to the policies so that when particular security work is being completed by the engineering teams, there is a direct line from that work to the organization's policies and goals.

The last big component that you will need to get from the organization is any roadmaps that are being developed or delivered on by the engineering, product, and security organizations. Understanding these will allow the application security team to align their work with the rest of the organization as well as ensure that when the application security roadmap is being built that it is considering the various other moving parts in the organization. For example, one of the goals of the application security roadmap might be to provide data encryption at rest across the organization. If the organization is in the middle of a cloud transformation, this will greatly influence the way that the application security team provides guidance and delivers on the data encryption project. It may also alter timelines, as resources might be constrained due to a rapid adoption of cloud technology.

7.2   Understanding the organization's security goals

Every organization has goals whether they are business or technology related. In most cases these goals are set at the highest level and are pushed down through the leadership of the organization, where each department or group then aligns their goals to the top-level goal. Security is no different. The application security team will often get their goals from the CISO or CSO of the organization who has aligned their goals to those of the organization. The goals from the CISO or CSO will usually be of the protect, defend, and enable flavors, where the security organization's goals will be to ensure that the business can deliver on their goals with the right controls to keep the organization safe.

7.2.1   The organization's goals

The business is working hard to understand what clients want, when they want it, and how the organization will meet the demand. The goals that are outlined by the top leadership will be ones that are there to address competition and provide a competitive edge over their rivals. Most software organizations attempt to meet three fundamental goals:

- Meet client requirements
- Deliver on time
- Keep quality and satisfaction high

Security plays a fundamental role in each of these goals for the organization. As you learned throughout this book, the application security team works with the development team to build requirements, ensure that software is delivered securely, and the vulnerabilities are detected early and patched. These security processes impact each of the organizational goals mentioned. When application security provides guidance on requirements or imposes their own requirements for the development team to meet, this can create a latency in the delivery if the development team was not anticipating the changes. This in turn impacts delivery dates and creates churn within the development process.

However, this can also help the development team and the product by creating a better sense of quality when security issues do not impact the reputation of the organization. Gone are the days where consumers do not care about the security of the products they use. Every consumer today is at least aware of the impact and importance of security when they are using services online—especially if those services require the user to provide sensitive or financial information.

> **NOTE** The Sophos Home survey "The State of Consumer Home Cybersecurity 2021" shows how concerned consumers are of security issues related to their data and privacy online. The survey polled 2,500 consumers around the United States and found that 91% of consumers are worried about online security threats like malware, viruses, identity theft, financial fraud, and ransomware (http://mng.bz/Xap9).

It can't be overstated how much security impacts a consumer's choice when looking at services, so when an organization provides reasons for the consumer to worry through lax security in their products, the concerns will perpetuate.

7.2.2 *The application security goals*

The security organization, and specifically the application security team's goals, are to provide the safe and secure delivery of software to the customers. The software can reside in several locations:

- Websites
- Mobile applications
- Payment systems
- Employee devices
- Customer devices

To be clear, attackers are constantly looking for ways to test the security of your applications regardless of where it is located. When your application can be accessed by an attacker either on the internet or on a device, the attacker will attempt to test the security through scanning tools, as well as through manual testing. Although we covered a lot of content so far in this book, the application security goals are actually quite simple:

- Protect the confidentiality, preserve the integrity, and promote the availability of data.
- Ensure the security and secrecy of the application's source code.
- Reduce the organization's risk by remediating vulnerabilities in internally developed and externally developed code.

That's pretty much it when it comes to the high-level goals that an application security team needs to achieve. The way these goals are reached is through the people, process, and tools that we have covered in this book.

7.2.3 *Aligning the business and security goals*

The business stakeholders depend on the security organization to provide information on how to achieve regulatory and security standards. The business is accountable to the regulations and standards, but they are often not well understood by the business, which leaves the security organization to interpret and define what and how the business should adhere to them. This often pits security against the business in the classic example of "security slowing down the business," when in reality the two need each other to achieve what is being required.

While the security organization focuses on making sense of the various frameworks and standards, such as ISO, NIST, SANS, and OWASP, to provide the protection that the organization needs, the business is focused on competitive advantages and speed to market as I described. Given that these two approaches are usually at odds with one another, it's important to find common ground. To do this, the security organization needs to put their concerns in the language of the business in order to get alignment and the support they need. Something like implementing a new security feature that not only addresses a security concern, but also reduces cost to the business or provides more efficiency can do this. As an example, the security organization may be pushing a single sign-on (SSO) solution.

> **DEFINITION** *Single sign-on* (SSO) combines multiple login options in one launch page so that a user needs to remember only one password. The technology behind it varies, but applications that support SSO will be able to integrate with a common or custom solution to allow users in an organization to use the launch page to access applications that are supported by the SSO.

There are security benefits to SSO but also business ones as well. The security is far more simplified, and users only have to manage one password as opposed to multiple. From a business perspective, the support organization will be spending less time handling password resets, which reduces downtime with productivity and IT support time.

One last important component of the business and security interaction is to ensure that there is a common language. Nothing is more frustrating than being in a conversation and saying the same thing, but using confusing and different language. Security people are guilty of doing this with not just business, but also with the engineering teams they work with. However, this does go both ways. An example is when a security person talks about a denial-of-service attack but can't put it in the context that the business understands. They may be more interested in knowing that a given service is unavailable or inaccessible but are not making the connection between the two. It's important for there to be a common taxonomy that is well understood, and for the security organization to use the terms that relate more to the outcomes of an attack, or a vulnerability as opposed to the specific technical terms for them.

7.3 Identifying the gaps

You're getting accustomed to your new role as the application security leader. You've done your initial review of what exists in the organization and what the goals are of the business and security. It's time to prepare a gap analysis in order to provide input into your roadmap.

> **DEFINITION** A *gap analysis* is the process of looking at the actual performance or state in order to compare it to a potential performance or state. The intention is to discover opportunities for improvement or identify gaps in the state. A gap analysis can be used at different stages and perspectives like organizational, business process, or technology.

In the case of a gap analysis on the current application security compared to the future state, the application security team will focus on discovering where they need to put their immediate efforts. They will also want to understand the risks and vulnerabilities in order to ultimately improve the security posture of the organization. If gap analysis looks and sounds familiar, it's akin to maturity models where a current state is defined, with a plan of action to get to a future state. However, in this case the approach is more tailored to the organization's needs.

7.3.1   *Finding the immediate gaps*

The organization that is looking to identify and close gaps needs to first identify what their goal is and the purpose of the gap analysis. There are several reasons for an organization to address application security and the gaps in their current approach. Each organization will have different drivers for addressing the gaps such as contracts, compliance, or customer driven. Table 7.6 shows some example purposes. If you're a widely diverse organization, you will have to adhere to several of these.

Table 7.6   Purpose of addressing open security gaps in the organization

Purpose	Reason
Compliance and regulation	There are plenty of compliance and regulation control frameworks out there. Some of the more common ones are HIPAA/HITECH, GDPR, CCPA, PCI DSS, SOX and others. Each of them are for specific industries and areas of concern. I'll touch on them soon.
Customer request	Organizations are in business because of customers. When the customer is requesting or demanding something, it is hard for the organization to ignore this and still stay in business.
Internal standard	The organization may be moving to a new architecture that requires all the products to adhere to a particular standard in order to work with the new architecture.
External standard	External standards like NIST, CIS, or ISO can require the organization to adhere to a specific set of requirements in order to follow the standard. In many cases, these are not required in order to pass a compliance audit, but they are often adhered to in order to raise the security of the organization.

For compliance and regulation, the industry you are in will dictate what you need to adhere to. For example, HIPAA/HITECH are two acts passed by the US Congress that are used in the health care space to address security and privacy as it relates to patient data. Any organization that handles health care data would be impacted by HIPAA. For those in the financial space, PCI DSS or SOX would apply in order to require the appropriate level of protection for data related to credit cards or financial accounting. More recently there has been a concerted effort by governments to address privacy around data being collected by organizations. This led to the CCPA and GDPR regulations that regulate the collection of personal data.

Customers often will request the adherence to either an industry standard, or their own requirements developed by their internal security organization. In some cases, the request may be to use client-specific hardware, segmentation of a particular client information from other clients, or the use of client-specific encryption techniques and technology. In other cases, the clients may simply require that the organization adhere to a particular standard or framework and then audit the organization periodically to prove that they are in compliance with the request.

With internal standards, the organization may need to make a change in technology that requires a change in the security standards and approach to something that they have been doing previously. A great example of this is the move to cloud by many different organizations. This change in deployment and operation has a large impact on the security standards that may already be in place. For instance, the way that encryption is managed in the cloud, using cloud native services, is much different than managing encryption when the organization hosts the encryption hardware and software internally inside of their data center. This change would lead to new standards that align to the best practices and standards that are specific to cloud services.

Lastly, for external standards such as NIST, CIS, or ISO, the organization can leverage these to inform their internal standards. These standards are not required but are instead used to guide the organization's security posture that aligns to a well-vetted and trusted set of standards. Some of the most well-known standards in the United States are those that are developed by NIST. As it relates to application security, NIST 800-53 (http://mng.bz/yazp) provides a wealth of information on security and privacy controls; however, it also dives into some of the tools and controls that are specific to application security such as RASP and IAST. NIST recommends that every organization should deploy RASP and IAST in order to secure their developed applications.

So, what does all of this mean for the organization that is looking to identify the gaps that impact their organization? The organization needs to determine whether there are any regulations that they need to adhere to. Do you store health care data? You're most likely affected by HIPAA and HITECH. Are you processing credit cards? Better look at PCI DSS and make sure you can meet the requirements. You may even need a formal audit depending on the amount of credit card data you process. It is also important to understand the contractual obligations in the organization. These are normally created in agreements with customers and will state what the organization must do in order to retain the business of the customer. Knowing this information will inform how the organization plans to identify and meet the demands of the regulations and their customers.

7.3.2   *Input into the gap analysis*

The application security team will need to ensure it has all the information in order to identify the current state. In section 7.1, I covered some of this needed information like what security tools and policies exist, and what vulnerabilities are known in the organization. However, to get a complete picture, the application security team will need additional data. The basic process that can be followed for the analysis includes first setting the scope. This is as simple as identifying the functions that are owned by the application security team. In most organizations those functions are

- Security scanning tools
- Internal and external penetration testing
- Run-time protection tools
- Standards, guidelines, and procedures
- Reference architecture

Some organizations may have other functions that fall under the application security team, but for the purpose of this section, we'll keep it scoped to these functions. As you progress through the gap analysis, you will take each of the functions that have been identified as in scope and attempt to determine the current state (table 7.7). For each of the functions, the current state will look slightly different, meaning there is no consistent metric for each.

Table 7.7 Current state goals for a given function

Function	Current state identification goals
Security scanning tools	What security tools exist in the organization and what percentage of coverage do they have across the organization?
Internal and external penetration testing	What internal and external penetration testing occurs and at what frequency? What tools are used by the internal team to perform penetration testing? What reports exist for both internal and external penetration testing?
Run-time protection tools	What run-time tools are being used in the organization, and what percentage of coverage do they have across the organization?
Standards, guidelines, and procedures	Where does the application security team store their standards, guidelines, and procedures (if they exist), and how do they align to the organization's policies?
Reference architecture	Where does the application security team store reference architecture documents, how do they align to industry standards, and are they shared across the organization?

Identifying and sticking to a scope will allow for the organization to ensure that it has enough resources and time to gather the information. This scope can always be revisited and expanded at a future date. Before the application security team embarks on gathering the information on the identified functions, they will want to highlight the functions that will be focused on for improvement. As an example, I'll use our favorite company Superior Products, where Dashing Danielle has been tasked with providing a gap analysis on the application security team. She takes the key functions that were described previously and knows that the application security scanning tools are a critical capability that should be reviewed first.

Dashing Danielle begins creating the gap analysis based on the scope of what the coverage percentage of scanning tools are in the organization. She creates a simple table that shows the products with the pipelines that are part of each product. From here, she works with the development teams to identify which security tools, if any, are integrated into the pipelines they operate and whether there might be plans in the near future to integrate them. With this information in hand, she is able to complete the table that shows which pipeline has the tools and which do not (table 7.8).

This is an extremely simple gap analysis, but effective in identifying the needed information. In reality, there might be additional information that the application security team might want in this analysis—for instance, which rules and configurations are set up in the tools. What is the alert process for the tools, and do the developers

Table 7.8 Security tools integrated into the product pipelines

Product	SAST	DAST	SCA
Stuff-For-You			
Pipeline 1	X		X
Pipeline 2	In-progress	X	
Stuff-For-Me			
Pipeline 3	X	In-progress	
Pipeline 4	X	In-progress	X
Things-You-Need			
Pipeline 5	In-progress	X	X
Pipeline 6	X		X

receive feedback on findings from the tools? These data points are extremely helpful when performing a gap analysis, as many security tools are not properly implemented or are not following a standard configuration developed by the organization. However, we will keep it simple for this chapter's purpose.

7.3.3 What to do with the gap analysis

Once a gap analysis has been completed, it's time to actually do something about it. As mentioned previously, the purpose of the gap analysis is to identify areas of improvement and begin to put together a path to those improvements. Depending on the initial purpose of the gap analysis, the organization will address the gaps based on some standard. They could be internal standards to improve security, or the standards could be a result of compliance or customer requirements as mentioned previously. For example, a customer may require that any software they use has been scanned by SAST. This is not an uncommon request in certain industries. In some cases, the organization will align to an industry framework in order to address customer and regulatory requirements. Something like NIST or ISO are good examples of where the organization can develop their standards and best practices for the purpose of benchmarking and targeting their gaps.

In order to close the gaps on certain functions or areas, the organization will require varying amounts of effort, time, and skill set. In the case of closing the gap on security tools, this will require effort from the application security team, the engineering teams, and the product teams since this will have potential impacts on the delivery of other priorities. Using Superior Products as an example, Dashing Danielle takes the information that she gathered as inputs that show the different pipelines that are not currently running the standard application security scanning tools. She works with the product owners and development teams to identify the amount of work that will be required to integrate the missing tools. Since there are three tools that are part of the application security scanning tool suite, Dashing Danielle puts together the plan that staggers the implementation of each tool since the same resources on the application security team will be required for each (figure 7.2).

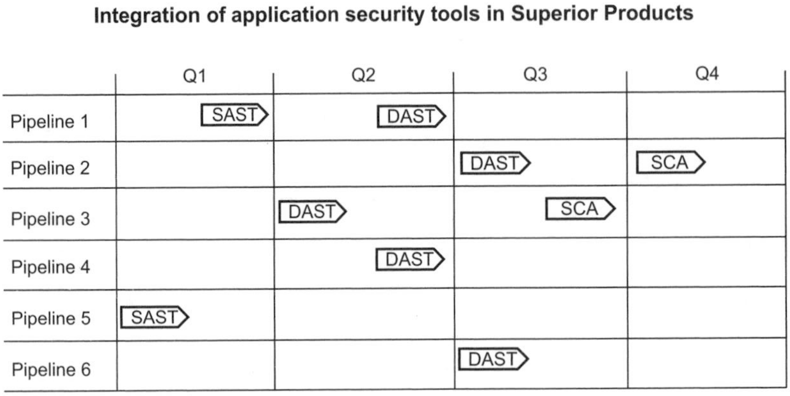

Integration of application security tools in Superior Products

	Q1	Q2	Q3	Q4
Pipeline 1	SAST	DAST		
Pipeline 2			DAST	SCA
Pipeline 3		DAST	SCA	
Pipeline 4		DAST		
Pipeline 5	SAST			
Pipeline 6			DAST	

Figure 7.2　Integration plan for application security tools

By the end of the year, Superior Products would have closed the open gaps in their application security toolset. This would raise the security posture of the organization through increased visibility into the vulnerabilities impacting all their pipelines.

> **NOTE** An important note here is that as Superior Products creates more pipelines when they have new products created, the tools would need to be integrated from the start to stay in compliance with the application security toolset.

Dashing Danielle performs this same exercise on each of the functions that were initially identified and develops plans to address each in the same manner that she planned for the application security tools. Each of these plans will go in the overall roadmap that I will cover soon.

7.4　Sample application security roadmap

Throughout this book, I have painted the picture of what a common secure software development life cycle looks like, how to understand where the gaps are in an organization, and ways to develop a closure of any gaps that are identified. But building an application security program goes beyond providing tools and uncovering vulnerabilities. The application security team will need to define ways to help make the code developed within the organization secure, while doing so with limited budget and resources. As I stated before, most application security teams cannot be sized large enough to meet the demands of the organization. This requires creativity by the application security team and force multiplication.

DEFINITION *Force multiplication* is a military term that is often used in other industries to mean leveraging tools, processes, and people in order to increase the potential impact of a team. In other words, getting more from less. A prime example of this is through automation techniques that allow a team to focus less on manual and repetitive tasks, freeing them up to focus on more critical and complex tasks.

Building a roadmap requires an understanding of the organization and the teams that make up the organization. However, there are some fundamental concepts in each organization that can take advantage of a well-developed application security roadmap. The key items to be addressed in this roadmap are

- Education
- Application security tools
- Engineering enablement
- Engineering alignment
- Future proof

For each of these roadmap items, the application security team will need to review the current state and develop a plan that raises the security of the current state. Some items will be inputs into others, especially as it relates to the engineering enablement and alignment. The application security team will want to take a phased approach to the roadmap where each phase can take weeks, months, or even quarters to complete. The timing is dependent on the size of the work and the resources and commitments from the organization.

7.4.1 Secure engineering education

I've mentioned previously that I am a big fan of security education. As a force multiplier, security education is one of the best. This allows for individuals to raise their knowledge in a given subject, therefore making them more effective in the role they are in. However, one of the goals of the application security team is to not just raise the security education of the engineering organization, but to also raise the application security team's own knowledge on key topics.

   The application security team will need to determine what, if any, training already exists in the current learning management system (LMS) in the organization. Most large organizations will have an LMS to deliver training of all kinds and levels to their staff. This will include things like sexual harassment, privacy, ethics, and other annual compliance related training. There is an opportunity for the application security team to leverage this LMS to deliver content from a third party or develop their own to be accessed in the LMS. In many cases, the organization will first approach the secure education training by creating their own internally developed training modules. This often is not sustainable, as the limited resources of the application security team have to maintain the content and keep it up to date. Often, out of maturity, the organization will contract with a third party and leverage their platform to deliver content. Ultimately, the application security team will need to develop an education roadmap (figure 7.3) to deliver the needed training to the engineering organization.

Education roadmap for the engineering organization

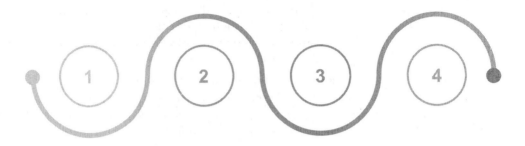

Phase 1

- Evaluate the current application security training in the LMS.
- Evaluate third-party training platforms specific to application security.
- Commit to engaging with third party or in-house developed training.

Phase 2

- Integrate the third-party solution into the LMS or as a stand-alone platform.
- Create the learning paths for each topic in secure development.
- Identify the roles and responsibilities for application security and engineering.

Phase 3

- Define the outcomes for every role in the training program.
- Develop metrics and reporting.
- Integrate the training platform into the security champions program.

Phase 4

- Reevaluate the number of seats/licenses in the platform.
- Mature the platform.
- Review the effectiveness of the training platform.

Figure 7.3   Secure development education for engineering

In the next phase of the secure engineering education roadmap, the application security team will review whether there is an ability to integrate into the current LMS system. Some training platforms will allow the organization to host their content within the organization-owned LMS while others will require the learners to access the content on the third-party platform. Knowing this will have an impact, as there may be additional setup in either case. Once the location has been determined for this content, the application security team will want to establish learning paths for the learners. This will be technology specific, domain specific, or both. Just as an example, the application security team may have the learning paths shown in table 7.9.

Table 7.9   Sample learning paths developed by the application security team

Domain or technology	Description
Web application security	More traditional training around items like the OWASP Top 10 and other web application–specific training.
Microservices	Training specific to how to deliver secure microservices in the cloud or in an on-premises data center.
Language specific	Training specific to languages like C#, Java, PHP, Ruby, and others. The application security team will obviously want to create training paths that include the most frequently used languages in the organization.

The application security team will also need to determine the roles that are included in the training. This is more difficult than just saying "all the engineers" in the organization. In many cases, tracking down the individuals who would qualify for this training can be unclear since roles are not always aligned to the individuals' function. For example, you may want to target training to those who develop code; however, that will be a broader group of people than "software developer." It will include some operational, quality assurance, and infrastructure resources as well.

Some pointers are to work with human resources to understand the role and title structure in the organization. This will get the team most of the way, but not all "engineer" roles will actually be ones who would be required to take training. The application security team can also work with the engineering organization to determine the users who actually commit code. This will provide a much more useful list of users who are actually working with code and would be required to take the training. As a last resort, the application security team can work with the engineering leaders in the organization to ask for their input on users who should be part of the platform.

The last two phases of education for secure engineering training are around the development of metrics and maturity using the platform, as well as integrating with a security champions team if it exists. (Security champions were covered extensively in chapter 5.) First, the organization can use a specific training plan to train a security champions group. That means that the application security team would create a plan that includes multiple disciplines and domains in order to give the champions enough training to be effective at providing guidance to the development teams they work with. The training should be formal and have an assessment at the end before the champion is certified.

The last part of the secure engineering education roadmap will be the continuous monitoring, reporting, and maturity of the platform. This will be a common theme with any roadmap, as you want to be able to show the improvement and benefits of the program as it is being adopted. In other words, what is the benefit of the investment? The basic metrics that should be collected pertain to the effectiveness of the training as well as the engagement. Are the engineers actually using the training platform? How often are they using it? And what are the average scores of the assessments? Are all worth tracking and reporting to leadership? Additionally, the application security team will want to evaluate the list of users in the platform periodically and ensure that there are no new roles or changes in the users that need to be adjusted over time.

7.4.2   Educating the application security team

Security training isn't just for the nonsecurity people in the organization. Security is a changing field, and the things that I was learning a decade ago about security have changed over that time. With this in mind, the application security team needs to ensure that it is keeping up with the ever-evolving security landscape. Just as important, the application security team needs to keep up with the evolving development landscape as well. New languages are being born at blinding speed, and then incorporated in a development team. The application security team can generally get by with basic engineering understanding, but at some point they will need to dive into the specifics of a language or perform a code review. Having a background in that language or basic knowledge will go a long way. To this end, the application security team needs to incorporate a training roadmap that evaluates their current level of competence and needed training (figure 7.4).

Education roadmap for the application security team

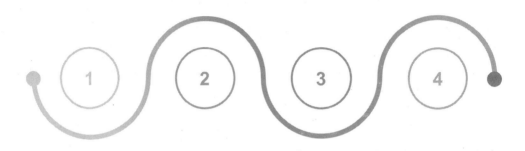

Phase 1	**Phase 2**	**Phase 3**	**Phase 4**
• Evaluate the current knowledge in the application security team.	• Review the current offerings in the LMS or other online platforms.	• Execute and track the progress of training and certifications among the application security team.	• Reevaluate gaps and changes in technology or team members.
• Determine the desired training and certifications that should be held in the team.	• Develop a training plan for the team that includes certifications.		• Repeat Phase 1.

Figure 7.4   Education roadmap for the application security team

For the education of the application security team, the organization will want to determine what is missing. This could be a simple gap analysis, as I covered earlier in this chapter, where the approach is to look at the current state and determine the desired state. It could also be as simple as talking to the application security team members to understand what skills they feel they lack. Not everyone is comfortable answering this question, as it might be perceived as a shortcoming; however, it's important to remember that technology and security are always changing, and staff have to change with them. One way to tackle this is to send out an anonymous poll or questionnaire to the team requesting feedback on potential gaps. The organization may also have requirements on certifications. For example, most formally recognized penetration testers should hold a penetration testing oriented certification in order to be able to perform a test. Additionally, leaders in the security space are often requested if not required to hold a broad security certification like the certified information systems security professional (CISSP) certification.

Once the team has determined its goals for training and certification through a formal gap analysis or an informal questionnaire, they can begin to look for ways to close the gap. There may already exist training in the LMS tool that is used by the organization, or there may also be sufficient training found freely on the internet. However, certifications will require more specific training and assessments. This will require time and expense to complete, and the organization needs to be prepared to meet that commitment.

The last two phases focus on execution and reevaluation. As I mentioned, training and certifications require time and money for the individual who is engaging in it. Depending on the certification, the individual may be able to take part in a bootcamp, which will condense the amount of time that is required but is often pricey. Once the team has been able to complete the identified training and certifications, it's time to reevaluate the landscape and determine whether gaps exist still. If so, rinse, wash, and repeat the phases.

7.4.3 Application security tools roadmap

As security threats change, so do the tools and techniques to address them. This means that often there is a better mousetrap being built somewhere. There have been a lot of advances in security tools from even 5 or 10 years ago, especially as it relates to application security. Ten years ago, if you were running anything more than SAST, you were ahead of most of your peers. Today, the number of tools coupled with advances in artificial intelligence and machine learning means that the detection and prevention security issues in the SDLC have dramatically changed. The application security team will be required to evaluate their toolset against current best practices and tools in the industry (figure 7.5) to ensure that they are staying up-to-date.

Application security tools roadmap

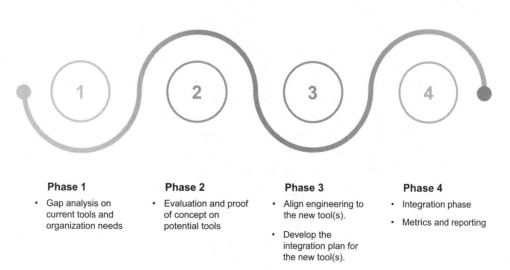

Phase 1
- Gap analysis on current tools and organization needs

Phase 2
- Evaluation and proof of concept on potential tools

Phase 3
- Align engineering to the new tool(s).
- Develop the integration plan for the new tool(s).

Phase 4
- Integration phase
- Metrics and reporting

Figure 7.5 Application security tools roadmap

As I covered in the use case example in this chapter, the application security team would approach the tooling roadmap through a basic gap analysis that looks at what is currently being used in the organization to detect security vulnerabilities like SAST and DAST as well as the protection tools that are being leveraged like RASP and WAF. The application security team will take the output from that gap analysis and begin to evaluate the tools and vendors that are available in the market. Some application security teams may take this opportunity to review the tools that they have deployed already to see whether they are getting the value that they expect from them. Additionally, some tools that they are evaluating may replace or overlap with the tools they are already leveraging.

Ideally the application security team will have short-listed a few vendors and tools from the evaluation that they can begin to complete a proof of concept (POC) with. It is critical to have clear requirements and expected goals and outcomes before embarking on a POC..Often, the vendor will tell you exactly what your problem is and how their tool will fix it. This may or may not align with your own organization's experience.

> **TIP** Just a word of advice and to put a finer point on working with vendors: Do not let them tell you what it is that you are trying to solve. You run the risk of getting tunnel vision with one particular vendor. That's why it is important to make sure that you have the requirements and outcomes defined before you speak with a vendor.

A successful POC will include engagement from the engineering organization. A tool that is sought by and evaluated by the application security team alone will lead to complicated integration when the engineering organization is only seeing it for the first time when they are asked to help integrate it. I've often found that in some security tools, the engineering team will find values in it and latch on to that aspect. This will certainly help with integration and selling the tool in the rest of the organization when it is coming from fellow engineering teams. With the help of the engineering teams that participated in the POC, the application security team can devise the requirements for integration as well as the amount of time integration will take with each team or development pipeline. With this in hand, the application security team can devise the integration plan with clear milestones.

The last phase is implementing the integration plan and ensuring that the metrics and results from the tools are being properly reported. Part of the integration plan should include integration with the defect tracking system in the organization that aligns with the engineering organization. In other words, the application security team should only integrate results from these tools into the tracking systems that are used by the engineering organization as opposed to something that is only used by the security organization. This will make tracking and metrics gathering much simpler. The results should follow the vulnerability management process that is defined in the organization.

7.4.4   *Aligning engineering and security roadmaps*

Enablement and alignment with the engineering organization sounds pretty fluffy. However, its importance shouldn't be overstated. The application security team is there to ensure that the engineering teams have the information and tools they need to develop secure software, so it's vital that they create the ecosystem that supports that effort. The application security team will need to build a roadmap that addresses this alignment (figure 7.6).

Engineering enablement and alignment roadmap

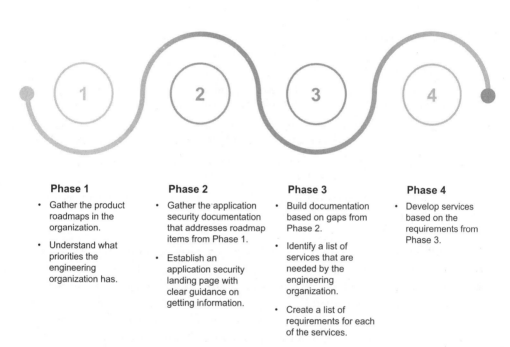

Phase 1

- Gather the product roadmaps in the organization.

- Understand what priorities the engineering organization has.

Phase 2

- Gather the application security documentation that addresses roadmap items from Phase 1.

- Establish an application security landing page with clear guidance on getting information.

Phase 3

- Build documentation based on gaps from Phase 2.

- Identify a list of services that are needed by the engineering organization.

- Create a list of requirements for each of the services.

Phase 4

- Develop services based on the requirements from Phase 3.

Figure 7.6   Enablement and alignment with engineering

The first phase here is to discover the product roadmaps that exist in the organization. This will help the application security team know what changes to the organization's technology or offerings are upcoming. Knowing this will be input into the subsequent phases. Additionally, product and engineering often have aligned priorities but different perspectives on how to meet those priorities. Engineering is in the business of doing, where product is in the business of selling. This means that the tools and processes used by engineering are more important for the application security team who wants to ensure that they are aligning their tools and processes with the teams developing code.

The application security team will then want to review their current tools, processes, and documentation and ensure that they have coverage with the product and engineering roadmaps. As an example, engineering may be looking to change the source code management (SCM) tool to a different platform. The application security team will want to review the new platform, ensure it meets the organization's security goals and requirements, and make recommendations where appropriate. These recommendations should be documented and available for the engineering team.

Enabling engineering means that the engineering teams have the information that they need to develop secure code when they need it. One simple way to accomplish this is by developing an application security landing page that is a one-stop-shop for all information related to application security. Some of the most common items you will find on an application security landing page are shown in table 7.10.

Table 7.10   Sample pages on the application security main page

Sample page	Description
Reference architecture	The well-defined standard security architecture that should be used in the organization as a starting point for all common architecture. For example, authentication flow.
Process documentation	The documentation related to the security processes in application security. For example, the process on generating secure symmetric encryption keys.
Services offered	The listing of the services that the application security team offers to the organization. For example, secure code review.
Contact methods	How to reach out to the application security team. This can be through Slack, email, or other communication channels.

Additionally, the landing page will want to have a simple section for keeping up-to-date with the latest changes, and updates from the application security team and the industry. How this landing page is developed and managed is up to the organization and the application security team. Not all suggestions will work in all organizations. However, the goal is to provide a single location to provide engineering resources the ability to access information that they need to develop secure code.

7.4.5   *Building for the future*

In the age of Scrum and Agile development, it is often hard to think about 6 months or several years down the road. There are some obvious big-ticket items that make sense to be part of a roadmap, but there are also a lot of small items that may only take weeks or months to complete. This is really what we think about as strategic versus tactical work in most organizations, and application security is no different.

When thinking about a roadmap in application security, there are a few things to consider. First, looking at the gap analysis that should be completed will guide your strategic thinking and goals. Perhaps there is a hole in your security tools coverage. Maybe there is an organization-wide directive to modernize authentication. Or, more likely these days, there is a multicloud doctrine in the organization and new development will leverage services from many different CSPs (cloud service providers). Each of these will require the application security team to align their work with the rest of the organization. Additionally, most security organizations consist of other functions like information security, network security, and the security operations center. With these peer teams, the overall security organization may have internal goals and directives that need to be met. For example, most organizations require annual audits and penetration tests, which will require support from the application security team.

When developing the roadmap, you are really attempting to present what the application security of the organization will look like in the next few years. This should be high level and consist of projects rather than specifics. It may be helpful to use either the gap analysis or even a more formal maturity model approach like BSIMM or SAMM (see chapter 5 for more information on maturity models). However, regardless of the approach, each year should build on the previous in terms of capabilities that are delivered.

Using our favorite organization, Superior Products, we can walk through an example with Dashing Danielle developing the roadmap for the next 3 years. She starts by gathering the current security posture and the organization's security goals, and performing a gap analysis. For the current security posture, she focuses on a few items that she knows are critical to the security of the software being developed and creates targets to be completed over the next 3 years:

- The current tool coverage in the organization in order to get to 100% coverage over 3 years
- The level of security training in engineering to ensure that all current and new engineers complete the application security training course
- The classification of data in the organization to feed into the security organization's encryption mandate
- How secure code reviews are occurring in the organization so that a code review platform and process can be developed and implemented
- How compliance and regulation are being integrated into coding to provide ease of audit
- How security testing is integrated into the testing process to reduce vulnerabilities being released into production

Additionally, there are several other projects that are being directed by the business as well as by the security organization:

- Ensure encryption of all PII and critical data at rest.
- Integrate with the security operations team and information security to provide a single pane of glass on vulnerability management.
- Provide secure development pipelines to a multicloud environment.
- Increase the coverage of internal penetration testing.

These items constitute the goals for the application security team, the security organization, and the broader business at Superior Products. This is a pretty short list, but there is intended slack so that as things change over the 3-year window, the application security team can revisit and modify their roadmap in order to realign. It is one of the complications of being a team that is largely dependent on the organizations it works with and their goals.

Exercise 7.1

Take a look at your own organization. If you have access to roadmaps and the application security team, review the information and think about how you would create an application security roadmap that raises the security of the developed software in your organization.

Dashing Danielle collects the information related to the current state and works with the other teams in the security organization and the engineering organization. She comes up with the current state and goals for a future state shown in figure 7.7.

Building a roadmap

Tool coverage

Current state	Three-year goal

• Current pipeline coverage with tools:
  • SAST: 45%
  • DAST: 70%
  • SCA: 30%
	• Three-year tool goal:
	  • SAST: 100%
	  • DAST: 100%
	  • SCA: 100%

Secure coding

Current state	Three-year goal
• Current secure training participants: 25% • Number of secure code reviews per release: 10% • Code coverage with security test: 30% • Security tools integrated into the cloud pipelines: 40%	• Current secure training participants: 100% • Number of secure code reviews per release: 75% • Code coverage with security test: 75% • Security tools integrated into the cloud pipelines: 100%

Data and vulnerability management

Current state	Three-year goal
• Data in the organization that has been classified: 20% • Critical and PII data encrypted at rest: 70% • Applications that receive internal penetration test: 60%	• Data in the organization that has been classified: 100% • Critical and PII data encrypted at rest: 100% • Applications that receive internal penetration test: 100%

Figure 7.7 Basic 3-year plan for Superior Products

Dashing Danielle then develops a basic project plan for each item to create goals, milestones, and risks (figure 7.8). She works closely with the engineering and the

Code review project plan—year one

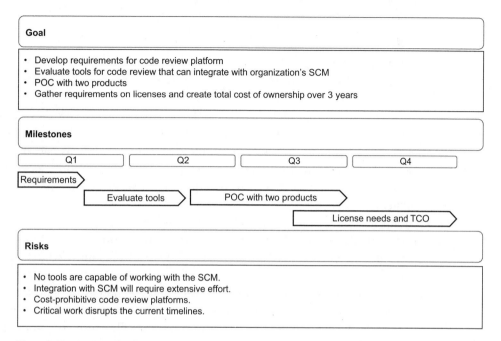

Goal

- Develop requirements for code review platform
- Evaluate tools for code review that can integrate with organization's SCM
- POC with two products
- Gather requirements on licenses and create total cost of ownership over 3 years

Milestones

| Q1 | Q2 | Q3 | Q4 |

Requirements

Evaluate tools

POC with two products

License needs and TCO

Risks

- No tools are capable of working with the SCM.
- Integration with SCM will require extensive effort.
- Cost-prohibitive code review platforms.
- Critical work disrupts the current timelines.

Figure 7.8   Basic project plan for a roadmap item

security peer teams to ensure that the targets are realistic and measurable. The first one she creates is for the code review platform that is part of the application security roadmap.

Figure 7.8 shows a very basic project plan and is used to help guide the application security team and the engineering organization on what the expected tasks are and the goals of the project. Additionally, it can be used to measure the progress over the year and ensure that the team is on track to complete the goals. By the end of the year, Dashing Danielle should have a recommendation on a tool, with projected costs over 3 years. This will be input into the following year's goals in the overall roadmap.

To be clear, creating, tracking, and implementing these roadmaps is not an easy task, and requires more than what the application security leader, or leaders, can do on their own. Where these roadmaps are most successful is when there is leadership buy-in as well as a project manager who is able to coordinate and drive the project with the help of the security leadership. Regular reporting on progress and risks also is required to ensure that leaders are aware of the progress and any roadblocks that might require senior leadership to remove. The bottom line is that these projects that are part of the roadmap should not be treated any differently than any other project in the organization. It is not uncommon for security projects in smaller organizations to not get the same attention because they are not part of the normal hierarchy of the business and development process. However, once the appropriate attention is paid to driving these projects, the organization will be more secure, which is a win for everyone.

Summary

- Creating a roadmap for application security first depends on the inputs from the current security posture. The organization needs to have a baseline of where it is before it knows where it wants to go.
- This baseline should include what tools already exist and how they are being used, what peers and partners are in the organization, what vulnerabilities already exist, and what additional inputs are required for the roadmap.
- Building the roadmap requires knowledge of the organization's security goals so that they can be aligned with the application security team and the overall security organization's goals.
- Inputs into the roadmap will help identify the gaps that exist through a process such as a gap analysis. With this in hand, the application security team will know what the immediate needs are and begin to identify the approach to closing the gaps.
- The application security team should use the gap analysis to build a roadmap that spans multiple years and addresses the immediate needs, midterm goals, and longer-term strategies that align with the overall security organization and the business.

Measuring success 8

This chapter covers

- Determining whether your application security program is effective
- Learning which metrics should be gathered and visualized
- Identifying who needs to know about the program's success
- Getting feedback from your clients
- Using your metrics to drive improvement

You've developed a program that addresses security at the different stages of the development pipeline. You have a roadmap that plots the midterm and long-term goals of the application security team going forward. But how do you know whether the program is effective and that all that hard work that you and your team have put in has paid off? Gathering metrics is a priority for any project or program to ensure that the returns are there from the initial purpose of the project. But metrics are also used to determine whether the project is on track and will complete with the expected outcomes.

For security projects, specifically, the metrics are not much different. You still want to know whether the project is on track and will have the expected outcome.

However, they are also used to determine whether the processes you have are working, whether the security posture of the organization is getting better, and whether the tools you use are effective. This can be helpful if you are looking at new tools to fill a gap or a competitor to a current tool so that you have baselines and an opportunity to compare current state with a potential new tool.

8.1   What to measure

We covered a lot of tools and process in this book, and each one will bring its own set of vulnerabilities and metrics. From a vulnerability standpoint, this can be noisy and time-consuming for those who must track and close the vulnerabilities. But from a metrics standpoint, with the intention of understanding whether the tools are effective or need *tuning*, the information from these tools is invaluable.

> **DEFINITION**   *Tuning* is not a specific application security term, but rather it is related to configuring a tool to run at optimal performance. However, in application security, tuning can take on a different connotation where the tool will be tuned to eliminate noise or false positives, manage alerts, and correlate with other tools to ensure accuracy.

Tools that are improperly tuned can create alert fatigue, where those that are responsible for responding to incoming alerts and notifications become less attentive to the potential findings. This is exacerbated by tools that create a lot of false positives, which leads to the reduction in confidence of the tool. As an example, SAST is notoriously noisy with false positives. Not that other tools are not, but SAST has been historically aggressive with over-reporting. This means that when the SAST tool finds a variable named `password`, it will flag it as a hardcoded password in the source code. This example is most likely not a hardcoded password, but having to triage each example of a variable named `password` will soon become exhausting. SAST tools are getting better at detecting these types of false positives, but work still remains.

When the tool vendor does not have a good solution for how to solve for the false positives—and to be clear the vendor will normally tell the organization that the tool is working as expected—then it is up to the organization to determine the integrity of the data coming from the tool.

> **NOTE**   I am painting with a very wide brush. Not all vendors will tell you to just deal with the false positives. It's in their interest to ensure that the tool works as expected and provides value to the customer. Additionally, not all tools create an abundance of false positives. However, if you intend to bring in a security tool, switch it on, and walk away from it, you will quickly find yourself in alert fatigue.

This is where good metrics will help the organization determine whether a single tool, or a suite of tools, offers the value that they need and paid for. So, which tools or processes should be measured to understand how to arrive at the best outcome?

8.1.1   Measuring the effectiveness of your tools

We use measurements to determine the effectiveness of our tools when we take the output from the tools and dig in to the *quantitative* and *qualitative metrics.*

> **DEFINITION** *Quantitative metrics* are those that are based and backed by actual numbers. An example would be how long it takes for the first-level support team to respond to a client issue. This is measured in minutes, hopefully, and will be an average based on a period of time. *Qualitative metrics* are those that are gathered through interviews, discussions, or questionnaires. These are less driven by numbers and more based on a gut feeling by the respondents. For example, a qualitative metric may be gathered by sending a survey to the engineering teams that work with the application security team to understand how pleased they are with the interaction with the application security team.

First, I want to clarify which tools we are talking about for the application security tools. These would be the following:

- Static application security testing (SAST)
- Dynamic application security testing (DAST)
- Interactive application security testing (IAST)
- Software composition analysis (SCA)
- Run-time application security protection (RASP)
- Web application firewall (WAF)

When it comes to measuring how well these security tools are working, you will focus on the quantitative metrics, as these will give you numbers that show two important aspects of your tools:

- How many vulnerabilities are being opened from each tool
- How many of these opened vulnerabilities are true positives versus false positives

Having this information in hand will allow your application security team to tune the specific tool that is being used and is introducing false positives.

8.1.2   Tuning the tools based on feedback

As an example, a SAST tool in the Superior Products organization was recently integrated into the development pipeline. Although Dashing Danielle has taken time to create custom rules in the SAST tool to handle some of the findings from the development team that participated in the POC, most of the rules and configurations are default from the vendor. For the wider organization, these default rules and configurations may not apply to their technology, code language, or processes. Dashing Danielle asks that the application security team take time to evaluate a set of findings through a spot audit. This means that the team will take a sampling of findings and begin to triage them to understand whether they are false positives and whether the tool needs to be adjusted to limit the false positives, as depicted in figure 8.1.

Providing feedback to the scanning tools

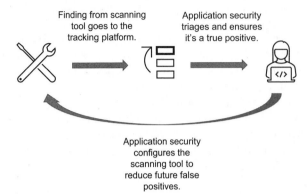

Finding from scanning
tool goes to the
tracking platform.

Application security
triages and ensures
it's a true positive.

Application security
configures the
scanning tool to
reduce future false
positives.

**Figure 8.1   Triaging output from
a scanning tool identifies tuning
opportunities**

During this spot audit activity by the application security team at Superior Products, they were able to discover that the SAST tool for Stuff-For-You, the organization's flagship product, flagged several examples of race conditions that can plague multithreaded code.

> **DEFINITION** *Threads* are a unit of execution in an application that is used to perform some task. When multiple threads are used, the application is considered *multithreaded*. Depending on the hardware, the threading can run in parallel. A race condition occurs when two or more operations complete out of sequence, creating a defect in the code.

However, the code where these issues have been found is not actually multithreaded when it is executed, and therefore the findings can be marked as not applicable. This allows the application security team to set that particular project for Stuff-For-You to safely ignore this category of findings from the SAST tool and eliminate them from future output.

Getting information related to false positives is great for understanding the amount of potential wasted time and effort related to these tools, but what about the actual effectiveness of the tool finding true positives? If the organization has several different scanning tools, like SAST, DAST, and SCA, in the development pipeline and the three tools generated 20 findings in their first week of operation, how does the organization know those are the only vulnerabilities impacting the application? Although, no matter how many tools you layer into the pipeline to discover vulnerabilities, you will never uncover all of the ones that impact the given application. These are considered false negatives. However, the other tools and processes should be used as feedback into the scanning tools as well. For example, it's not uncommon to look at findings from a penetration test, or one that was identified from an external source, and ask the simple question of why the issue was not found in existing tools.

A good example of using other tools and processes to identify false negatives is by taking the findings from an external penetration test and reviewing the configuration in your DAST or IAST tools to determine why the issues were not found in them. At Superior Products, their annual external penetration testing engagement discovered several vulnerabilities in the Stuff-For-You product. One of the most curious was that XSS was found in the application. Considering that there are SAST and DAST tools that are used in the pipeline, the application security team was unsure how this would have slipped past both of those tools.

Dashing Danielle works with the application security team and the development team to look at how the DAST and SAST tools are being used and what code is being scanned. Through this effort, she is able to determine that the particular model that was tested during the penetration test is actually not being scanned by either the SAST or DAST tool. Through configuration, the project was omitted in the code base because the code was being replaced by newer code that used more modern techniques. However, this code was still being delivered to production while the new code is developed and tested. This is a prime example of misconfiguring the security tools in a way that leads to the organization unknowingly being exposed to vulnerabilities.

Although we've talked about the scanning tools and how they should be tuned, the protection tools that are used in the run-time environment also need to be considered. The organization may have a WAF or a RASP deployed in their environment to detect and block known vulnerabilities as they attempt to attack the organization. With these tools, the tuning that is appropriate is to ensure the following is not occurring:

- Legitimate traffic is not being blocked.
- Illegitimate traffic is not getting through.

Both of these cases have real impact on the organization. Stopping your customers from accessing your sites will certainly raise concerns with them, maybe as much as letting an attack through your protection tools. How most application security teams address this is through a staged approach to integrating the protection tool. For example, in Superior Products, the application security worked with the Stuff-For-You team to integrate a WAF with their production domain. Before they did this, they first integrated the WAF for one of the Stuff-For-You pre-production environments. This allowed both the application security team and the engineering team to test whether the traffic that flows through the WAF is providing value and is not interfering with normal traffic. However, once they integrated the WAF with the pre-production domain, they quickly found several issues related to dropped traffic and a reused digital certificate. The team was able to quickly resolve the certificate reuse by procuring a unique certificate for the domain. However, the drop in traffic took additional troubleshooting for the application security team. It was eventually determined that there were DNS changes that needed to be made on a forward proxy with one of the biggest customers of Stuff-For-You. Superior Products reached out to the client and was able to resolve the DNS issue. Traffic improved and the application security team was able to begin monitoring for potential malicious activity.

Because the WAF was enabled on a pre-production domain in the initial stages, the likelihood of external attacks was nonexistent. The domain was not publicly exposed, meaning there was no ability to see real-world attacks from external sources. The application security team, however, was able to automate security testing with their DAST tool and leverage their penetration testing skills to simulate attacks against the WAF. Through this effort, the team was able to determine that the bad traffic that was expected to be blocked as well as the good traffic that the application was expecting was all in order. After 2 weeks of testing in the pre-production environment, the lessons learned and the data that was gathered provided enough confidence to move to the production domain with minimal impact.

Although getting the WAF integrated with the production domain is considered the final step in integration, there is still ongoing work that needs to be done to tune these types of run-time protection tools. The organization must have a means to handle the following:

- *Newly discovered attacks in the wild.* These are attacks that may be able to circumvent the run-time tool and leverage an attack against an application.
- *Changes to the run-time protection tool rules.* The vendor will have updates available on a continuous basis as things in the technology world change. These updates are often pushed automatically, but it depends on the vendor and product.
- *Environmental changes.* As the organization changes, their threat landscape and risk profile changes with it. A change in technology with the web server that is behind the WAF may require a change in the patterns used to detect attacks. For example, the run-time environment may have changed from Java to Rails, which could eliminate several classes of vulnerabilities.

What is important is for the organization to have a process to monitor and adjust their run-time tools as things change and as different needs arise. Using these processes to monitor, gather metrics, and feed that back into the run-time tool can help the organization ensure it is running in a manner that does not negatively impact the organization. However, the effectiveness of the security processes goes beyond tool tuning.

8.1.3 *Measuring the effectiveness of your processes*

Organizations run on processes. Large organizations will even have processes on how to create and manage processes. From a security perspective, the processes that the application security team are most concerned with are the ones that relate to the security scanning tools, vulnerability management, penetration testing, and security education. Although every organization is different and will have separate processes, depending on the maturity of the organization, these are the basic ones you will see in an application security team and the ones I will focus on here.

8.1.4   *Measuring the mean time to remediate*

As discussed previously in the chapter, tuning your security tools will help ensure you are getting quality results from the tool. But measuring the effectiveness of your process around your tools is equally critical. One metric for the effectiveness of your tools is to review the amount of time it takes for the engineering teams to close out found vulnerabilities, as shown in figure 8.2. This means that when a finding is produced from the security tool used in the pipeline, how long does it take to be triaged by the application security team, assigned to a development team, and deployed to production?

Time to resolve for a given vulnerability

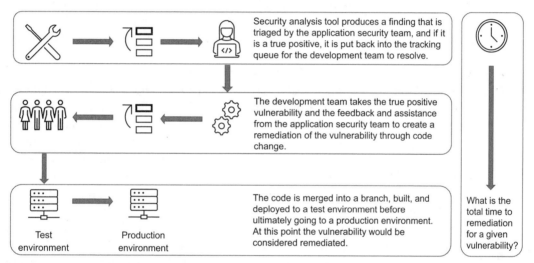

Figure 8.2   What is the time to remediate a vulnerability

This type of metric is often called the *mean time to remediate* (MTTR). This means from the time the issue was discovered to the time that it was remediated and deployed into production, often measured in days. Having this metric is critical in knowing how well your vulnerability management processes are working and how well your development teams understand what is being asked by them. Some common issues that can cause delays with the MTTR are

- Not having the right points of contact in engineering
- Not having enough information to resolve the issue
- Not having the right priority on the open vulnerability
- Not having a well-tuned development pipeline that allows for the fast release of code
- Not having quick access to retesters

Each of these issues will drag down the organization's ability to close out a vulnerability in a timely manner, and leave it exposed for longer than necessary. Furthermore, the organization is typically introducing new vulnerabilities on a daily basis depending on how their security tools are set up.

8.1.5 *Optimizing the mean time to remediate*

To have the effective processes in place to tackle a vulnerability, the organization has to consider what they would do in the event of a critical vulnerability that needs immediate remediation. This is not an uncommon occurrence in the security world. New vulnerabilities come out that can require the organization to drop everything and remediate. A great example of this was the Log4j issue I mentioned in chapter 7. This required immediate remediation by any organization that was using Log4j in their logging process. Once the application security team, or the broader security organization, found out what the exposure was in the organization, they then began working with the engineering teams to formulate a path forward.

Using Superior Products as an example, the process of getting a newly discovered vulnerability to remediation would need to first identify the organization impact—in other words, which applications are impacted by this vulnerability found in the specific tool. At Superior Products, they maintain a registry of the owners of each of the applications in each of the scanning tools they operate. This includes a distribution list email address, and the appropriate ticket tracking system that applies to this solution. Internally, the application security team needs to have a service level agreement (SLA) on how quickly they will acknowledge and triage an issue found in a scanning tool. The application security team will triage the issue to determine whether it is a true positive and then send the ticket to the tracking system or an email to the distribution list. In the ticket, the application security team will include all the relevant information needed to remediate the issue, including links to more information or training.

Once the development team receives the information, depending on the criticality of the issue, they will begin to work toward a remediation. They, too, will have SLAs associated with remediating the issue. As mentioned in previous chapters, the organization will have developed a time to fix associated with each found vulnerability that is aligned with the criticality. With the remediation steps and the timeline defined for them, the engineering team will begin to develop the remediation that aligns the remediation time with the release schedule for the application. This means that for a critical vulnerability that needs to be resolved within 30 days, the remediation code should be released in a patch that is released within that time frame. During the time the development team is working on the remediation, the application security team will develop the retesting process that should include manual steps as well as potential automated testing scripts that will test whether the vulnerability is still present in the application once the remediation code is deployed. From here the remediation code will follow the same path as any other code release in the sense that it will be built and deployed following the standard pipeline practices that the development team follows (figure 8.3).

Mean-time-to-resolution optimization

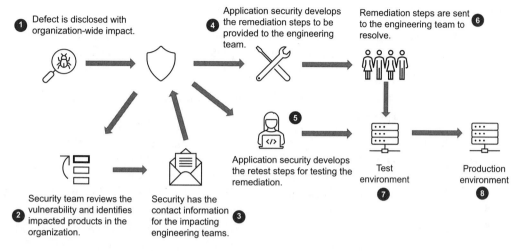

Figure 8.3 Optimizing the MTTR

This workflow can get more complex when you are juggling multiple vulnerabilities. Most organizations are not lucky enough to work only one vulnerability at a time. They will have dozens in their backlog to slot for upcoming releases with varying criticality. Each criticality will have a time to remediate a target that is set by the organization. Aligning all of these to the release, and still managing to be within the time to remediate timelines, is not an easy task. To find the organization's mean time to remediate, per criticality, the organization can take aforementioned inputs of each vulnerability and put together something similar to table 8.1.

Table 8.1 Sample MTTR for low through critical vulnerabilities

Vulnerabilities		Time (Days)			
Criticality rating	# Closed vulnerabilities	Time to remediate	Shortest time	Mean time	Longest time
Critical	5	30	2	20	38
High	12	60	17	37	56
Medium	23	90	24	50	75
Low	40	365	63	169	275

Having this information in hand is an important input into the overall metrics that are needed by the organization to understand how efficient they are at closing particular criticalities. I talked about both the tool and the process data collection to help an organization understand its application security effectiveness, but there are other pieces of data that an organization will want to gather.

8.2   *Gathering effectiveness with KPIs*

Programs are generally put in place to drive new processes and products or to solve a problem for the organization. With an application security program, the organization will want to see improvement in a few *key performance indicators* (KPIs).

> **DEFINITION**   A *KPI* is a way for an organization to measure the effectiveness of a long-term goal.

Organizations will have KPIs for many different goals that they are working toward, especially as it comes to the business side where they want to see how effective they are being at meeting customer requirements. However, in the engineering, and specifically the application security world, the KPIs will focus on how effective the program is at stopping vulnerabilities and having a quicker reaction to discovered new ones. To this end, the application security team should focus on developing the metrics and align them to goals that address the following:

- How the business risk is reduced over a given time period (month, quarter, annual). This relies on the business having identified the open vulnerabilities, assigned criticality to them, and put them into the context of business risk.
- How quickly the organization can resolve open vulnerabilities from initial identification to remediation in production. This is what I covered in the previous section.
- How frequently vulnerabilities are being reintroduced in an application. For example, an application may have discovered multiple SQL injection vulnerabilities in the same project. Unless the root cause is being addressed, these will continue to be introduced.
- How much coverage the application security program has in terms of the security tools it uses (SAST, DAST, IAST, WAF, or others). This will be an overlay of the known development pipelines and run-time environments with the tools that are integrated with them.

Whereas every organization will have different KPIs they may want to track, these are fundamental ones that will be effective in measuring how well the application security team is doing in reducing the overall risk of the organization. So, how can you create these KPIs?

8.2.1   *Building the KPIs*

Creating a KPI measurement process can be simple or complex depending on how deep the organization wants to get with the data. For the KPIs I will use for measuring the success of the application security program, I will keep it relatively simple given that the measurements are qualitative in nature and simple to measure. The four KPIs that I outlined previously can be summed up into the following labels:

- Open vulnerabilities
- MTTR
- Reintroduction of vulnerabilities
- Application security coverage

For each of these KPIs, the application security team will start by outlining the criteria of the KPI that they need to capture information on. They will start with a simple document that captures the relevant information, as shown in table 8.2.

Table 8.2   Sample KPI data collection

Objective		Result		
Description	**Type**	**Source**	**Frequency**	**Targets**
Number of vulnerabilities opened should be reduced to be within business risk	Quantitative	Application scanning tools and penetration testing	Weekly	Lower than the acceptable business risk

Gathering this information will guide the future data collection and aid in the reporting of progress toward the goals.

> **NOTE**   To be clear, gathering this information is not for the faint of heart. Ideally the organization will have automated ways of collecting this information. Without that, the team, or individual tasked with collecting this, will quickly become overwhelmed, disorganized, and discouraged as they have to wrangle with all the sources to collect it.

For this particular case, the organization is looking to reduce the overall vulnerability count in the organization. The vulnerabilities will be identified in the scanning tools that the organization has in place, and the KPI data will be refreshed weekly. The target, or goal, of this KPI is to be within the predefined business risk threshold.

An owner of the KPI needs to be identified for the collection and reporting of the progress toward the goal. In the case of the open vulnerabilities KPI, the ownership is with the application security team since they have the broad view of the scanning tools and can easily report at the organization level. At Superior Products, Dashing Danielle has been put in charge of collecting the weekly metrics and sharing them with stakeholders from the security, engineering, and business organizations on a weekly basis. This is informally done through a weekly email notification. However, as the KPI collection and reporting matures, this will change over time to become a more robust method of reporting to the stakeholders.

8.2.2 *Setting KPI targets*

Once the KPIs have been identified, the organization needs to address its desired targets for the given KPI. In many cases, this may be driven by outside pressures such as regulatory, contractual, or other demands. The simple target for the previous example in table 8.2 was that the organization will keep the open vulnerabilities within the business's acceptable risk. This assumes that the acceptable risk has been properly classified and agreed upon by the business and security organization. In chapter 6, I talked about the level of risk that the organization has identified as its acceptable level. This should be in line with what the target of the open vulnerability KPI is.

Taking another example with the MTTR, the organization will first gather its baseline metrics for the MTTR that currently exists. In the example in table 8.3, the organization has decided they will target a 14-day MTTR for critical vulnerabilities. This means that the average time from declaring a critical vulnerability a true positive to the remediation code running in production should be 14 days or less.

Table 8.3   Sample MTTR KPI

Objective		Result		
Description	**Type**	**Source**	**Frequency**	**Targets**
MTTR for critical vulnerabilities	Quantitative	Defect tracking tool	Weekly	MTTR for critical vulnerabilities will be within 14 days

The application security team will use the defect tracking tool in the organization to track the progress of each of the true-positive critical vulnerabilities that are discovered. Although the development teams are resolving vulnerabilities, new ones will be discovered, triaged, and put into the queue for resolution. The overall tracking of critical vulnerabilities will look something like table 8.4.

Table 8.4   Tracking of critical vulnerabilities

Vulnerability	Date opened	Version deployed	Date deployed	Number of days to remediate
SQL injection in Project 1	Dec. 7, 2022	Patch 4.1.8	Dec. 20, 2021	13
SQL injection in Project 4	Dec. 2, 2022	Patch 4.1.8	Dec. 20, 2021	16
XSS in Project 3	Dec. 10, 2022	Patch 4.1.9	Dec. 27, 2021	17
Path traversal in Project 2	Dec. 20, 2022	Patch 4.1.10	Jan. 3, 2022	14

The MTTR for these four vulnerabilities is 15 days. This is significantly less than the SLA of 30 days for critical vulnerabilities, but not within the KPI metric that the organization wants of 14 days. Using these metrics, the organization can make some improvements.

8.2.3 Driving change based on KPIs

Now that the organization has targets, has collected the information, and knows what its goal is, it's time for them to drive to get their KPIs in line with the targets. To do this, the team responsible for driving the KPI will be required to provide several reoccurring functions that will assist in driving down the KPIs:

- *Regular and automated metrics gathering.* The organization will want to ensure that it can gather the metrics quickly, regularly, and with confidence that the data is accurate. This last part is critical. Many organizations fail to ensure the quality of their metrics when they start gathering them. Specifically, finding all sources of data, eliminating stale and duplicate data, and finding owners for the data.
- *A clear set of stakeholders that have the ability to effect change in the way the KPI is managed.* If I take the example of the KPI that looks to provide application security coverage across the organization, these stakeholders are the leaders in the engineering organization that need to buy in to the disruption. This is because they will need to assist with implementing the tools and pledge to resolve vulnerabilities that are discovered.
- *Assign KPIs as goals for individuals and leaders in the organization.* This is an oftenoverlooked part of driving KPIs. When individuals have a stake in the KPI and are capable of effecting change with the KPI, then the organization is more likely to hit its targets. This can be as simple as making certain KPIs part of an individual's annual review and goal setting. However, it is important to ensure that the individual is capable of meeting the requirements of the KPI.
- *Make the KPIs visible and available to all stakeholders.* Don't be ashamed of your KPIs; they need to be front and center, and regularly reviewed by the stakeholders. If you look at an example of personal finance, an individual will regularly check in with their budget, their accounts, and where they are on their financial goals. KPIs are no different.

I will use our favorite organization, Superior Products, to illustrate how an organization can work to drive change with a KPI. Here, the application security team has been given the ownership of the KPI that is set to reduce the reoccurrence of closed vulnerabilities. This one is difficult since metrics around recurrence will require more processing than getting general metrics from the application security tools. The team will be required to look for opened vulnerabilities in the same projects, with the same vulnerability type. This is not as simple as finding multiple SQL injections in the Stuff-For-You application, although that is a criterion; rather the application security team will need to identify vulnerabilities that reoccur across all applications and projects. This also includes ones that are similar to previously closed ones. Today, that may be an exercise in manual review of opened and closed vulnerabilities to determine ones that are similar.

Dashing Danielle has been tasked with building the plan for addressing the recurrence of vulnerabilities KPI. Her first goal is to gather the metrics from the available tools in the application security program. Her focus is on the SAST, DAST, and penetration test results to begin with since the organization has these three tools and processes widely implemented. In order to test out her processes, she decides to focus on one type of vulnerability first. In this case, she decided to concentrate on XSS. These are found frequently through the application security program's tools and processes.

She uses labels in the scanning tools and reviews the penetration testing reports to locate all known XSS vulnerabilities that have been found in the past 12 months in the three products that Superior Products sell, as described in table 8.5.

Table 8.5   Superior Products' XSS findings over 12 months

Product	SAST	DAST	Penetration test
Stuff-For-You	1	6	2
Stuff-For-Me	2	4	1
Things-You-Need	1	3	3

Over the past 12 months, each application has had several XSS vulnerabilities identified. Many of them were already closed, but newer ones are being opened in the same applications over time. Dashing Danielle first looks to remove any duplicate findings in each of the applications. It is not uncommon for the various tools to identify the same issue in the same set of code. Next, it is critical to determine whether the issues are true positives or not. As I talked about in previous chapters, many tools will produce false positives. Even a penetration test can produce a false positive.

With the true results in hand, Dashing Danielle sets out to locate vulnerabilities that are reoccurring over time. For example, in the Stuff-For-Me application during the annual penetration test, a XSS vulnerability was identified. Dashing Danielle looks back at the previous year's penetration test to determine whether it was identified there and reopened. She determines that this is a new finding in the penetration test. However, while reviewing the specific issue in the report, she finds that the DAST tool had uncovered this specific finding months before the penetration test, and the vulnerability was closed by the development team with a partial fix in place that passed the DAST scan. However, the application security team was not able to retest the closed vulnerability, and it was never formally tested until the penetration test. This highlights a gap in the process that led to the reopening of a vulnerability.

The previous example is pretty abstract and requires the insight of a subject matter expert (SME) in the application security team to determine. Other findings will be more obvious. For example, in the Things-You-Need application, there was one XSS finding from the SAST tool. Dashing Danielle does some research on the issue and discovers that the same project in Things-You-Need has seen several XSS issues opened and closed throughout the year. This leads Dashing Danielle to believe that the development team has been unable to create code that is secure from XSS. With this information in hand, Dashing Danielle can work with the development team to have a small workshop that focuses on protection mechanisms around XSS. She also works with the SAST vendor to include more specific resolution text when the tool discovers a XSS vulnerability. This means that the developer will be presented with specific fix recommendations and links to internal resources to resolve XSS.

With this new, more targeted approach, Things-You-Need saw fewer recurrences of the XSS vulnerabilities and has been able to address newer ones before they are deployed to production. This is a simple example but should get you thinking about how you would drive a similar KPI in your organization.

> **Exercise 8.1**
> Take the application security KPI and describe what the objectives are and how you would drive this adoption in your organization.

8.3 Getting feedback

Up to this point, I have been talking about quantitative metrics. However, qualitative metrics are key to the success of the program as well. This is where feedback from your peers and partners helps you gauge how well your application security program is working. This comes down to asking basic questions related to the experience engineers have with the program and the way that the engineers interact with the controls and tools that the application security team has put in place. Some examples of qualitative questions that the application security team should ask are

- Is the guidance received on remediating software vulnerabilities clear?
- How accessible are the results from the scanning tools?
- Is your code well tested for security vulnerabilities?
- Do you understand the business risk level of your application?

Each of these questions will provide the application security team with context on how well the application security program is doing, and more importantly, how well the development teams can access the information that they need regarding the security of their application.

> **NOTE** One important callout here is on how accessible the scan results are to the development teams. This is a sticky subject since many organizations do what they can to limit the accessibility to the data due to its sensitivity. I'm a firm believer that this information should be made available to the people who are responsible for developing and deploying the remediation of the vulnerability.

The feedback should be aligned back to the KPIs, the goals, and the needs of the organization. This means that just as the organization gathers qualitative metrics such as the open critical vulnerabilities, the organization will want to also know what the developer's experience is with the application security program. So, how is this information collected?

8.3.1   *Getting feedback from conversations*

One easy way to collect information from your peers and partners in the engineering organization is to simply ask. As I mentioned earlier in the book, I often ask my peers and partners in the engineering organization what their biggest security concerns are. What I didn't tell you is that I often also ask how my team is doing and what the interaction is with my team members and engagement model. It can be as simple as asking whether the engineering teams know how to engage with the application security team. You'd be surprised by how some process that your team spent months working, and even had a launch party for, is unknown to those that are supposed to use it. This is often due to the lack of a well-formulated communication around the process, and the inability to block circumvention by possibly just asking someone on the team to provide a quick favor.

> **NOTE** As much as many of us try to get away from it, email is here to stay. In your organization, you may have a spiffy ticketing system where anyone can open a ticket to your team to request support. However, as many of us are familiar, a quick email to a member of your team will shortcut this spiffy tool and make it so that the work is quickly lost to any oversight. This is often due to the fact that it is hard to change habits. Or is it related to the possibility that not many are aware of the ticketing system and how to use it? Direct emails to someone is often a way to circumvent a defined process.

Having a conversation with your peers and partners can help direct traffic to those tools and processes that are in existence to support the engineering team and make your team's life easier. Prior to entering these conversations, it is helpful to understand some of the challenges that your team is facing and address them through qualitative questions. Using the example I gave with the ticketing system, it would make sense to simply ask your peers and partners whether they know how to engage with the application security team and whether they are aware of the ticketing system that makes everyone's life easier. This is a great way to get the feedback that you are looking for while engaging with those the application security team is there to support.

One drawback to this method is that it doesn't scale well, as you can only collect information as quickly as you can hold these types of conversations. Additionally, it's difficult to operationalize that information in your team. In the case of the lack of awareness with the ticketing system, this will take good old-fashioned advertising. However, there are more scalable ways to get feedback.

8.3.2   *Getting feedback from surveys*

A scalable way to get feedback from many respondents in a short period of time is through surveys or online services. Although you miss the human connection that allows you to ask additional questions when you notice the respondent has more information to provide, you are able to send a survey or provide an online interaction to a much wider audience in a shorter period of time. This is useful in the case where you may have just made a change to a process or an interaction point and want to get feedback as early as possible.

One huge advantage of reaching a broader audience is that this will lend credibility to your feedback. Getting feedback from a select few through interview or casual conversation is not as powerful as getting feedback from a larger audience of those who are most likely more involved in the day-to-day activities that you are looking to get feedback on. For example, you may want to discover how comfortable the development teams are with the SAST tool that is used in a particular application pipeline. If you are a leader and have this conversation with your peer, they may not have the context or information as to how their team is using the tool and how effective it is. Worse, you might only get the negative feedback that the leader has heard from their team.

There are two main methods of getting feedback from surveys. One is through general communication via email or other electronic communication that you can send to a distribution list, or groups of people. Although this is pretty easy to implement by just creating a series of questions and sending them to a list of people, it is difficult to track and aggregate the responses. As long as the audience is small, this can still be effective and should be used in the case where you are looking for specific feedback on a specific topic. For example, perhaps you are looking to get feedback on a reoccurring meeting that is used to communicate security architecture. A simple email communication soliciting feedback from the meeting attendees will suffice.

For more complex questions that need to go to an even larger audience, an online survey using a platform like SurveyMonkey can help. Instead of trying to collect and track the information through emails, these survey platforms can help the team build complex surveys and deliver them to dozens, hundreds, or even thousands of people. The use of these surveys can help the application security team understand the broader strategy around their program. For example, at Superior Products, the application security team created a survey that they wanted to send to the engineering organization to get an understanding of the engineering team's familiarity with the general vulnerability management processes in the organization. The team developed a survey in an online platform that was then sent to several hundred developers in the organization. The questions in the survey were

- How familiar are you with severity levels for vulnerabilities that are found in your application?
- How familiar are you with the OWASP Top 10?
- Do you understand the threats and risks that apply to the application you develop?
- Do you have the material and training needed to close a vulnerability found in your application?
- How confident are you at being able to close a vulnerability found in your application?

With answers to these questions, the application security team is able to get a sense of the confidence level of the developers and their ability to address vulnerabilities in their applications, as shown in figure 8.4.

Difference in qualitative feedback

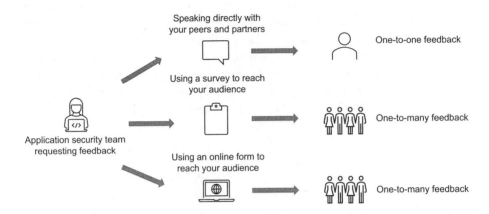

Figure 8.4   Methods of qualitative feedback

Regardless of the method being used to collect this qualitative information, it is important for the organization to then be able to act upon it by building the findings into their processes. For example, it is possible that the results from the online survey show that most of the engineering organization does not have enough information to resolve vulnerabilities when they are found in their application. The application security team may have a very nice landing page, with links to training, whitepapers, and helpful guidance. However, based on the feedback from the survey, that information is not getting into the hands of those who need it. This would likely lead to the application security team spending time and effort to get the information out to the rest of the organization through a communication blitz.

8.4   *Security scorecard*

The concept of a security scorecard, or security nutrition label, is not new. In fact, it has been talked about mostly in the internet of things (IoT) space since the rapid adoption of connectivity in everyday products, which has brought about significant security and privacy concerns. However, we are far away from having a label slapped onto applications that we use. Take, for example, a mobile app that you download and install on your mobile device. It is unlikely that the app developer will enthusiastically showcase a poor security score alongside their age rating.

For this to work in the real world, a third party would need to provide a seal of approval similar to something that Underwriters Laboratories does for product safety. You might also be thinking about audits that are performed by third parties that provide a report on compliance like SOC (system and organization controls) and PCI (payment card industry). Although these audits are necessary, they do not often get into the details of the application and its specific security posture. This is where I would like to focus more on how an organization can use the security scorecard concept to raise awareness within the organization of the security posture of their applications. To be clear, until we get to a utopia where a third party assesses and assigns a security score to an application, this exercise is kept internal to the organization to simply raise the security of their products.

Inside of an organization, a security scorecard will look similar to the KPIs or maturity models that I covered in section 8.2. The major difference is that the security scorecard will focus more on the tactical aspects of the application itself rather than the broader vision of the organization. For example, one of the criteria of the security scorecard might be the Transport Layer Security (TLS) version supported by the application. The lower the version that is supported, the lower the score for the application. Similarly, using weak encryption would reduce the overall score of the application. Like most of the other journeys in technology and security, it starts with collecting the data and getting oriented.

8.4.1 Preparing for the scorecard

The first step in a security scorecard is identifying what should be measured and how to connect that to a score for the application. Collection should be automated and repeatable with little to no manual steps. As an example, consider the collection of the TLS version for the application. This should be done through scanning tools, or online tools like SSL Labs.

> **NOTE** Just a word of caution against using online tools to perform scans or reviews of your technology. This can be concerning, especially when it comes to intellectual property. Some online services may keep information regarding your interaction with them. Often these services will provide documentation on what they collect and how it's used. It's important to be familiar with how this might impact your organization and opt out if possible. Your best, most secure option is to use an internal tool that the organization has tighter controls over.

The creation of the metrics that will be used to make up the scorecard should align to the business risks and what is important to the organization. Things like TLS versions and security are always good markers, but if the organization doesn't have any publicly exposed applications for customers or the applications that are exposed do not process sensitive information, then maybe this is less of a concern. Additionally, the organization may see that code quality has a direct connection to the vulnerabilities that are released to production. In this case, they will want to ensure that code quality metrics are included.

Our favorite organization, Superior Products, implemented a security scorecard with Stuff-For-You as a start. Once again, Dashing Danielle was tasked with this project, and she first sought out to understand what is most important to the organization from a security point of view. Given that the application is an e-commerce platform, there are several items to focus on:

- The security of the data related to personally identifiable information (PII) and financial information
- The privacy of the data as it relates to customers' browsing and purchase history
- The confidence and reputation of the application
- The integrity of the shop and the items that are sold through the marketplace

This gives Dashing Danielle enough guidance on what criteria should be part of the scorecard. Based on this, she can surmise that the scorecard should minimally focus on data protection like the use of encryption at rest and in transit with strong encryption algorithms as well as a hashing technique used to ensure the integrity of the data in the database. Vulnerabilities that impact data as it is transmitted or sits at rest will be weighted higher than others. Additionally, because the organization is concerned about the reputation of the site, Dashing Danielle also includes any vulnerabilities or design decisions that put the availability of the application at risk. She knows that this list will expand over time, but this is a good start with Stuff-For-You and allows her to start getting the process going.

> ### Exercise 8.2
> What criteria or metrics do you believe your organization should focus on given its industry and types of applications?

Now that Dashing Danielle has high-level criteria in mind, she can start to ensure that she can collect this information in an automated and repeatable manner so that it is able to be called on demand and updates in real time. Both of these are requirements of the scorecard. She develops the scorecard criteria, their source, and the frequency of updates shown in table 8.6.

Table 8.6 Criteria of the security scorecard in Superior Products

Criteria	Source	Frequency
TLS version supported	Network level scan from the network team	Daily
TLS cipher suites supported	Network level scan from the network team	Daily
Checksum of critical database	Database team	On demand
Data in the relational database is encrypted using Superior Products' encryption standards	Database team	On demand
NoSQL (nonstructured data) containing sensitive information is encrypted at rest	Site reliability engineering (SRE)	On demand

Table 8.6 Criteria of the security scorecard in Superior Products *(continued)*

Criteria	Source	Frequency
OWASP Top 10—A02 Cryptographic Failures	Vulnerabilities identified in scanning or manual review and logged in the defect tracking tool	On demand
OWASP Top 10—A03 Injection	Vulnerabilities identified in scanning or manual review and logged in the defect tracking tool	On demand
Availability and DDoS-related vulnerabilities	Vulnerabilities identified in scanning or manual review and logged in the defect tracking tool	On demand

The criteria that are listed as on demand can be run as needed when generating a score. The items that are run daily will have, at most, a 24-hour lag in data as these criteria scans take time to execute and cannot be called on demand. This is acceptable in the Superior Products case since the TLS cipher suites and versions do not change frequently. In most cases, this would change perhaps annually or quarterly. Now that Dashing Danielle has the criteria of the scorecard that Superior Products would like to initially focus on, it's time for her to assign scores to the criteria.

8.4.2 Weighting the scores for the scorecard

Just as chapter 6 covered releasing code based on risk, an analogous approach will be taken to define the security score of an application. This requires the organization to understand what the criticality is to the organization of each of the applications. Table 8.7 shows the way an organization should classify the criticality of an application.

Table 8.7 Application importance in an organization

Importance	Description of the application importance
Critical	Critical applications are vital to the operations of the organization. These are applications that require the highest level of uptime and would result in significant financial loss or critical damage should the application become unavailable or should its data be breached. A critical application could be a clinical application used to administer doses of medication to patients.
Important	Important applications are ones where uptime is expected, and the data maintained by the application would pose a severe impact to the organization should it become exposed or unavailable. An important application could be one that provides supply chain management services within an enterprise.
Support	These applications are used widely in the organization to provide some service that relates to the operation of the organization. Downtime and breach of data would have a mild impact on the organization. For example, an application that provides client support functions would not pose a significant risk to the organization.
Internal	Internal applications, as the name specifies, are applications that are only used internally within the organization. These applications are used to assist with the internal operations of the organization such as customer relationship management tools. Although they may seem important, these types of applications usually have workaround methods, and their uptime and data pose a mild risk to the organization.

The criticality of the application becomes a mathematical factor when determining what the actual scorecard is. This means that it becomes an additional criterion when determining the overall score.

From a simplistic point of view, the organization can then use a basic weighted scoring method in order to determine an overall score for the product. Because not every criterion carries equal weight in the score, it is important to rank them by importance. At Superior Products, Dashing Danielle works with the security organization, as well as the engineering and business teams to rank the scorecard criteria. Based on this review, Dashing Danielle comes up with the following list of ranked criteria:

- Application criticality (20%).
- TLS version supported (10%).
- TLS cipher suites supported (10%).
- Checksum of critical database (5%).
- Data in the relational database is encrypted using Superior Products' encryption standards (15%).
- NoSQL (nonstructured data) containing sensitive information is encrypted at rest (15%).
- OWASP Top 10—A02 Cryptographic Failures (5%).
- OWASP Top 10—A03 Injection (5%).
- Availability and DDoS-related vulnerabilities (15%).

Now that weights are assigned, it's time to look at the data and create the actual scorecard.

8.4.3 Creating the scorecard

For each of the criteria in the scorecard, there needs to be a method of mapping it to the weighted score. What I mean by this is that not each of the criteria are identical. Some are "off or on" like the adherence to a specific version of TLS. Others have a range of possible inputs like the count of a specific vulnerability. The table for the scorecard input and weights should now look more like table 8.8.

Table 8.8 Criteria with weights and possible inputs

Criteria	Weight	Possible input
TLS version supported.	10	Binary
TLS cipher suites supported.	10	Binary
Checksum of critical database.	10	Binary
Data in the relational database is encrypted using Superior Products' encryption standards.	20	Binary
NoSQL (nonstructured data) containing sensitive information is encrypted at rest.	20	Binary

Table 8.8 Criteria with weights and possible inputs *(continued)*

Criteria	Weight	Possible input
OWASP Top 10—A02 Cryptographic Failures.	10	0->n
OWASP Top 10—A03 Injection.	10	0->n
Availability and DDoS-related vulnerabilities	10	0->n

Although this can make the scorecard complex, it also gives a bit of flexibility in the way that the scores are defined. The binary criticalities are a bit trickier since it is either on or off, 1 or 0. This means that you will need to assign a value to whether the criteria are implemented or not. Taking TLS version support as an example, if the application has the TLS version configured that is in line with the organization's standards, let's say TLS version 1.3, then this would be considered fully implemented, and the application would receive a score of 1. If it is not implemented, then the application would receive a score of 0 for those criteria.

Lastly, for the 0->n criteria that relies on an ever-changing group of vulnerabilities, these should be put into groups of acceptable vulnerabilities. For example, for the A02 Cryptographic Failures criteria, the organization may decide to use a grouping that aligns with their risk and may come up with a grouping of 0, 1-5, 6-10, 11-15, >16. Additionally, the organization can consider the severity of the vulnerabilities in the criteria in order to create additional score levels.

Exercise 8.3

As I mentioned, the way the scores can be created really depends on the organization and what matters most to them. However, even in the examples I've given, there are shades of scores. Take a moment to think about how you can further break down the score for the TLS-supported cipher suites and how you can create a score that is more nuanced than an A or F.

For the scorecard to work effectively, the criteria would need to be made into a percentage or grade that aligns with a common educational grading system of A, B, C, D, and F for each of the criteria. This allows for an overall score to be averaged and presented as the score for the application. The organization can use any other method to present the score so long as it is agreed upon and well understood within the organization. If an item is binary, the "on" would be a 100 or A, and the "off" would be a 50 or F. For the other items with multiple possible scores, the organization should use a grouping strategy that assigns a score for each group. From the previous example of groups like 0, 1-5, 6-10, 11-15, >16, the 0 would signify a 100, or A, the 1-5 would be an 80 or B, and so forth.

At Superior Products, Dashing Danielle builds the security scorecard by collecting the information for each of the criteria. She creates a script that pulls all the information and places it into a format that can be calculated and then presented in a dashboard that will be used for the remaining products in Superior Products. Using a basic weighted grade calculation, she can get an overall score, or grade, for Stuff-For-You and present it in the dashboard (figure 8.5).

Basic scorecard for Stuff-For-You

Application name: Stuff-For-You
Application criticality: Important

Criteria	Weight	Score
TLS version supported	10	A
TLS cipher suites supported	10	F
Checksum of critical database	10	A
Data in the relational database is encrypted using Superior Products' encryption standards	20	A
NoSQL (nonstructured data) containing sensitive information is encrypted at rest	20	A
OWASP Top 10—A02 Cryptographic Failures	10	D
OWASP Top 10—A03 Injection	10	C
Availability and DDoS-related vulnerabilities	10	B

Figure 8.5   Sample security scorecard for Stuff-For-You

There is a lot of refining that can be done here, but this provides a quick score for the application that tells the consumer several things. One, it shows where the application is in overall security. Two, it shows where the application can focus its effort to raise the grade and where they are doing well. Additionally, the weights provide context on what is important to the organization. The organization can take this and build additional criteria as well as more granular criteria that will help create a more robust scorecard.

Summary

- Building an application security program will raise the security of your applications in the organization, but without measuring the effectiveness of the program, the organization will not know how well it is working and where to make improvements.
- There are two high-level measurements that the application security program should consider taking. One is how well your tools are working and the other is how well your processes are working.

- Building a set of KPIs is a common approach to measuring success and areas of improvement. This starts with identifying the KPIs that are important to the organization, followed by setting targets. Once the KPIs are identified and targets set, the organization can move forward with closing gaps.
- Gathering feedback on the application security program can be done formally or informally through surveys or conversations with peers. This is a great way of hearing back from the community of peers and partners on their interactions with the application security team and program. Using this feedback, the application security team can build additional enhancements to the program.
- Creating a security scorecard is a method of getting a quick glance at the security posture of an application and allows for the organization to focus on security items that matter most to them. These scorecards can be tailored to fit the capabilities and targeted security posture.

Continuously improving the program

This chapter covers

- Exploring modern and advanced techniques for application security
- Supporting future changes in the application security space
- Avoiding common pitfalls with an application security program

Your application security program is up and running. It's humming along. Vulnerabilities are down. Engineers are getting ahead of the security issues that are impacting their application, and things are looking great. This is the point where most application security leaders begin to think about what's next. Although there will be the desire to just keep going with what the team is doing, security and attackers do not stay still. There is an ever-evolving landscape of security issues, and attacks only get better.

Whereas fighting vulnerabilities should be the organization's primary focus, your program should be designed in such a way that the regular influx of vulnerabilities should not be cause for alarm. Your program will have the people, process, and technology in place to manage the vulnerabilities to closure within the timelines established by the organization. Even when a zero-day vulnerability comes in that doesn't have a patch that can be deployed to resolve, you have built the communication channels, you know where your data and applications are, and you have the appropriate run-time protection tools in place to provide mitigation until a fix can be deployed.

Now that vulnerabilities are no longer something to fear, it's time to look at some more advanced topics in the security space that will help you understand how attackers are thinking about your applications and ways for you to stay ahead of that by building resilient architecture.

9.1 *Keeping ahead of the attacker*

There is a very common phase in defense, whether it's physical or cyber. It goes something like this: "The attacker only has to be right once; the defender has to be right every time." As systems get more complex with an increasing amount of exposure points, the attacker quickly has a target-rich environment to play in. In chapter 2, I showed the different attackers that are looking for ways into an organization's applications. Figure 9.1 is a reminder of the threat actors, the likelihood that the organization would face that threat actor, and the organization's level of challenge in defending against the actor.

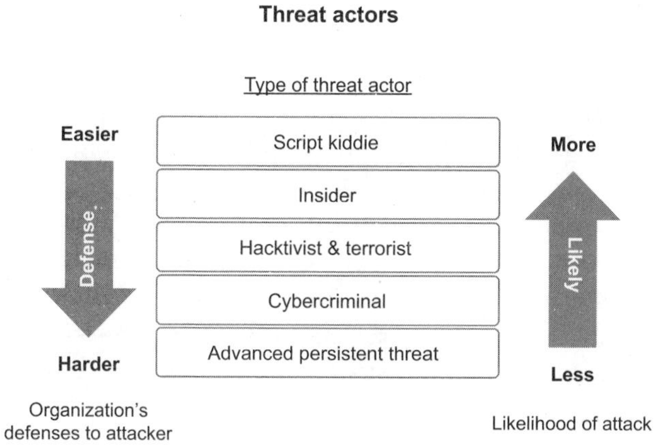

Threat actors

Type of threat actor

Easier		More
Script kiddie		
Insider		
Hacktivist & terrorist		
Cybercriminal		
Advanced persistent threat		
Harder		Less

Organization's defenses to attacker

Likelihood of attack

Figure 9.1 Threat actors based on likelihood of attack and ability to defend

Although some of these attackers leverage automated tools to infiltrate the organization and their skill level is not high—for example, the script kiddie—other, more sophisticated attackers will use a multitude of methods to compromise an organization. The more advanced the attacker, the more difficulty the organization will have in protecting against the attack. This is where a layered defense will support the organization in fending off most attacks. Although the organization will put the controls in place to protect against an attacker, the attacker will have their own methods they use in order to compromise the organization.

9.1.1   *MITRE ATT&CK*

Despite what Hollywood might tell us about how attackers compromise a system, the reality is far more mundane. An attacker is not likely to rappel into your data center, or your cloud service provider (CSP), bypass all your physical security, and slip a USB device into a server sitting on a rack. I'm not saying it is not possible; I'm just saying it is the least likely scenario. Honestly, the far more likely scenario is a hardcoded password or one that is written down or shared and leads an attacker to be able to compromise a system. Attackers will always look for the weakest link or the easiest way in.

MITRE has developed a framework for the various steps that an attacker takes to go from reconnaissance to exfiltration of an organization. This knowledge base is called the MITRE ATT&CK framework (https://attack.mitre.org/).

> **NOTE**   MITRE is a not-for-profit organization that focuses on research and development in support of US government agencies. For our purposes, just know that MITRE supports cybersecurity practices.

The ATT&CK framework covers a broad range of different techniques that an attacker can use, but by no means are the techniques intended to show a complete list or a map of what every attacker does. In other words, attackers will leverage some, all, or none of the techniques identified in the matrix when they are attacking an organization. However, one of the key benefits of the framework is its ability to assist in developing threat models and mitigation techniques that are specific to the way that attackers behave.

RECONNAISSANCE

The basic ATT&CK framework starts with reconnaissance where the attacker is able to gather information by scanning and searching through public information that might be available about the target person or organization. From the application security perspective, the application will want to reduce information that can be made available about the organization or application by reducing the exposure of their source code or documentation where available. The organization should also ensure that any web server does not provide any information above what is necessary in their HTTP headers (e.g., Server, X-Powered-By, and X-AspNet-Version) and that all non-used ports are closed.

RESOURCE, ACCESS, AND EXECUTION

The attacker will then pivot to gathering hardware and cloud resources to perform their attack, gaining access and executing scripts where practical. This can be accomplished through weaknesses in the infrastructure and hosts that are running, including web, application, and database servers. Once the attacker has gained access to these resources, they will attempt to deploy their tools and scripts to further compromise or gain additional access to other resources. The primary entry point here is through the network where the attacker can land on a host that doesn't have the appropriate security controls on, such as least privilege access, closed ports, and ensuring that software is patched and up-to-date. Additionally, the organization should monitor for indicators of compromise through logging and monitoring controls.

PERSISTENCE, ESCALATION, AND EVASION

If the attacker is able to gain a foothold on a host, they will then look to ensure that they have persistence on the machine. They can do this through creating new accounts, hiding their activity, setting up tasks and jobs, and modifying the system. They will then look to escalate their privileges by trying to gain access to administrative accounts or system accounts in order to be able to perform more extensive persistence. They will also use this to evade defensive techniques that the organization may have in place by modifying processes and workflows, like authentication workflows. Where possible, they will modify the system and the tools used to monitor and block their activity. Again, the organization will want to focus on ensuring that their defenses include secure configuration on their hosts, servers, and network appliances, as well as having the appropriate logging and monitoring in place to detect malicious activity. Hashing is also a key capability that can be used to ensure that files are not tampered with—especially log files since many attackers will look to hide their activity.

CREDENTIAL ACCESS AND DISCOVERY

Part of the escalation of privilege will be attempts to gain access to credentials or account access by impersonating another account. Once the attacker is able to gather credentials, they will enter a discovery phase where they attempt to locate services and information across the organization's systems. If they are able to do this without setting off alerts, they can gather a fair amount of information.

> **NOTE**   Think about the accounts you use on your database servers or web servers, and imagine that account being in the wrong hands. What can that attacker do?

LATERAL MOVEMENT AND COLLECTION

The attacker then will look to move laterally across the network or organization. This means that they will find other openings in the organization through phishing attempts or using tools to take over sessions or remote services. This allows them to move from a less juicy target to one that has more potential for additional compromise. The attacker will use the machines that they were able to compromise to begin to siphon data from them or the network. It's possible that the attacker will look for data on the machine itself that they might be able to steal, as well as on some of the machines that may have access to the network traffic in which they can sniff and potentially grab more data.

COMMAND AND CONTROL AND EXFILTRATION

Having all this data is useless unless the attacker knows how to get it out of the network. This is where command and control (C2) and exfiltration come in. The attacker will attempt to look for ways to get the data out of the network through obfuscation and encryption where the tools on the network may not be able to determine what is being removed from the network. Attackers are also patient and know that certain activity will raise alarms, like the sudden and massive movement of large datasets from the network. They will attempt to hide any exfiltration data by staying below network throughput thresholds so as not to raise any alarms and moving data between different servers to further obfuscate their activity.

LATERAL MOVEMENT, COLLECTION

In the last phase, the attacker attempts to disrupt the system through destructive methods such as data wiping, destruction, or encrypting; account access removal; or corruption. The goal of the attacker is to interrupt the availability or create an integrity compromise.

Most pieces here in the ATT&CK matrix (figure 9.2) are mitigated through vigilance, tooling that is special purpose built to look for these issues, and a strong team of defenders. However, the applications built by the organization have to take some responsibility as well. Leaving vulnerable code in an application open to an attacker is often too easy of a target to pass by. A simple set of unencrypted credentials in a configuration file, a private key hardcoded in source control, of a default password on a web server are all means of entry for an attacker who might already be on your network.

MITRE ATT&CK matrix

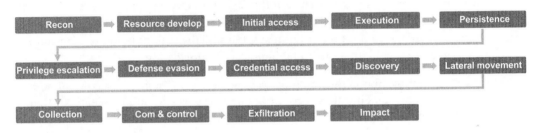

Figure 9.2   MITRE ATT&CK matrix

9.1.2   *Cyber Kill Chain*

Similar to the MITRE ATT&CK matrix, the Cyber Kill Chain framework (http://mng .bz/aPdj) was developed by Lockheed Martin and was intended to provide a quick glance at the types of attackers and their process for compromising a system. The usual suspects exist as they did in the ATT&CK matrix. However, in the Cyber Kill Chain, there are several tactics, techniques, and procedures (TTP) that are highlighted to give the defender an idea of where an attacker may look to strike.

RECONNAISSANCE

The first step in the Cyber Kill Chain is reconnaissance, where the attacker will attempt to gather information on the organization, system, or network that they are attempting to compromise. This is often done through gathering public information on the organization, perhaps through online profiles on professional sites, through information spread at conferences, or just through basic searches online. However, the reconnaissance techniques can get more sophisticated by leveraging tools that can crawl the internet looking for openings in the target system. Shodan is a prime example of a reconnaissance tool used for this purpose.

WEAPONIZATION AND DELIVERY

Once the attacker has identified enough information regarding the target, they will begin to develop the exploit into a payload that can be delivered to the target.

> **DEFINITION** An *exploit* is a piece of code that takes advantage of a vulnerability. A *payload* is what delivers the exploit to the target.

The attacker may have to go through several iterations of obfuscation in order to evade any detection tools that are in place at the organization. Often, they will craft specific exploitation code that is custom to the organization in order to slip past the defenses. Next, the attacker is able to deliver the malicious payload with the exploit to the target. This can be through an email with a malicious attachment, USB device, social engineering, or using a weakness in an application to have a user at the organization redirected to an attacker-owned site that can then download malicious code. Given that systems today are more and more complex, the opportunity to slip a payload into the organization are many.

EXPLOITATION AND INSTALLATION

Once the exploit can get through the defenses and deliver the payload, the initial exploitation of the system is complete. This allows the attacker to install software to the system that will give the attacker the opportunity to further exploit the system, pivot to another machine, siphon data, interrupt processing, or simply monitor traffic and activity.

COMMAND AND CONTROL AND ACTIONS

The last steps are the command and control (C2) activity that gives the attacker the ability to send data to and from the attacker-controlled C2 servers. These servers act as a platform for the attacker to deliver additional commands during the compromise. Finally, the attacker will have remote access to the target system through these TTPs, where they will be able to perform their original goals for the compromise.

So, what does all this have to do with development security? Organizations have a reliance on perimeter tools to identify and uncover indicators of compromise (IoC) as they are seen in the network, and the developed application is the most exposed part of their operations. Consider an organization that creates SaaS products that are deployed to a CSP and accessed by their customers around the world. The most accessible part of the organization's offering is not the hardened infrastructure in the CSP; you could argue that the organization can misconfigure this and leave an opening, but the most likely scenario is an unresolved vulnerability in the application that is being exposed to the customers. It is therefore imperative that the organization understands how an attacker can leverage an exposed vulnerability in an application and use that to further compromise the organization. Understanding the TTP is one thing, but what about the specific types of vulnerabilities?

9.2 *Threat catalogs*

Threat catalogs are useful in identifying the various threats that can impact a system. The simple way to think about threat catalogs is that they are a method of identifying generic security threats. They can be specific to a type of architecture, or more broadly across technology. The OWASP Top Ten (https://owasp.org/Top10/) is considered a threat catalog, as it identifies the ten most prevalent security threats to web applications. OWASP also maintains several other top ten style lists related to mobile applications and APIs. MITRE maintains a catalog called the common weakness and enumeration (CWE). The MITRES's Top 25 is a listing of 25 software and hardware weaknesses that can lead to a system breach. OWASP has specific focuses like web and mobile applications, whereas the CWE is more broad-based so that it is more generic and can be applied to a broader range of systems regardless of how they are accessed.

> **NOTE** NIST SP 800-30 and ISO27005 also list threats in a catalog. These are used more broadly within information security and are not scoped specifically to technology as in the MITRE CWE and the OWASP Top Ten lists.

The goal of these threat catalogs is to provide a means to identify the various threats that can be found in the systems and the implementation of the systems. They are not meant to show what the only possible threats are, but instead are there to show some of the common and well-known threats that exist. Organizations can add and remove additional threats as they see fit or as the landscape changes for that organization, the technology they use, or industry they are in.

9.2.1   Applying the OWASP Top Ten

If you are running an application that is accessed over the internet, chances are you are exposed to the various issues that are found in the OWASP Top Ten web application security risks for 2021. Table 9.1 outlines the most prevalent security issues that impact a web application.

Table 9.1   OWASP Top Ten web application security risks for 2021

Risk	Description
Broken access control	Allows an attacker to circumvent authorization to access data and functionality that they otherwise would not be able to access.
Cryptographic failures	These are failures in the implementation and application of encryption and can include not applying encryption at all.
Injection	Injection attacks can be SQL injection, or others like cross-site scripting, command injection, and query injections.
Insecure design	Risks that are designed into the application can be dangerous, as they are difficult to unravel once the application is implemented.
Security misconfiguration	Misconfiguration happens when a configuration setting allows for an attacker to perform a compromise. A simple example of this is using a default password that is well known on a network reachable system.
Vulnerable and outdated components	Applications are multiple components combined to build the overall application. Each component can have their own vulnerabilities and weaknesses in them and requires strong patch management.

Table 9.1 OWASP Top Ten web application security risks for 2021 *(continued)*

Risk	Description
Identification and authentication failures	Failing to use strong authentication techniques provides an attacker an easier way to compromise a system that is not using standardized identify frameworks and federated identity management.
Software and data integrity failures	To work securely, the development pipeline needs to ensure that software has been tested for tampering. This is completed by doing integrity checks like verifying the hash of software it is using.
Security logging and monitoring failures	Logging and monitoring of critical events that can lead an organization to detect and respond to a security threat reduces their risk of a security event becoming much larger.
Server-side request forgery (SSRF)	SSRF occurs when an application does not validate the remote resource destination that it is being asked to fetch resources from. This can lead to an attacker redirecting the application to a malicious site.

USING THE TOP TEN TO CATEGORIZE VULNERABILITIES

The Top Ten web application risks can be applied in several ways. One of the primary methods of using the Top Ten is to categorize vulnerabilities that are found in penetration testing or scanning tools. Whether it's a penetration test or output from a scanning tool, the findings will leverage the OWASP Top Ten to describe the issue, provide guidance on how to prevent the issue, and describe methods of attack that can leverage the vulnerability as described in the sample report in figure 9.3. This helps with a common taxonomy for how to describe a vulnerability, which helps cut down on confusion and provides a reference point for more information.

Sample vulnerability report using OWASP top ten

Risky code: SQL injection

```
string strQuery = "SELECT * FROM users
                    WHERE username = '" + strUser + "'
                    AND password = '" + strPwd + "'";

ExecuteQuery( strQuery, db_connection );
```

Reason for the risk:
- Attackers can take advantage of the lack of input sanitization that allows for the attacker to send data that can influence the behavior of the application.

Remediation steps:
- Use parameterized queries and stored procedures that avoid concatenating stings to execute queries.

Potential attacks:
```
Input: - Adam'--

SELECT * FROM users WHERE username = 'Adam'--' AND password = ''
```

Figure 9.3 Sample scan report showing an SQL injection finding

USING THE TOP TEN FOR PENETRATION TESTING

Penetration testers use many tools and methods for testing, but they can also use the OWASP Top Ten as guidance into their activities. For example, a penetration tester may be tasked with testing the frontend UI of a web application. They can review the OWASP Top Ten as a starting point as they test the application looking for weaknesses. The guidance provided by the OWASP Top Ten can also help the tester create automated scripts or hone existing tools. Last, the tester can use the OWASP Top Ten as a reference when creating the output report with the results from their test. This additional information will help the receiver of the report understand what the risk is, how it can be leveraged, and more importantly, how it can be resolved.

USING THE TOP TEN TO DETERMINE TOOL EFFICACY

The OWASP Top Ten can be used to determine the efficacy of security scanning tools that you may be evaluating or running. When vendors are showcasing the capabilities of their tool—for instance, a SAST tool—they will often describe how the tool discovers vulnerabilities related to the Top Ten. It is often prudent to ask a vendor, if they don't offer this information up, whether they detect the OWASP Top Ten. However, this should never be the sole criteria for determining the effectiveness of a scanning tool.

USING THE TOP TEN TO CREATE REQUIREMENTS

The OWASP Top Ten can also be used in developing security requirements for developing software. This is helpful considering that security requirements are often not integrated early in the development life cycle due to the fact that security requirements are not written by the same team that writes the functional requirements. The security requirements are often written and managed by the application security team.

OWASP's APPLICATION SECURITY VERIFICATION STANDARD

OWASP maintains a project called the application security verification standard (ASVS), which is a list of statements that can guide a tester on how to verify the security of a web application. For instance, one of the statements is "Verify that a password strength meter is provided to help users set a stronger password." These verification statements use the OWASP Top Ten as well as the community of security practitioners that helped develop the ASVS (http://mng.bz/gRVe).

Something like the OWASP ASVS can help the application security team and engineering teams understand what requirements should be written to cover the security concerns for the application. However, the ASVS is written for the benefit of the tester of an application by using the term *verify* before every statement. Using this language means that in order to derive true requirements from it, the team will need to change the language from a testing statement to a functional requirement.

- *ASVS statement*—Verify that a system generated initial activation or recovery secret is not sent in clear text to the user.
- *Security requirement*—When the system generates an initial activation of a user, it will not send recovery secrets in clear text.

This is a simple transformation of the testing statement to a requirement. Each organization will have a separate approach, terminology, and structure to how their requirements are written. However, this approach cuts down on a lot of the guesswork for requirements writing and provides a listing of security guidance that is backed by a community of security professionals through OWASP.

Last, the OWASP Top Ten can and should be used to determine the threats while performing review activity. This can be achieved either formally or informally. An informal approach would be to keep the OWASP Top Ten close by as reference while reviewing a design or code review and then simply asking whether the design or code has protections against broken access controls, cryptographic failures, injection attacks, and so on, through all ten vulnerabilities in the list. In a more formal manner, the organization may take the approach of having a checklist and required proof that the design or code is free from the vulnerabilities in the Top Ten. The proof could be a clean scan report from a security scanning tool or a penetration test that was completed that shows the lack of vulnerabilities.

9.2.2 Applying the MITRE CWE Top 25

Similar to the OWASP Top Ten risks, MITRE created a threat catalog called the common weakness and enumeration (CWE) Top 25. As I stated previously, this list goes beyond the OWASP list of just web application vulnerabilities and extends to a broader category of vulnerabilities that impact an overall system. It may seem like some of these are out of scope in the application security space; your application runs on a system that could be exposed to these vulnerabilities, and in some cases, your application may be the window into those systems. For example, an injection vulnerability in your application that allows an attacker to attempt a remote code execution could imperil the system or provide the attacker an opportunity to pivot to another system with additional weaknesses. Inversely, a weakness in a system could lead an attacker to compromise or change data that is used by your application. For example, think of a case where the database has a vulnerability that allows an attacker to have privileges to alter the data in the database or take it offline. This would have a huge impact on the application that depends on that data. The CWE Top 25 (http://mng.bz/epD9) is in order of prevalence and severity. Some examples from the Top 25 are

- *Improper input validation*—The application receives data from a user that does not go through proper validation and sanitization, allowing for an attacker to influence the behavior of the application.
- *Cross-site request forgery*—The attacker is able to get the server to make an unintentional request to a resource due to the lack of validation of the request.
- *Exposure of sensitive information to an unauthorized actor*—The exposure of sensitive information to an actor that does not have permission to view the information.

Similar to the OWASP Top Ten, this catalog of the most prevalent security issues found in software can be used to measure the effectiveness of the software security tools that are being used in the organization. Most security tools will provide a corresponding

CWE number associated with its finding, which will provide more information on what the issue is and how to resolve it. The Top 25 can also be used when reviewing code, design, or architecture by looking for the weaknesses during the review.

As an example, we can look to Superior Products where Dashing Danielle has been asked to review code in the Stuff-For-You application. The developer created a new integration with a third party that requires the exchange of XML through an authenticated web service. Dashing Danielle sits with the developer to review the code and ensure that proper security is in place. She focuses her attention on several of the MITRE Top 25 issues that would be relevant in this case, namely the ones associated with XML, credentials, authentication, and authorization. With these in mind, Dashing Danielle asks to see how the XML is being parsed and realizes that there are no checks being done to ensure that the application does not access files on the web server that are not supposed to be exposed. She suggests that the developer add an allowlist for the only files and locations that should be accessed by the XML parsing function when it processes XML input from the third party.

The MITRE Top 25 can also be used as guidance in penetration testing and other manual security tests where the tester can use the list to identify weaknesses that they should be looking for. In this effort, MITRE provides information for each CWE they list that contains examples of how to exploit the weakness, and detailed technical information on mitigations throughout various stages of the development life cycle. A tester, whether doing a penetration test or informally testing the application, can use this information to guide their activity and build test cases to evaluate whether the application is exposed to a given weakness.

Other threat catalogs exist, and new ones are being developed with the intention of providing organizations the ability to focus on a small set of high-impact weaknesses and vulnerabilities. They are not meant to be a complete list. As in the case of the MITRE CWE, there are many more CWEs associated with system weaknesses. Additionally, the OWASP top risks are not the only ones that can impact a web application. However, these short lists can help the organization prioritize their efforts to remediate. More importantly, the information that is available in these catalogs can enable the developers and architects creating new features to build security into the product early in the life cycle.

9.3   *Staying ahead of engineering*

One of the biggest challenges that the application security team, or any security team, has is staying in front of the engineering organization and their desire to move fast with new technologies. Often the technology being pursued can be bleeding edge with little to no supporting documentation or empirical evidence of its effectiveness. However, the desire to find something that fits a need and leverage it as quickly as practical are the hallmarks of a fast-moving engineering team. Throughout this book I have covered the ways that development teams move rapidly to deliver value to their customers. Whether through the Agile methodology or by using a continuous integration/continuous deployment (CI/CD) pipeline, the development team can deploy software multiple times a week, a day, or an hour. With this rapid development and deployment, the application security team often finds itself overstretched and outmatched.

9.3.1 *Keeping up with the coding languages*

This has implications for any team that wants to ensure that security is built into the development process and life cycle. The challenges arise when the application security team falls behind in terms of the skills that are being used by the development teams. This can relate to the coding languages being used or the deployment technology that is leveraged to deploy software to an environment.

> **NOTE** Although the numbers vary widely, there are hundreds of programing languages in existence today. There are a small number, comparatively, that make up the widest share of usage, but the opportunity still exists for nonstandard languages to be used in an organization. This can put the application security team on their heels if the organization does not require standardization on languages used.

The application security team, when it does have staff with experience in software engineering, can find that the experience is outdated with some of the newer software development languages that exist. You can refer to chapter 5 on the makeup of an application security team, including how staff with development experience fit into the team. This may not seem like a big deal, considering that the application security team is often not expected to write code or develop software. However, there are two issues here. One is the fact that the application security team will lose some of its authority when performing code reviews. Without working knowledge of the language, it becomes more difficult to identify issues in the code that could become security vulnerabilities. Second, when making recommendations on remediation or when interpreting results from scans or penetration tests, the application security team will want to provide examples in the language that is being used. Ideally, the example will be specific to the actual application to leave as little room for interpretation as possible.

So how does the application security team stay ahead of this? The short answer is through training. As I mentioned, the application security team members do not need to develop software, but simply staying up-to-date with the coding languages that are being used in the organization, attending training, and upskilling where necessary. The application security team should also look to hire new staff with the desired skills. Where the current staff can train to learn new skills, hiring a new employee with the skills you are looking for is a way to shortcut that skill gap. Of course, this depends on your team's ability to hire truly qualified people.

9.3.2 *Keeping up with the technology changes*

Keeping up with the software languages is often not enough. There is also the potential skill and tool gaps when a given technology decision is made in engineering without the consultation of the security organization. This can occur with regard to things as simple as the source code management (SCM) tool that is used to manage the source code, the integration tool used to build the software and integrate testing tasks, or the deployment technology and tools used to deploy to the running environments.

The primary concern with these technology choices is that the security tools owned and operated by the security organization may not integrate well or may need additional work to integrate with. In some cases, it may just require a change in the connector technology between the security tool and engineering tool. As an example, the organization may be looking to adopt a new SCM tool. The application security team will need to review their current tool chain that they use in the development life cycle and understand the effort required to integrate with the new SCM. In most cases, this particular example would only impact the SAST, the IaC scanner, and the SCA tools, as these tools scan code in a nonrunning state and integrate well with SCMs.

An additional concern is with the security tool's ability to work with particular technology stacks and languages. This is more evident with tools like SAST where, in order to perform the scan of code in a nonrunning state, the SAST tool needs to have the ability to understand the language and the patterns of that language. This will often limit the SAST tool's ability to scan many languages and instead focus on a subset of a handful of languages. With this limitation, the application security team can find itself with a SAST tool that is not capable of scanning a language that is brought into the organization. This is not limited to just scanning tools. Containerized or virtualized technologies can often make it difficult to operate agents with the appropriate visibility into the running application. This limitation means that security tools that require agents to be installed may not work in a container or virtual machine. This can force the application security team to review other options for tools that exist that may offer that support or look for other compensating controls.

Last, the technology being chosen could be beyond the expertise of the application security team, which reduces their ability to provide oversight and guidance to the engineering organization. Nothing made this more evident than the move to cloud by many organizations. Most application security folks prior to the great cloud migration were focused on protecting software that was operated in the organization's own data center. The migration to cloud brought on an additional level of complexity, where the engineering teams could now select services from the CSP and have code running in minutes with worldwide access. This is pretty freeing for engineering teams, but extremely frightening for the security folks who need to attempt to provide protection. This means that application security teams have to suddenly become well versed in cloud or leverage the knowledge of their counterparts in engineering to help solve security problems.

Once again, training and hiring for the needed skill set can help close the gaps when it comes to missing technology expertise. However, the application security team should get their hands dirty on the technology as well. This can be done by being tightly coupled with the engineering teams during proof of concept (POC), where the application security team has the chance to raise questions and concerns in order to have them addressed. They will also have the opportunity to kick the tires on the product to give them a better understanding of how it works and how it can integrate with their current tools.

9.3.3   *When hiring and training aren't enough*

Budgets can bring into reality the limitations that an organization has when it comes to addressing skill sets. Many organizations cannot simply go out and hire staff with the proper skill set or send their staff to training in order to learn new skills. As with most things in application security, the team will have to get creative with their approach in addressing the technology gaps between application security and the engineering organization.

The application security team has several options for addressing this gap, and one of the easiest ways is to ensure that they are part of the technical conversations, planning sessions, and roadmap building. Being a part of these forums allows the application security team to be present to not only represent the security interests of the organization, but to also learn from the engineering organization about changes and upcoming technology decisions as they are being made. Knowing what the engineering organization is working on, what their goals are, and what their strategy is goes a long way in developing ways to integrate security.

BUILDING A PARTNERSHIP WITH THE ENGINEERING ORGANIZATION

An approach to advance this partnership is to ensure that application security has built and maintains relationships with their counterparts and decision makers in the engineering organization. I've found that doing something as simple as sharing the application security roadmap with the CTO or business leaders helps foster an exchange of ideas and opens up the opportunity for the application security team to solicit feedback on their direction. It also becomes easier for the application security team to request technology and business roadmaps from their counterparts to better understand where the organization is heading. Some things that the application security team will want to look out for in these roadmaps include the following:

- New products being presented by the business that will need SDLC security integration.
- New approaches or technologies that alter the way that software is developed or deployed to an environment.
- Consolidation of products by the business, which can mean efficiencies but also the carryover of technical debt and legacy code.
- Sunsetting of products and the timeline for the decommission. This often means that the product could be neglected and lead to security vulnerabilities not being resolved.

Understanding these data points will help the application security team align their plans, tools, processes, and roadmaps to the organization's own path forward.

INTERCHANGEABLE TOOLS

Another method of addressing the skills and tools gap is by ensuring that the tools, processes, and technologies are as fungible as possible.

DEFINITION   The term *fungible* gets used a lot in engineering, usually in reference to staff and the ability to swap engineers in and out of projects because of their skill set. However, tools can also be fungible if they are loosely coupled with the processes and technology in the organization. This allows the organization to avoid vendor lock-in and move to a different vendor should their initial vendor not meet expectations.

A prime example of how having a fungible tool set can help the organization address staying ahead of engineering is when running a run-time protection tool like a WAF. There are various deployment models for a WAF, namely on premises and cloud. In a cloud deployment, the organization can more easily swap vendors or choose a multivendor approach that ensures that you have the ability to move from one vendor to another in the event that pricing becomes a point of contention, or even if technical limitations with one vendor become a factor. However, in general, it is good security practice to remove a single point of failure, in this case a vendor, and be able to move from one vendor to another. There is, of course, switching costs that can be incurred every time you move vendors, as well as the loss of potential bulk savings when using a single vendor. This cost needs to be balanced with the overall strategy and the need for diversity in tools and the ability to scale and leverage different technologies when trying to meet the goals of the engineering organization.

The last point I'll make on staying ahead of engineering is to find ways to pair up with the people who do actually know what they're doing and are working in the newer technology that the application security team needs to upskill in. There is a concept called *paired programming* that is sometimes used in software development teams. The purpose of paired programming is to have two developers working together in a single development environment to develop a solution or a feature. Similarly, it would not be out of place for the application security engineers to take opportunities to sit with a developer who is working with a new technology that the application security team has interest in so that they might learn more about the technology and potentially get a hands-on demonstration of how it works.

9.4   *Stop chasing the shiny new tool*

Don't get me wrong, there are a lot of great tools out there to solve a lot of security issues that face an organization. There are tools to uncover vulnerabilities, block them, and auto-remediate them, and don't forget about the artificial intelligence, machine learning, and blockchain. Needless to say, there is a time and place for tools to be used to address a given use case, but some teams tend to look for tools to solve every problem where there might be a simpler solution.

Bringing in another tool can lead to overlap of functionality and the organization paying for more than it needs. This occurs more frequently when someone in the organization discovers a tool that suits a particular need without regard for the current tools available, or without a plan to unravel one tool in favor of another, which can lead to redundancy. For example, the organization may determine that it has a gap in data classification, which is used to input into a data encryption process that encrypts data based on the classification level of the data. The application security team may solicit a request for proposals that can help the team compare capabilities between multiple vendors. A proof of concept may ensue, and eventually a purchase may be made for a particular tool that provides data classification. Several months after the tool is in operation, it may be brought to the application security team's attention that there already exists capabilities to meet the need in another tool that has been in operation in the organization. How does the application security team handle this?

9.4.1 Use a capability matrix

One approach to identifying the abilities of your tools is to build a simple capability matrix. This requires a firm understanding of the tools that the team has, and what their purpose is. From here, the team can identify the capabilities that it is looking to address as well as what capabilities the tools actually have. A capability matrix can be as simple or as complex as the team needs it to be. One of the primary purposes of a capability matrix is to highlight what the tools can do so that information is readily available when evaluating new tools.

When creating your capability matrix, start with the tool inventory that exists in the team. For the application security team, in order to keep it simple, I'll use the standard scanning tools that I've used throughout the book. Once the tool inventory has been created, the team will want to build out what capabilities those tools have. This does not have to be a complete or exhaustive list, as it is a living document that should be updated as the toolset changes and needs change.

Figure 9.4 is a simple matrix that helps identify the various capabilities that exist in the toolset that the application security team has. It is then used to understand what tools can provide what coverage in the SDLC or the overall defense-in-depth of the software.

Simple application security capability matrix

Tool	Run-time protection	Uncover OWASP Top Ten risks	Jira ticketing integration	Requires an agent installation	Source code management integration	OSS scanning	SaaS/On-prem
Static application security testing		X	X		X		On-prem
Dynamic application security testing		X		X		X	On-prem
Software composition analysis		X	X		X	X	SaaS
Interactive application security testing	X	X		X			On-prem

Figure 9.4 Capability matrix with application security tools

A similar matrix should be used when comparing the capabilities of a given type of tool. For example, the team may be looking to replace a current scanning tool like the SAST tool or may be evaluating new tools to meet a particular need. In this case, the application security team will want to create a capability matrix that is more granular to the specific tool. Here, the matrix can be used to measure the different SAST tools that are being used or evaluated in the organization. Again, it is important to build out the capabilities based on what is important to the organization. In figure 9.5, some of the tools may be specific to one organization while others may be more concerned with different tools or capabilities. Once the organization's key capabilities are identified, it is easier to evaluate new tools and determine whether they meet the needs of the organization.

Static application security testing capability matrix

Tool	Integration with Visual Studio	Integration with Eclipse	Integration with Jira	Integration with GitHub	Custom rule creation	Support for in-house languages
SAST-Tool1	X	X	X		X	X
SAST-Tool2	X		X	X		X
SAST-Tool3		X	X		X	
SAST-Tool4	X	X	X	X		X

Figure 9.5   SAST capability matrix

9.4.2   *Managing the tool and vendor*

Once a decision has been made on a tool or even if the organization already has a tool in place, it's important to continuously evaluate the effectiveness of the tool and vendor. It's not uncommon for an organization to be surprised by a feature that exists in a tool that they already have in-house because there was no awareness or communication regarding the feature. Most vendors will keep regular meetings and conversations with the team that operates the tool and ensure that the team is kept up-to-date with changes in capabilities and features as well as support in the usage of those features.

Regardless of the frequency of the conversations with the vendor, it is critical for the application security team to ensure that they ask to see the roadmap for the tools that they have in-house. This will often lead to an update of the capability matrix as the roadmap evolves. For instance, it is not uncommon for a SAST tool to address customer requests for additional language support. Let's say that the SAST tool in the organization currently supports Java and .NET for scanning of source code; however, the organization has an abundance of PHP code that the vendor currently does not support and therefore leaves a blind spot in the organization. Simply asking for the roadmap for the next several months or quarters may keep the organization from making a decision to move off of the vendor and potentially incur switching costs or loss of productivity.

NOTE The vendor will often move more rapidly on customer requests when they hear those requests from more than one customer. Additionally, the vendor will often weight their roadmap in favor of the larger accounts. If you're lucky enough to be a big spender with a vendor, then you are likely to be able to get them to move more rapidly on your requests for additional features.

The last point I'll make is that the team will want to continuously monitor the effectiveness of the tools they are using to ensure they are getting the value out of it. In chapter 8, I talked about how to measure the effectiveness of the tools you have. With this information, the application security team will want to ensure that it is constantly evaluating this effectiveness and providing that feedback to the vendor. The vendor has every desire to see their tool succeed in your environment, and they will do what they need to do to ensure you have a good experience.

Whether you use a capability matrix or work closely with your vendor to ensure you are getting the most out of your tool, the organization wants to ensure that it is looking at tools with all the information it has available. This means that they are well informed about the current capabilities of their tools and that they are getting the most out of them. There is a saying that I have heard many times: "Don't go to the grocery store on an empty stomach." The reason is that you are likely to buy or spend more because you are hungry. I don't want to reduce making a large purchase with multiyear implications to be as simple as going to the grocery store, but the analogy is similar. Don't make a purchase without all the information. This leads to chasing the shiny new tool. However, there are times that you'll go to the grocery store on a full stomach and know that you still need to buy milk.

9.4.3 Buy the shiny new tool

You have done your due diligence, you have worked with the vendor to get their roadmaps and current features, you have built out your capability matrix both for what the application security team should be doing and for the tools they use to do it, and still you know that there is a gap in the organization when it comes to protecting the software. One example of this is that in many organizations, run-time security of their software is somewhat new—especially in the context of application security. As a function, application security has largely spent its time focusing on code scanning, penetration testing, and finding vulnerabilities early and often. This is the shift-left approach to application security.

Shifting to the right means that more effort is being placed later in the SDLC. Specifically, run-time tools like WAF and RASP are gaining traction. Although each of these has been around for quite some time, many organizations are just now beginning to operate them or are in the early stages of integration. This is where an organization has a greenfield for finding a tool to fit an open need.

However, it is still critical for the organization to ensure that the tool they purchase will fulfill the need of the capability they are attempting to accomplish. This should be done by leveraging the capability matrixes mentioned previously, by running a successful proof of concept and proof of value, and by successfully adopting and integrating the tool. One word of caution is that the organizations will often underestimate the integration of security tools. The uniqueness of security tools is the fact that they are often needed to work with many different engineering teams with varying processes and technologies. A good example of this is with something like an interactive application security testing (IAST) tool. These tools depend on being integrated with the code and the testing suite that is being used by the engineering team. This can vary by teams within the organization, creating a snowflake integration where each team is unique enough that it is difficult to have a standard approach to adoption. Although this is a simple caution, there will always be a need to close a gap in the defense of the organization, and often those gaps need to be filled by a tool. The last thing the organization wants is to have a gap in the defenses that leads to a breach.

9.5   *Preparing for the worst*

Despite their best efforts, organizations still get breached. Granted, it's not always due to an issue in an application that is developed by the organization, but the application security team will more often than not still need to play a role in any attack or breach that may occur. This is primarily due to the fact that applications need to run on systems that comprise hardware, software, and third-party tools and that have network dependencies. At any time, attackers can compromise not only the application, but also any of the components that the application runs on.

Figure 9.6 shows some of the components that create the ecosystem around a developed application in an organization. This is not a complete list and depends on the architecture and technology stack of the given application. Figure 9.6 assumes a data center deployment, as opposed to a cloud-style deployment where the technology stack and the various services used will be different. However, it is imperative that the organization has identified the assets, tools, technologies, and services used in the development and operation of their application.

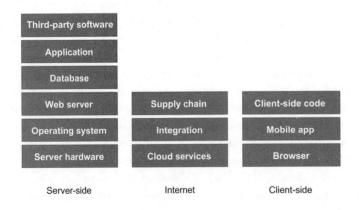

Application technology stack

Server-side	Internet	Client-side
Third-party software		
Application		
Database		
Web server	Supply chain	Client-side code
Operating system	Integration	Mobile app
Server hardware	Cloud services	Browser

Figure 9.6   Application technology components

DEFINITION *Asset management* is a term that is used in technology that defines the process around managing the assets within the organization. An *asset* is anything that the organization deems to have value. This can be hardware, software, data, and even people. Often this listing of assets is stored in a database for easier management.

During the case of a potential cyberattack, the first thing that any organization will ask is: "What is our exposure?" Having a solid asset management strategy is the first step in answering that question. However, it goes beyond simply knowing what the organization has and extends into knowing what versions are being used and ownership of assets. Often when a new vulnerability is released that impacts a given library or component, there will be a series of versions that are impacted and ones that are not. Additionally, each version may have different mitigations and remediation techniques that can be leveraged in order to remove the vulnerability. For instance, in the Log4j vulnerability in late 2021 and early 2022, multiple versions were impacted; however, there were several recommendations on how to resolve the issue, depending on version, due to the usage of certain functions in the code. Many organizations were using more than one version, leading to confusion on how best to approach the remediation when a simple upgrade wouldn't work due to technical or customer constraints. Table 9.2 shows CISA's recommendations (www.cisa.gov/uscert/ncas/alerts/aa21-356a) on mitigation and remediation of the Log4j CVEs that were collectively known as *Log4Shell*.

Table 9.2 Log4shell mitigation and remediation recommendations from CISA

Version	Mitigation/remediation
Log4j versions 2.12.1 and 2.13.0 through 2.15.0	Upgrade to version 2.16.0
Java 8 or later	Upgrade to version 2.17.0
Java 7	Upgrade to version 2.12.3
Log4j versions 2.17.0 and below	Remove jdnilookup.class

As you can see, it quickly became complex to know what versions were impacted by what, and how to provide the remediation and mitigations recommended. In many cases, a simple upgrade to the latest version was not practical. Customers may have to update their own internal code if there was integration with your software where the upgrade to the latest version would be a breaking change. Add in the fact that information was flowing fast, and it was sometimes hard to know what was the right mitigation at the time. This is where robust asset management becomes critical. This enables the application's technical and business owners to act on relevant information to track the issue to closure.

Regardless of the asset management strategy at the organization, another critical tool to respond to a security event is the ability to contact the right people. One of my mentors when I was getting into security told me that you always want to know who to call when things go sideways. This is not unique to security, since many of us who work in technology know that when you want something done it's better to call Jill or Bob because they can get it done quickly. It's the type of thing that makes managers cringe and angry, but it's the reality of working in technology.

However, this is the type of line of communication that is often needed in time-sensitive events like a production outage or a security event. In some cases, it can be an all-hands-on-deck event that requires staff from multiple disciplines and teams to attempt to bring the event to a resolution. And knowing who to contact and how to get them to engage in the event can be the difference between a well-contained security event and a breach.

The last point I'll make on preparing for the worst is the need for the security tools that you have in place to aid in the occasion of an ongoing security event. Yes, these tools are good at uncovering security vulnerabilities that can then be sent to engineering to resolve. However, these same tools can be used to identify exposure, test for vulnerability, and validate fixes that are deployed, as shown in figure 9.7. When asset management tools are not available, the application security tools can be used to detect exposure. For instance, if a new CVE is released that shows a popular library used in your organization is now vulnerable to a critical flaw, the application security team can review the tools they have at their disposal to identify the exposure and use of the library. They can then use their testing tools, whether automated or penetration testing tools, to identify whether the vulnerability can truly be exploited. If so, they can then use these same tools to identify whether a patch that has been applied is effective at resolving the issues. Additionally, the application security team, if they are operating the run-time protection tools like a WAF or RASP, can use these tools to create rules,

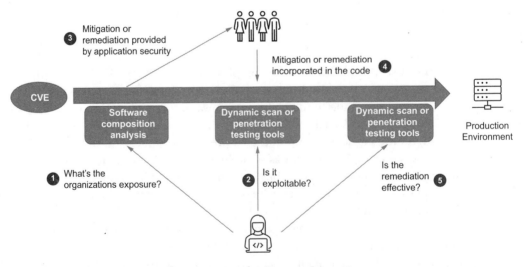

Figure 9.7   How application security tools participate in a security event

assuming the vendor has not already created and released ones, to block attacks that attempt to leverage the vulnerability.

The organization can always apply more defenses, or more tools for detection and alerting, but the hard truth is that all organizations will be breached at some point. Some may have been breached today and don't even know it. As a security industry, we are moving away from the idea that stopping attackers is the best approach to cybersecurity, and instead we're moving to the concept of detect and respond. This allows the organization to be resilient to attacks as they happen and have the tools, processes, and people in place to respond accordingly. Consider the way that organizations prepare for production issues. We know that we can't stop production issues from happening; we can only change the way we respond. I hope this book has shown how you and your organization can respond to software vulnerabilities throughout the development process and that you are more prepared to take on that challenge.

Summary

- Using matrices such as MITRE ATT&CK and Cyber Kill Chain provides a glimpse into how attackers leverage simple openings in a system or software in order to compromise an organization and lead to a breach.
- Threat catalogs are a primary method of measuring the efficacy of a tool and a way to have a common language around known weaknesses and vulnerabilities in software.
- Threat catalogs can be used as guidance for quality assurance testers and penetration testers to provide them steps to take to review the security of software.
- Engineering teams move quickly, and it is often difficult for the application security team to stay ahead of them. It is important for the application security team to maintain their skills through training and work closely with the engineering teams they partner with.
- Tools are used broadly throughout the organization and the application security team. However, the application security team needs to be sure that the tools they are implementing provide the value they are expecting. More importantly, the application security team needs to avoid redundancy in their toolset.
- Organizations can only do so much to keep attackers out. It is critical for them to know how best to respond to a cybersecurity event when it occurs. This can be done through processes, tools, and clear lines of communication to the engineering organization and peers in order to respond rapidly and contain a cybersecurity event.

appendix
Answers to exercises

Chapter 1

EXERCISE 1.1

Using APIsecurity.io (https://apisecurity.io/tools/audit/) to perform a security audit on OpenAPI JSON files. This tool will identify relevant information in your JSON file as it pertains to code quality and security. Using the Microsoft's Visual Code (https://code.visualstudio.com/) plug-in, you will find the identified security items when they exist in the JSON file in the OpenAPI section in the left hand column.

Follow the instructions to identify security issues that may exist in a JSON file used for OpenAPI: http://mng.bz/WMO4.

EXERCISE 1.2

You have three options here with the Touchpoints. The first is the Architecture Analysis, which requires security expertise to be integrated at the design time in order to identify risks and provide remediation. This is a similar case with the Code Review Touchpoint, where the security team will be required to identify and provide guidance on insecure code that is discovered. In most organizations, the most appropriate approach is to leverage scanning tools to test applications and provide the reports back to the development team so that they may resolve the identified issues. Although this requires some cost to implement, there are many free tools that can be used to identify security issues. OWASP offers an open source dynamic security testing tool called ZAP and a source code analysis tool called Dependency Track. Additionally, Defect Dojo can be used to coordinate the findings in each of these tools. For many less mature organizations, the Security Testing Touchpoint makes the most amount of sense.

EXERCISE 1.3

Take a look at a recent story: https://threatpost.com/menswear-zegna-ransomware/179266/. In this case, a popular clothing brand, Zegna, was a victim of a ransomware attack in August 2021 by the RansomExx operation. Zegna claimed to have restored their systems through the backups and cloud providers that they use and resisted the pressure to pay the ransom.

Although it is often not shared how the attackers were able to get into the system, once identified, Zegna used an external third party to assist in the forensic activity to remove the ransomware, ensure that the attackers were not able to regain access, and restored their systems. Although these attacks are difficult to fend off, it's important for the organization to have the means to identify attacks, respond to them, and if needed pull in a third party to assist with the recover. As most security people will tell you, it is never wise to pay the ransom.

Chapter 2

EXERCISE 2.1

Often, we collect data from end users with the expectation that the data will be used now or in the future. However, when we collect sensitive information like a social security number or other personally identifiable information, it can put the organization and the end user at unnecessary risk. When the organization collects this information, it can make them an unnecessary target for attackers or expose them to additional costs in the case of a data breach. When sensitive information like this is exposed, the organization often has to spend additional money to supply the affected users with some type of monitoring service. Often the easiest thing to ask is, "Should this information be collected, and is there value to the business or application?" If there is no immediate need for the data, it's a good idea to pass on collecting it. Future potential use is not a good enough reason to collect it today.

EXERCISE 2.2

The OWASP Risk Rating Methodology provides the ability to walk through the factors that are associated with a particular risk. There are a few methods of walking through the risks. One of the easiest ways is through the online tool at www.owasp-risk-rating.com/. With this tool, it is simpler to quickly identify a basic risk calculation that takes into account the likelihood and impact of a given risk. As an example, we can take the risk of a remote code execution on a clinical application in a hospital. This is pretty vague, but for this exercise, we can use our imagination to fill in the blanks.

First, we need to find the likelihood factors that relate to the threat agent and vulnerability details. Taking the threat agent first, we can assume that a higher skill level would be required to craft an exploit. This assumes that there is not a publicly available exploit already existing. With motive, and opportunity, this would need research on the actual attackers who would want to take advantage of this vulnerability. Assume that the attacker would want to extort a hospital for payment, so the threat actor would be a cybercriminal. This means that the size would be smaller but not nonexistent, and their motive would be to receive some monetary value. Lastly, the opportunity really depends on the exploit itself and whether there are any compensating controls in place to limit its exposure.

Let's move to the vulnerability factors. The discovery, exploit, and awareness really depend on the specifics of the vulnerability, but we can assume that public and automated tools exist to discover this. We can also assume this because once a vulnerability is public, automation for discovery quickly follows. However, likewise, so long as the organization has good security tooling in their defenses, detection signatures will be added, which helps the organization identify attackers looking to exploit the vulnerability. Based on this, the likelihood comes out to a medium.

Lastly, we need to understand the impact of this risk, which focuses on the technical impact as it relates to the confidentiality, integrity, availability, and accountability of the impact. In this case, the hospital is concerned mostly about the confidentiality and availability of the system and data. A remote code execution will certainly put the confidentiality of data at risk, assuming that the code execution leads to excessive access to the system and underlying data. The system could also be brought down with the intention of forcing the hospital to pay to restore services. These are the technical impacts, but there are also business impacts. These focus more on the financial implications that might lead to lawsuits or other possible violations. In this case, the hospital has to consider any HIPAA violations that may occur, as well as financial damage as it relates to lost revenue or reputational damage. With these factors in consideration, we can find that this is a medium-impact risk.

Although what was described is one example, there are a multitude of different ways to think about the risks that are posed to an organization when a vulnerability in their system or application is found. Even this particular one, a remote code execution, can vary, depending on the application, controls, and specifics.

Chapter 3

EXERCISE 3.1

Once you download and install either Microsoft Threat Model (http://mng.bz/82zZ) or Threat Dragon by OWASP (https://owasp.org/www-project-threat-dragon/), create a basic drawing that depicts a workflow with a browser and a web server with an interaction between the two. Using this simple stencil, the tool will identify several possible threats. One will be spoofing of the browser or user as it accesses the web server. This means that the session the user has while accessing the web server may be hijacked by an attacker to spoof the user. To protect against spoofing, a robust authentication mechanism needs to be in place to ensure that the web server can properly identify the user. Depending on the criticality of the application, this might mean adding multifactor authentication to ensure sensitive workflows are protected.

EXERCISE 3.2

Take a CVE from the NVD (https://nvd.nist.gov/vuln/full-listing) and use it as an example for this exercise. One option is https://nvd.nist.gov/vuln/detail/CVE-2022-0939. Get familiar with the details of it and what the CVSS score is. In most organizations, the CVSS score is only used as an indication of severity, but once a review is completed on the vulnerability, that score may change internally within the organization. This often occurs because the CVSS score does not take into account the compensating controls that the organization may have. Looking at the CVE I mentioned above, it is a server-side request forgery (SSRF) in GitHub, and the CVSS score is rated as 9.9. However, using the CVSS calculator (www.first.org/cvss/calculator/3.0), the score may be altered based on the organization's internal compensating controls. Perhaps the organization is only just beginning to utilize GitHub, and as of now, they do not host any repositories with code while they complete a proof of concept. Therefore, there is no threat to the organization's code. Other organizations may have far greater exposure to this vulnerability and will keep the 9.9 CVSS score in order to drive other mitigations to reduce the threat.

EXERCISE 3.3

You can find a sample job description here for a penetration tester: http://mng.bz/E01o.

EXERCISE 3.4

Bug bounty programs are a great way to solicit security testing from a larger audience of testers. Often these programs will source testers from all over the world, which allows for a wide range of capabilities and techniques. However, the organization will want to ensure that there are clear rules of engagement with dos and don'ts. To get started, you can get the Cybersecurity and Infrastructure Security Agency template on a vulnerability disclosure program: http://mng.bz/N5eN.

Chapter 5

EXERCISE 5.1

Application security teams can be organized in many different ways and can be large or small. Their goals can change per organization and industry. For instance, think about an organization that develops software for medical devices versus one that develops software consumed by end users over the internet. One resource for application security teams is the build security in maturity model (BSIMM), which uses the term *software security group* (SSG) (http://mng.bz/DDNn). If you don't have a team internally in your organization, take a look at the BSIMM to understand the scope of the SSG and what they do.

EXERCISE 5.2

One quick example of a standard is an encryption standard that outlines what the acceptable encryption levels are allowed to be used in the organization. Take a look at NIST's example encryption standards and guidelines to help guide your journey in creating standards: http://mng.bz/lRo6.

EXERCISE 5.3

Looking at the architecture diagram for access to the application through the API gateway, one simple requirement is to implement multifactor authentication on the application login. This requirement can be stated as: the user must complete a multi-factor authentication challenge when authenticating to the application.

Chapter 6

EXERCISE 6.1

Using the template for risk definition, we can choose another risk to highlight and assign a value to it.

Risk	Definition	Cost of risk
Ransomware that encrypts a production database for 48 hours.	The production database is critical to the operation of the business.	Every hour that the production database is unavailable costs the business $10,000.

EXERCISE 6.2

When thinking about the services that can be offered, consider how best to automate typical security services. One thought is a service for API URL testing that will identify security issues and return a report on findings and remediations.

Chapter 7

EXERCISE 7.1

In this exercise, it's important to align the application security roadmap to the organization's overall roadmap. A quick example of this is perhaps the organization is moving to a multicloud deployment for their applications. The application security roadmap will need to align to this strategy and begin to ensure that they have the tools, training, and expertise required to support the multicloud strategy. This may mean performing proof of concepts on cloud-native tools in each of the cloud locations to ensure that security services are available to meet the required security controls.

Chapter 8

EXERCISE 8.1

In this exercise, you should think about a KPI that was listed in the book or think of one on your own. One example is to measure the total security testing coverage of the organization's applications. Similar to the concept of code coverage as it relates to unit tests, the security testing coverage should be applied to the lines of code, the projects, and the deployed application stack that is used to run the application. The organization should aim to achieve 100% coverage, but first it is important to understand where the testing coverage is today. This is an exercise in reviewing the application security toolset and identifying its coverage for each application.

EXERCISE 8.2

Depending on the industry your organization is in, the security scorecard will look different. Think about a medical organization that has an application that tracks medication dosages given to patients. It is critical that data maintains its integrity and is not tampered with. Security metrics that ensure the integrity of the data will be of key focus. This could mean that the criteria like integrity checks on data in the database and access control to the data would be the highest priority.

EXERCISE 8.3

Setting an organization-standard version of TLS is one step in ensuring that the organization is securing its data in transit and that it's in line with the industry best practices. But the organization can go beyond the simple TLS version of 1.2 or 1.3 and dig into the cipher suites that are being used. Look at Mozilla's information on cipher suites and the version of TLS (http://mng.bz/BZ20). Keep the modern and intermediate compatibility cipher suites as a goal for the scorecard and assign a value for each adherence.

index